"PROHIBITED PERSONS"

Abuse of Undocumented Migrants, Asylum-Seekers, and Refugees in South Africa

Human Rights Watch
New York · Washington · London · Brussels

Copyright © March 1998 by Human Rights Watch
All rights reserved.
Printed in the United States of America.

ISBN 1-56432-181-9
Library of Congress Catalog Card Number: 98-84835

Addresses for Human Rights Watch
350 Fifth Avenue, 34th Floor, New York, NY 10118-3299
Tel: (212) 290-4700, Fax: (212) 736-1300, E-mail: hrwnyc@hrw.org

1522 K Street, N.W., #910, Washington, DC 20005-1202
Tel: (202) 371-6592, Fax: (202) 371-0124, E-mail: hrwdc@hrw.org

33 Islington High Street, N1 9LH London, UK
Tel: (171) 713-1995, Fax: (171) 713-1800, E-mail: hrwatchuk@gn.apc.org

15 Rue Van Campenhout, 1000 Brussels, Belgium
Tel: (2) 732-2009, Fax: (2) 732-0471, E-mail: hrwatcheu@gn.apc.org

Web Site Address: http://www.hrw.org

Listserv address: To subscribe to the list, send an e-mail message to
majordomo@igc.apc.org with "subscribe hrw-news" in the body of the message
(leave the subject line blank).

Human Rights Watch is dedicated to
protecting the human rights of people around the world.

We stand with victims and activists to prevent
discrimination, to uphold political freedom, to protect people from inhumane
conduct in wartime, and to bring offenders to justice.

We investigate and expose
human rights violations and hold abusers accountable.

We challenge governments and those who hold power to end abusive practices
and respect international human rights law.

We enlist the public and the international
community to support the cause of human rights for all.

HUMAN RIGHTS WATCH

Human Rights Watch conducts regular, systematic investigations of human rights abuses in some seventy countries around the world. Our reputation for timely, reliable disclosures has made us an essential source of information for those concerned with human rights. We address the human rights practices of governments of all political stripes, of all geopolitical alignments, and of all ethnic and religious persuasions. Human Rights Watch defends freedom of thought and expression, due process and equal protection of the law, and a vigorous civil society; we document and denounce murders, disappearances, torture, arbitrary imprisonment, discrimination, and other abuses of internationally recognized human rights. Our goal is to hold governments accountable if they transgress the rights of their people.

Human Rights Watch began in 1978 with the founding of its Europe and Central Asia division (then known as Helsinki Watch). Today, it also includes divisions covering Africa, the Americas, Asia, and the Middle East. In addition, it includes three thematic divisions on arms, children's rights, and women's rights. It maintains offices in New York, Washington, Los Angeles, London, Brussels, Moscow, Dushanbe, Rio de Janeiro, and Hong Kong. Human Rights Watch is an independent, nongovernmental organization, supported by contributions from private individuals and foundations worldwide. It accepts no government funds, directly or indirectly.

The staff includes Kenneth Roth, executive director; Susan Osnos, associate director; Michele Alexander, development director; Cynthia Brown, program director; Barbara Guglielmo, finance and administration director; Patrick Minges, publications director; Jeri Laber, special advisor; Lotte Leicht, Brussels office director; Carroll Bogert, communications director; Jemera Rone, counsel; Wilder Tayler, general counsel; and Joanna Weschler, United Nations representative.

The regional directors of Human Rights Watch are Peter Takirambudde, Africa; José Miguel Vivanco, Americas; Sidney Jones, Asia; Holly Cartner, Europe and Central Asia; and Hanny Megally, Middle East and North Africa. The thematic division directors are Joost R. Hiltermann, arms; Lois Whitman, children's; and Dorothy Q. Thomas, women's.

The members of the board of directors are Jonathan Fanton, chair; Lisa Anderson, Robert L. Bernstein, William Carmichael, Dorothy Cullman, Gina Despres, Irene Diamond, Adrian W. DeWind, Fiona Druckenmiller, Edith Everett, James C. Goodale, Jack Greenberg, Vartan Gregorian, Alice H. Henkin, Stephen L. Kass, Marina Pinto Kaufman, Bruce Klatsky, Harold Hongju Koh, Alexander MacGregor, Josh Mailman, Samuel K. Murumba, Andrew Nathan, Jane Olson, Peter Osnos, Kathleen Peratis, Bruce Rabb, Sigrid Rausing, Anita Roddick, Orville Schell, Sid Sheinberg, Gary G. Sick, Malcolm Smith, Domna Stanton, Maureen White, and Maya Wiley. Robert L. Bernstein is the founding chair of Human Rights Watch.

ACKNOWLEDGMENTS

This report is based on research conducted in South Africa by Peter Bouckaert, Orville Schell Fellow in the Africa division of Human Rights Watch, and consultants Busani Selabe of the University of the Witwatersrand Refugee Research Programme (RRP), Jonathan Klaaren of the University of the Witwatersrand Faculty of Law and the Centre for Applied Legal Studies (CALS), and Jeff Handmaker of Lawyers for Human Rights (LHR). The report was written by Peter Bouckaert, based on an earlier draft by Busani Selabe and additional work by Bronwen Manby, counsel in the Africa division of Human Rights Watch, and Chris Dolan, formerly of the RRP. Bronwen Manby wrote the appendix on the obligations of South Africa under International law, the section on domestic legislation (based in part on work done by Jonathan Klaaren), and edited the report. The report was also edited by Peter Takirambudde, executive director of the Africa division, Binaifer Nowrojee, counsel, Wilder Tayler, general counsel, and Jeri Laber, senior advisor. The section of the report addressing conditions of detention was further edited by Joanne Mariner, associate counsel and the coordinator of prison work. Ariana Pearlroth, associate of the Africa division, Lucinda Saunders, intern in the Africa division, and Patrick Minges, publications director, provided invaluable production assistance.

Human Rights Watch would like to thank its many NGO partners who contributed to the report by offering their opinions and by facilitating interviews and visits. In particular, we would like to thank Lee Anne de la Hunt of the University of Cape Town Law Clinic; William Kerfoot and Catrin Verloren Van Themaat of the Legal Resources Centre (LRC); Sheena Duncan and Alison Tilley of the Black Sash; and Vincent Williams of the South African Migration Project (SAMP) at the Institute for Democracy in South Africa (IDASA). Jonathan Klaaren of CALS assisted in the writing of the report, provided legal analysis, and participated in a number of visits and interviews in the Johannesburg and Mpumalanga border area. Jeff Handmaker of LHR also contributed legal analysis, and helped set up and conduct our interviews in the Pretoria area. Busani Selabe of the RRP conducted some of interviews and visits for this report, and Chris Dolan and Nicola Johnston of the RRP allowed us access to their extensive research files. Human Rights Watch would also like to thank the many South African officials who agreed to be interviewed for this report and who facilitated access to detention facilities.

Human Rights Watch recognizes with appreciation funding for work on South Africa from the Netherlands Organization for International Development Cooperation (NOVIB).

Most of all, we would like to acknowledge the many undocumented migrants, asylum-seekers, refugees and others who agreed to speak with us and provide information for this report.

CONTENTS

I. SUMMARY 1
  Abuses Against Undocumented Migrants in South Africa 2
  Abuses Against Asylum-Seekers and Refugees 3
  Xenophobia and Abuse of Foreigners 4
  The Stalled Policy Debate 6

II. RECOMMENDATIONS 7
  Recommendations to the Government of South Africa 7
  Recommendations to the State Institutions Supporting
    Constitutional Democracy 13
  Recommendations to the Office of the United Nations High
    Commissioner on Refugees (UNHCR) 13
  Recommendations to the Southern African Development Community
    (SADC) 14

III. INTRODUCTION 15
  Migration to South Africa Today 19
  Brief History of Migration to South Africa 22
    Labor Migration to South Africa 22
    The Destabilization of the Frontline States by the Apartheid Regime. 24
    The Repatriation of Mozambican Refugees 29
    The SADC Amnesty 31

IV. THE TREATMENT OF UNDOCUMENTED MIGRANTS IN SOUTH
  AFRICA 36
  Labor Exploitation 36
  Abuses During the Arrest Process 43
    The Agencies Involved in the Detection of Undocumented Migrants. 43
    Abuses Committed During Detection and Arrest 49
      Arbitrary Identification Procedures 49
      The Destruction of Documents 54
      Bribery, Extortion and Theft during the Arrest Process ... 55
      Physical Abuse During the Arrest Process 61
    Threats to Academic and Journalistic Freedom 64

Conditions of Detention 67
    Lindela Facility 69
        The Intake and Processing of Detainees 71
        Accommodation 71
        Food 72
        Telephone Access 73
        Abuse of Inmates by Guards 74
    Prison Facilities 85
        Pretoria Central Prison 86
        Johannesburg (Diepkloof) Prison 87
        Pollsmoor Prison 89
    Police Cells 93
    Military Detention 98
    Unlawful Long-term Detention of Undocumented Migrants 98
    The Deportation Process: The Train to Mozambique 102

V. THE TREATMENT OF REFUGEES AND ASYLUM-SEEKERS IN SOUTH
    AFRICA 109
    Asylum-Seekers in Detention 110
    Corruption in the Asylum Process 111
    Arbitrary, Uninformed Decisions 114
    Rubber-Stamp Appeals Process 117
    Police Abuse of Refugees and Asylum-Seekers 118

VI. XENOPHOBIA AND ATTACKS AGAINST MIGRANTS 123
    Xenophobic statements by officials 123
    Attacks Against Foreign Hawkers 127
    The Alexandra Riots against Foreigners 135

VII. THE STALLED POLICY DEBATE 137

APPENDIX A:
    SOUTH AFRICA'S OBLIGATIONS UNDER INTERNATIONAL AND
    DOMESTIC LAW 141
    South Africa's Obligations under International Human Rights Law 141
        The Rights of All Persons, Citizens and Non-Citizens 141
            The Rights of Detainees Generally 144
            The Rights of Deportees 144
            The Rights of Migrant Workers 145
            Reduction of Statelessness 146

The Rights of Asylum-Seekers and Refugees 147
    The Definition of a Refugee 148
    The Right of Non-Refoulement 149
    Procedures for Determining Refugee Status 150
    Other Rights of Refugees 152
    Detention of Asylum-Seekers and Refugees 153
Domestic Obligations 156
  Constitutional Obligations 156
  The Aliens Control Act 160
    The Deportation Process 161
      Prohibited Persons 161
      Legal Entry into the Country 162
      Identification of Prohibited Persons 164
      Removals 165
      Detention of Deportees 165
      Appeal and Review of Immigration Decisions
      and Detention 166
    The Asylum Determination Process 170
      Processing of Asylum Applications 170
      Application 171
      First Interview 171
      Processing of Applications 172
      Decisions 173
      "Refugee Generating Countries" 174
      "Manifestly Unfounded" Applications 174
      Appeal 175
      Representation 175
      Rejected Applicants 176

APPENDIX B:
ORGANIZATION OF AFRICAN UNITY CONVENTION GOVERNING
THE SPECIFIC ASPECTS OF REFUGEE PROBLEMS IN AFRICA . 177

APPENDIX C:
DECLARATION ON THE HUMAN RIGHTS OF INDIVIDUALS WHO ARE
NOT NATIONALS OF THE COUNTRY IN WHICH THEY LIVE . . . 185

APPENDIX D:
INTERNATIONAL CONVENTION ON THE PROTECTION OF THE
RIGHTS OF ALL MIGRANT WORKERS AND MEMBERS OF THEIR
FAMILIES 190

I. SUMMARY

Although South Africa, since the first democratic elections in 1994, has made remarkable progress towards establishing a free and democratic society based on respect for the human rights of its own citizens, foreigners have largely failed to benefit from these developments and remain subject to serious abuse. Anti-foreigner feelings have also increased alarmingly. Politicians, the press, and the South African public commonly blame foreigners for exacerbating social problems such as rising crime, unemployment, or even the spread of diseases, and undocumented migrants have been subject to abuse by officials from the Department of Home Affairs, the police, and the army, as well as by the general public. In general, public attention has been focused on the allegedly socio-economic impact of migrants within South Africa, despite the absence of evidence to confirm these. In the process, attention has been diverted from the suffering and exploitation experienced by aliens as a result of official policies and xenophobic attitudes. This report seeks to document the experiences of foreigners in South Africa, including undocumented migrants, legal residents, asylum-seekers, and refugees, in order to add their voices to the debate on migration in South Africa. Human suffering should not be ignored in a country that only recently emerged from a system that degraded basic human rights and human dignity.[1]

Human Rights Watch conducted an investigation of the treatment of undocumented migrants, asylum-seekers, and refugees in South Africa in 1996 and 1997. During the course of our missions, we visited several areas of the country, including Johannesburg and Pretoria, the Northern Province and Mpumalanga border regions with Mozambique, and Cape Town. We interviewed foreign farm workers, migrants in detention, asylum-seekers, refugees, hawkers, repatriated Mozambicans, and representatives of nongovernmental organizations (NGOs), as well as officials from the Department of Home Affairs, the South African Police Service, the Department of Correctional Services, the South African National Defence Force, and the Mozambican Department of Labor. We visited a number of detention facilities, including the private Lindela detention facility in Krugersdorp; Pollsmoor, Pretoria Central, Johannesburg Central (Diepkloof), and

---

[1]In this report, we use the term "undocumented migrants" to refer to all persons who entered South Africa without passing through formal border control procedures. The South African authorities normally refer to such people as "illegal aliens," a term Human Rights Watch considers objectionable because of the way it dehumanizes those with irregular immigration status.

1

Modderbee prisons; and a number of police stations. Our findings indicate pervasive and widespread abuse of migrants in South Africa.

Abuses Against Undocumented Migrants in South Africa

The South African economy, especially its farming, mining, security, and construction sectors, relies heavily on the cheap and easily exploitable labor of undocumented migrants, mostly from Mozambique, Lesotho, Zimbabwe, and Swaziland. Undocumented laborers on farms work for a pittance, on average about 5 rands [U.S. $ 1 at an exchange rate of five rands for one U.S. dollar] per day. Because of the illegal immigration status of their workers, farmers can exercise tremendous power over them. Human Rights Watch interviewed a number of child laborers, some as young as fourteen, and our research indicates that physical abuse of farm workers is common. Police rarely investigate or prosecute farmers for abuses, and in some instances contribute to the exploitation of farm workers by deporting them without pay on the request of farmers who have employed them. In one instance, Human Rights Watch interviewed three young farm laborers who described how they had been kept on a white-owned farm against their will, without any accommodation, and were regularly beaten to make them work harder. After two weeks, they were finally paid at the rate of 5 rands [U.S. $1] per day, only to have their money stolen by the foreman who then called the police to have the young laborers deported.

South Africa has been deporting an increasing number of migrants each year since 1994, and reaching close to 200,000 people in 1997. Suspected undocumented migrants are identified by the authorities through unreliable means such as complexion, accent, or inoculation marks. We documented cases of persons who claimed they were arrested for being "too black," having a foreign name, or in one case, walking "like a Mozambican." Many of those arrested—up to twenty percent of the total in some areas by our calculation—are actually South African citizens or lawful residents, who often have to spend several days in detention while attempting to convince officials of their legitimate status.

Assault and theft by officials during the arrest process seems disturbingly common. We interviewed several persons who claimed to have been beaten and robbed of valuables by members of the army or police and obtained evidence of several other such cases. In some urban areas, especially Johannesburg, police often suggested a "fine" or a bribe as an alternative to arrest and deportation. One person told Human Rights Watch how the police had volunteered to drive him to a bank automated teller machine (ATM) to withdraw the money for a bribe, while two others told us how they were forced to pay for a beer drinking party and to give the arresting officers additional "beer money" before being released.

After arrest, suspected undocumented migrants are brought to a place of detention where they often wait for long periods before being deported. Human Rights Watch interviewed some people who had been unlawfully in detention for more than four months and documented a case in which a suspected undocumented migrant had been detained for more than a year. Migrants awaiting deportation are held at a private detention facility called Lindela, as well as at prisons, police stations, and army bases. Conditions of detention are usually far below internationally accepted minimum standards. Places of detention are often severely overcrowded, meals are insufficient, bedding was dirty and vermin-ridden, and detainees did not always have regular access to washing facilities. At Pollsmoor prison, migrants in detention often share cells with criminal suspects and are frequently robbed of their possessions and clothes by these criminal suspects.

At the private Lindela facility near Johannesburg, operated on behalf of the Department of Home Affairs by the Dyambu Trust, Human Rights Watch found numerous serious human rights abuses. Most troubling, we interviewed and photographed more than ten people who claimed to have been beaten by security personnel in three separate incidents in the week prior to our visit, and we obtained medical reports documenting their injuries. A young man from Lesotho had been brutally beaten over a period of several hours after complaining to security guards about the theft of his music tapes by security personnel. Although the Lindela management was aware of some of these incidents, no internal investigation appeared to have been instituted prior to our request for an investigation. The number of beds at Lindela was significantly lower than the average number of persons detained at the facility. Detainees also described many instances of corruption involving officials of the Department of Home Affairs at the facility and complained to Human Rights Watch about the quality of the food, the lack of phone access, and rude and violent behavior by the guards.

Repatriation to their home country is the final chapter in the journey of most arrested undocumented migrants. In some areas, deportees were not allowed to gather their often substantial belongings before being deported, thus virtually guaranteeing that they would return again to South Africa. Several people told Human Rights Watch about their experiences on the twelve-hour train ride to Mozambique, where they were verbally and physically abused by police guards, and where a substantial bribe often provided a final opportunity to escape deportation by being allowed to jump from the moving train.

Abuses Against Asylum-Seekers and Refugees
South Africa only began to abide formally by international refugee law after signing a Basic Agreement with United Nations High Commissioner for Refugees

(UNHCR) in 1993. South Africa became a party to the Organization of African Unity (OAU) and United Nations (U.N.) refugee conventions in 1995 and 1996, respectively. The treatment of refugees and asylum-seekers in South Africa does not fully comply with international refugee law. There is no legislation implementing the South African government's obligations under these documents, so all refugee-handling procedures are governed by internal regulations of the Department of Home Affairs, leaving ample room for confusion and abuse of process. Human Rights Watch interviewed several asylum-seekers who had been in detention for up to three weeks at police stations, waiting for officials from the Department of Home Affairs to interview them. We discovered extensive corruption in the refugee determination process, with Home Affairs officials demanding bribes for the scheduling of interviews and for the granting of permits.

In addition to the impact of pervasive bribery and extortion, the refugee determination process is flawed in several respects. First, officials often make arbitrary, uninformed decisions that are inconsistent with the requirements of the U.N. and OAU conventions and guidelines for their implementation. Asylum-seekers from a number of African countries, including Angola, Mozambique, Tanzania, and Malawi, appear to have their asylum applications turned down as a matter of course. Refugee applications are determined by a panel which does not itself hear the applicants. Until recently, applicants denied asylum were not furnished with reasons for the denial, a practice which has now been rectified. Denied asylum-seekers can only appeal to a one-person appeal board which appears not to provide a genuine review of the case.

Xenophobia and Abuse of Foreigners

In general, South Africa's public culture has become increasingly xenophobic, and politicians often make unsubstantiated and inflammatory statements that the "deluge" of migrants is responsible for the current crime wave, rising unemployment, or even the spread of diseases. As the unfounded perception that migrants are responsible for a variety of social ills grows, migrants have increasingly become the target of abuse at the hands of South African citizens, as well as members of the police, the army, and the Department of Home Affairs. Refugees and asylum-seekers with distinctive features from far-away countries are especially targeted for abuse.

Human Rights Watch interviewed a number of refugees and asylum-seekers who claimed to have been assaulted by police. In one case, a Ugandan refugee told us how she had been arrested and violently thrown into a police van, then subjected to vile language and rough handling as she was transferred from one police station in Cape Town to the other. A Nigerian refugee hawker in Cape Town showed us his wounds from a recent scuffle with the police, in which he was manhandled and verbally abused for insisting that a police officer who had asked him for his papers identify himself first.

At least one asylum-seeker, Jean-Pierre Kanyangwa of Burundi, has died after apparently being beaten in police custody. Kanyangwa was arrested by police in Cape Town at about 11 a.m. on June 2, 1997, and was brought to the Department of Home Affairs at about 2 p.m. the same day in a bad condition. He was suffering from stomach pains, had urinated in his pants, and reportedly told a fellow Burundian that he had been beaten by the police. The police sergeant who brought Kanyangwa to the offices of the Department of Home Affairs refused to take him to the hospital, saying it was now a refugee problem, and left. Kanyangwa died from a ruptured spleen on his way to the hospital. A murder docket into the case has been opened.

Foreign hawkers, often asylum applicants with temporary residence permits, have repeatedly been the targets of violent protests and other forms of intimidation as local hawkers attempt to "clean the street of foreigners." During repeated violent protests in Johannesburg, South African traders and ordinary criminals have brutally beaten foreign hawkers, and stolen their goods. Hawkers interviewed by Human Rights Watch who were the targets of such abuse universally complained to us that the police had done little or nothing in response to their complaints. In many areas around Johannesburg, such as Kempton Park and Germiston, foreign hawkers have had to abandon their trade after repeated attacks and looting incidents in which the police failed in their duty under both international and domestic law to protect all persons. Human Rights Watch interviewed members of a large community of Somali asylum-seekers who had been forced to abandon their trade and who told Human Rights Watch that they now never left their overcrowded and impoverished compound unless they were in a large group, in order to protect themselves from attacks by hostile "locals."

A xenophobic climate in South Africa has resulted in increased harassment of migrants. Many people interviewed by Human Rights Watch described how they had been verbally abused by South Africans, and told to "go home." In some cases, verbal abuse led to physical attacks. In the township of Alexandra near Johannesburg, for example, Malawian, Zimbabwean and Mozambican immigrants were physically assaulted over a period of several weeks in January 1995, as armed gangs identified suspected undocumented migrants and marched them to the police station in an attempt to "clean" the township of foreigners. Similar but less extensive incidents continue to occur regularly in South Africa, and foreigners have received little protection from the police and other institutions.

The Stalled Policy Debate

The Aliens Control Act which currently governs all aspects of migrants control in South Africa is an archaic piece of apartheid legislation, at odds with internationally accepted human rights norms and the South African constitution. South Africa still remains without legislation specifically covering refugee determination procedures. In order to remedy these deficiencies, the government appointed a task group to draft a "Green Paper" policy document as a first step in drafting new legislation.

Many of the recommendations contained in the ensuing Green Paper on International Migration, finalized in May 1997, would help remedy the institutional and legislative deficiencies which are partly responsible for the human rights abuses discussed in this report. However, it appears that the reform process has stalled, and with the 1999 general elections appearing on the political horizon in South Africa, the window for migration and refugee legislative reform is rapidly closing. Without legislative reform, it will be difficult to address the problems and abuses existing under the current system, as many of these problems and abuses stem from fundamental deficiencies in the current legislation. In the meantime, without reform, Human Rights Watch fears that foreigners in South Africa will continue to suffer major and systematic human rights abuses.

II. RECOMMENDATIONS

Recommendations to the Government of South Africa

Human Rights Watch makes the following recommendations to the South African government, to be implemented by all agencies involved in migration policy and its enforcement. In all its policy initiatives and official statements, the government should make it clear that all individuals in South Africa, regardless of their immigration status, are entitled to respect for their basic human rights. The government should take steps to ensure that all agencies involved in migration control in South Africa emphasize the promotion and protection of human rights in the fulfillment of their responsibilities to enforce South African immigration laws.

General

- The government should immediately take steps to bring South African immigration law into line with internationally recognized human rights norms and the South African constitution, in accordance with the recommendations contained in the *Draft Green Paper on International Migration.*

- Members of the government, including ministers, should publicly condemn harassment of or attacks on foreigners, and call for tolerance, understanding and respect for the human rights of all those living in South Africa.

- South Africa should ratify the International Covenant on Civil and Political Rights and its protocols, the International Covenant on Economic, Social and Cultural Rights, and the Convention against Torture and Other Cruel, Inhuman or Degrading Treatment or Punishment, and bring domestic law and practice into conformity with these treaties.

- South Africa should sign and ratify the International Convention on the Protection of the Rights of All Migrant Workers and Members of Their Families and bring domestic law and practice into conformity with this treaty.

- South Africa should sign and ratify the International Labor Organization (ILO) Convention concerning Migration for Employment (Revised 1949, No. 97), and the ILO Migrant Workers (Supplementary Provisions) Convention (1975, No. 143), and bring domestic law and practice into conformity with these treaties.

7

- All efforts should be made to prevent practices of racial discrimination in the application of migration and refugee policy.

Refugee Protection

- The government should develop an independent process for refugee status determination. As proposed by the *Green Paper on International Migration*, refugee status determination should be the domain of an impartial and independent expert authority with a sound familiarity with the legal and empirical realities of human rights protection, insulated from political intervention.

- Refugee legislation should provide in detail not only for the procedures for determining refugee status, but also for the substantive rights of refugees and asylum-seekers. The central purpose of such legislation should be to grant international protection to those who need it. Both procedural and substantive provisions of refugee legislation should be based on the U.N. and OAU refugee conventions and other international instruments as a minimum framework.

- Refugee legislation should provide for determination of refugee status in accordance with the guidelines contained in the UNHCR *Handbook on Procedures and Criteria for Determining Refugee Status*, on the basis of a hearing at which the applicant is given an opportunity to make his or her case directly to the person or persons who will make the first instance decision whether or not to grant refugee status. In the event of rejection, reasons must be given and a reasonable period to prepare and file an appeal must be granted. Appeals should be heard by a properly constituted body, with independent status. The right to an interpreter, to submit documents in any language, to use legal representation and to present a case in person should all be specified.

- Refugees in South Africa should have the right to identity and travel documents indicating their status; asylum seekers should also be given documentation indicating that an asylum application has been filed and that the holder may remain in the country pending determination of the application.

- Refugee legislation should provide explicitly for the protection of unaccompanied minors, and should aim to respect as far as possible the principle of family unity in line with the recommendation of the Final Act of the conference that adopted the 1951 U.N. Convention, and should guarantee other rights provided in international human rights and refugee law and in South Africa's constitution.

- South Africa should recognize the especially vulnerable position of women by explicitly including gender-based persecution, including sex-specific abuse, as grounds for granting asylum, and should adopt guidelines to assist asylum adjudicators to evaluate gender-related persecution.

- Legislation should provide that asylum-seekers should in general not be detained, but if they are, detention should be only on the basis of the grounds contained in the UNHCR *Guidelines on the Detention of Asylum Seekers*. Detention of asylum-seekers should be subject to judicial approval and supervision. Detained asylum seekers should have the right to contact a legal representative and a family member or friend, and to be informed of that right and given the means to make such contact.

- In accordance with the 1951 U.N. Convention, the assimilation and naturalization of refugees should be facilitated. Those who have been settled in South Africa for a long time—including, for example, the Mozambicans in South Africa recognized as refugees on a group basis until December 31, 1996—should in particular be eligible for permanent residence status where possible.

Preventing Abuse by Government Officials
- The law should provide clear protections against arbitrary arrests, searches and seizures in the apprehension of undocumented migrants, including procedures to be followed by police and immigration officers: for example, rules should be drafted to determine when an individual may be stopped and asked for his or her identity documents and to ensure that individuals who do not have documentation with them are given an effective opportunity to produce it.

- The government should take immediate steps to end the pervasive corruption in the handling of undocumented migrants, asylum-seekers, and refugees by the Department of Home Affairs, South African Police Service, South African National Defence Force, and other agencies.

- Senior officials in each agency responsible for implementing migration policy should make it clear that abuse of undocumented migrants, asylum seekers and refugees is inconsistent with South African and international law and will not be tolerated. All allegations of abuse by government officials should be investigated thoroughly, and the responsible officers should be brought to justice.

- All uniformed police officers should be required to wear clearly visible and readable identification badges which state their name and an identification number. Officers requesting documents or detaining persons should be required to identify themselves by name, rank, and identification number when asked to do so.

- Persons being repatriated should be allowed to retrieve their belongings in South Africa prior to repatriation. All efforts should be made to facilitate and ensure that persons being repatriated are able to return to their home countries with their possessions.

- The border fence between South Africa and Mozambique should no longer be electrified, in light of the continuing reports of electricity-related injuries at the border fence.

- Effective procedures should be established where they do not already exist, and publicized, to enable refugees, asylum seekers, and undocumented migrants, as well as South African citizens and residents, to file complaints, without fear of retaliation, against officials of the Department of Home Affairs, the South African Police Service, the South African National Defence Force, and all other agencies involved in migration control. Such complaint procedures should take into account the need for rapid determination of complaints if individuals are in the process of deportation, while also providing for an independent review of the process.

Detention of Suspected Undocumented Migrants
- All efforts should be made to minimize the period undocumented migrants and asylum-seekers spend in detention. In accordance with the Body of Principles for the Protection of All Persons under Any Form of Detention or Imprisonment, undocumented migrants who are apprehended and held in custody must have "an effective opportunity" to have their case reviewed "promptly" by a judicial or other authority. Continued detention should be on the basis of specified conditions, and should be subject to periodic review and to a maximum time limit. The current practices, allowing for the judicially unsupervised detention of undocumented migrants for an initial period of thirty

days, are inconsistent with international human rights standards and the provisions of the South African constitution.

- Detention conditions for undocumented migrants and asylum-seekers should conform with international and domestic standards, including the U.N. Standard Minimum Rules for the Treatment of Prisoners and the Body of Principles. In particular, undocumented migrants in detention and asylum-seekers are entitled to clean and adequate bedding, prompt access to medical treatment, adequate washing facilities, three meals a day at regular intervals, and, at a minimum, one hour of exercise per day.

- Those who are held in custody simply pending deportation should be held in separate places of custody from criminal suspects or convicts. All efforts should be made to hold undocumented migrants in dedicated detention facilities, offering material conditions and a regime appropriate to their legal situation and staffed by suitably-qualified personnel.

- Conditions in places of custody for deportees, whether in dedicated facilities, police cells, prisons or elsewhere, should be subject to inspection by an independent authority. Independent non-governmental organizations should also be allowed to inspect these facilities in order to ensure compliance with international and domestic standards.

- Detainees who are foreigners should have the right to obtain their own legal representation, to contact a family member or friend, and to a state-provided interpreter in official interviews or hearings by state officials, and to be informed of these rights and given the means to make contact with a family member or friend.

- Where undocumented migrants are held in places of custody operated by private bodies, such as the Lindela facility operated by Dyambu Trust, the government must ensure that such facilities are operated in accordance with international and domestic law. Delegation of the task of operating such facilities does not absolve government of ultimate responsibility for the acts done on its behalf, and procedures should be in place to ensure close government oversight.

- In particular, clear rules of conduct and disciplinary rules for security guards at private facilities should be instituted, and all guards should be trained in appropriate disciplinary procedures and rules applying to the use of force. Any incidents involving the use of force by guards should be fully investigated and reported to the Department of Home Affairs and, where appropriate, the South African Police Service. The failure by security guards to report incidents involving the use of force should be an infraction subject to disciplinary proceedings.

- The government should ensure that information is made available to undocumented migrants in custody setting out in clear and simple language their rights and the available avenues for redress if any of these rights are violated. This information should be translated into several languages commonly spoken by undocumented migrants, such as Shangaan, Shona, French and Portuguese, and should be prominently displayed at offices of the Department of Home Affairs, police stations, army offices, offices of the Internal Tracing Units, and all facilities used for the detention of undocumented migrants. In addition, contact information of organizations that can provide legal and other assistance should be displayed.

- In order to prevent arbitrary expulsions, procedures should be put in place which allow migrants to appeal deportation orders. These appeal procedures should be easily accessible and should not significantly extend the period of time spent in detention. Migrants who have been issued with a deportation order should be informed of their right to appeal, and information explaining appeal procedures in clear and simple language should be easily available in several languages commonly spoken by undocumented migrants, such as Shangaan, Shona, French and Portuguese.

Protection of Foreigners from Violence
- The police, army and other security forces should develop and adopt specific policies for the protection of foreigners from violent attacks from whatever source, recognizing undocumented migrants as a particularly vulnerable group.

- The police should investigate all incidents of assault or other offenses committed against foreigners. All persons are entitled to the protection of the police services on an equal basis, regardless of nationality.

Preventing Exploitation of Migrant Labor
- Integrated policies by different state authorities should be developed and implemented to end the abuse of undocumented migrants and use of coercive

labor practices by employers: in particular, the immediate investigation of such allegations and the prosecution of employers who engage in such practices. All reasonable steps should be taken to ensure that employees are paid for work performed prior to their deportation.

Education and Training

- Public officials interacting with refugees and undocumented migrants, including immigration officials and police with responsibilities in this area, should receive specific training relating to the rights of refugees, asylum seekers and undocumented migrants, and the human rights of all persons.

- Public education campaigns should be devised and implemented directed at reducing xenophobia and increasing tolerance and respect for the human rights of asylum seekers, refugees and migrants generally.

Recommendations to the State Institutions Supporting Constitutional Democracy

- The Human Rights Commission, the Commission for Gender Equality, and the Youth Commission should monitor the situation of undocumented migrants, asylum seekers and refugees as especially vulnerable groups in South African society and should conduct campaigns to inform and educate the South African public about the rights of foreigners.

- The Independent Complaints Directorate, responsible for investigation of complaints against the police, should pay special attention to complaints of police abuse against foreigners, and should take note of the particular vulnerability of those with irregular immigration status in investigating such allegations of abuse.

Recommendations to the Office of the United Nations High Commissioner for Refugees (UNHCR)

- UNHCR should continue to work closely with the South African government and concerned NGOs to ensure that respect for human rights is an integral part of the new refugee policy currently being developed and that the 1951 U.N. Convention and the 1969 OAU Convention are fully implemented.

- UNHCR should continue to monitor, investigate, document, and make public any abuses committed against asylum seekers, refugees, and other migrants residing inside South Africa.

- UNHCR should do all in its powers to facilitate access to asylum seeking procedures, including, where necessary, the development of sub-offices in key locations such as Cape Town, Johannesburg, and Durban.

- UNHCR should all in its powers to ensure that asylum-seekers and refugees are given full documentation.

Recommendations to the Southern African Development Community (SADC)
- SADC should seek regional solutions to the problem of undocumented border crossings in the region, and encourage cooperation among member states in the area of migration policy.

- SADC should also address the issue of refugee accommodation on a regional basis, and encourage burden sharing among member states in the area of refugee accommodation.

- SADC should establish a permanent committee to monitor the treatment of undocumented persons, refugees, and asylum-seekers in the SADC member states, and make the treatment of migrants by member states a standing issue on the Community's agenda.

III. INTRODUCTION

During the apartheid era,.the regime tried to implement its vision of an all-white South Africa by stripping "African"[2] South Africans of their South African citizenship and attempting to remove them to remote and desolate "homelands."[3] To control the movement of non-white South Africans to its "white" cities, the apartheid state imposed a system called influx control, with a vast supporting bureaucracy. All Africans who traveled beyond the confines of their "homeland" were required to be in the possession of a pass, and inability to produce the pass on demand would lead to immediate arrest and deportation. Kader Asmal, a long-term human rights activist and the present Minister for Water Affairs and Forestry, described the impact of the pass law system in a recent book:

> The laws restricting the right of Africans to free movement in their own country caused terrible suffering to many more than did the laws prohibiting interracial marriage and sex. The pass laws, restricting the physical movement of Africans to those areas endorsed in the pass books that they were required to carry, resulted in over 381,000 Africans being

---

[2]South Africa's complex racial classification system divided the population into different racial groups, which included "African" (of solely African ancestry), "Asian" or "Indian" (largely descended from indentured servants brought from the Indian subcontinent, but also including more recent Asian immigrants), "coloured" (of mixed ancestry), and "white" (of European ancestry). Persons were provided with different civil and political privileges depending on the racial category they found themselves in, with whites enjoying the most extensive civil and political privileges.

[3]During the apartheid era, South Africa had sought to create a series of nominally independent homelands in order to implement its policies of apartheid, or "separate development." Each homeland was envisioned to belong to a distinct ethnic group; for example KwaZulu was seen as the homeland of the Zulus. In the implementation of this design, many South Africans were stripped of their South African citizenship, and forcefully removed to their homeland, often a place they had never before seen. The independence and legality of the homelands was universally rejected by the international community. As South Africa reached its historic negotiated settlement for a transition to a democratic government, it was decided to re-integrate the territories of the homelands into the territory of South Africa. As many homeland residents had been stripped of their South African identity documents, it became necessary to issue them with new South African identity documents. As discussed in this report, in the chaotic and rushed re-registration process, many non-South African homeland residents were able to obtain South African identity documents.

arrested in the year 1975-76, at the height of their use; and in over 12 million arrests over the period from 1948 to 1985.[4]

These laws exposed blacks to lives of humiliation and insecurity. Passes had to be produced upon the demand of any authorised official, a term that was defined to include any police officer and that, in practice, included any white who felt like harassing a black.[5]

Dr. A.B. Xuma, then president of the African National Congress (ANC), complained that "flying squads, pick-up vans, troop-carriers, and mounted police are all abroad irritating and exasperating Africans by indiscriminately demanding passes [and] handling them in an insulting and humiliating way."[6] The movements and migrations between urban and rural areas, which were largely a response to the policy of creating homelands, defied the heavy-handed tactics of influx control and pass laws. They were finally abandoned in 1986.

South Africa has made great strides in its efforts to establish a democratic, human rights centered society since the historic all-race elections of 1994. Yet for foreigners living in South Africa today, life continues to be fraught with difficulties disturbingly similar to those faced by black South Africans under the influx control system. South Africa has become increasingly xenophobic in recent years, with a large percentage of South Africans perceiving foreigners—especially, almost exclusively, black foreigners—as a direct threat to their future economic well-being

---

[4]Kader Asmal, Louise Asmal, and Ronald Suresh Roberts, *Reconciliation Through Truth: A Reckoning of Apartheid's Criminal Governance* (Cape Town: David Philip Publishers, 1996), p. 80.

[5]Ibid., p. 129.

[6]William Beinart, *Twentieth-Century South Africa* (Oxford: Oxford University Press, 1994), p. 152. Nelson Mandela similarly condemned the pass law system in his statement during the 1964 Rivonia Trial: "Pass Laws, which to the Africans are among the most hated bits of legislation in South Africa, render any African liable to police surveillance at any time. I doubt whether there is a single African male in South Africa who has not at some stage had a brush with the police over his pass. Hundreds and thousands of Africans are thrown in gaol each year under pass laws." Nelson Mandela, "Statement during the Rivonia Trial, April 20, 1964," in Thomas Karis, Gail M. Gerhart, and Gwendolen M. Carter, *From Protest to Challenge: A Documentary History of African Politics in South Africa 1882-1964, Volume 3: Challenge and Violence 1953-1964* (Stanford, CA: Hoover Institute Press, 1977), p. 795.

and as responsible for the troubling rise in violent crime in South Africa. Foreign hawkers are routinely attacked on the street, and criminals seem to believe that they have the right to steal from foreigners. In certain townships such as Alexandra, near Johannesburg, the homes of migrants have been burned to the ground, and they have been told to leave the area or be targeted by violence.

Although Human Rights Watch recognizes the right of the South African state to regulate the entry and movement of foreign nationals within its borders in line with international law, we are concerned about the methods used to achieve this end. During our investigation, we interviewed numerous people who alleged that they had been beaten by police, army, or detention facility officials, and who often showed clear signs of recent violence. At least one asylum-seeker has died apparently after being beaten by police officers while in custody. Detainees also often complained about having money or other possessions stolen by officials when they were taken into custody. We received many allegations of bribery and corruption of police officers and home affairs officials.

In many detention facilities for undocumented migrants, Human Rights Watch found the conditions deplorable. Most were severely overcrowded. Some were lice-infested, unhygienic, smelly, and very dark and dank. At Pollsmoor, detainees received only two meals per day and had to wait for seventeen hours after their dinner at 3 p.m. until their morning meal at 8 a.m. Migrants were often arrested and brought to the detention facility with only the clothes on their back and were thus forced to remain in detention for long periods of time with only one set of clothes. Some of the persons interviewed by Human Rights Watch had been in detention for more than three months without money or a change of clothes. At Lindela, several inmates claimed they had been assaulted by security personnel and bore the marks of recent beatings. At Pollsmoor prison, detainees alleged that they had many of their possessions stolen by the criminal suspects with whom they were forced to share cells when they first arrived at the prison.

Many of the migrants interviewed by Human Rights Watch expressed a deep disappointment with the way they had been treated by the South African authorities, and by the South African public in general. One Nigerian refugee contrasted his own treatment at the hands of the South African police and the South African public with the way South African exiles where received in African countries during the apartheid struggle:

When I was young, we always talked about our brothers in South Africa
and that we wanted them to be free. If a South African came to Nigeria,
we welcomed him as a brother. The local people must learn about us.[7]

Benneth Mabaso, who claimed to be South African and alleged that his ID book
had been destroyed by the South African police the week before our visit because
he had a Mozambican inoculation mark, complained that,

We are still treated like under the apartheid system, always asking for our
pass even though we are South Africans. Pass, pass, pass. It is still the
same. It is very sad.[8]

Indeed, troubling similarities exist between the old apartheid pass law enforcement
system and the current migrants control system. Pass law violations were the most
common criminal charge during the operation of the influx control system. Today,
arrests for violations of the Aliens Control Act clearly outstrip all other arrests. In
1997, the Department of Home Affairs "repatriated" 176,351 "illegal aliens," a
startling average of 485 per day. The same institutional structures once responsible
for enforcing influx control laws—including the Department of Home Affairs, the
police, and the army—now enforce the system of migrants control. Most
disturbingly, the heavy-handed tactics associated with influx control continue to be
used to control migrants. Finally, despite the heavy-handedness and systematic
abuses, the system of migrants control is as ineffective in controlling migration as
influx control was in controlling the movement of black South Africans.

The new South Africa has seen a marked increase in the profile of migration
related issues in the mass media. Much of this coverage is uninformed and
perpetuates untested assumptions about the negative impact of migrants on the
economy and on crime and drug abuse levels. There is little coverage of the
systematic abuse of human rights in the implementation of the aliens control
system, nor is there informed coverage of the underlying issues of labor
exploitation which the current system clearly perpetuates. This report aims to
redress one of these imbalances, and focuses on the systematic abuse of migrants
at all stages of the aliens control system. South Africa has pledged itself to the

---

[7]Human Rights Watch interview with Akinjole A.J. "Giant," Nigerian hawker,
Cape Town, December 11, 1997.

[8]Human Rights Watch interview with Benneth Mabaso, Komatiepoort Police
Station, December 2, 1997.

creation and nurturing of a vibrant democratic society committed to a culture of human rights. In his inauguration speech, President Nelson Mandela pledged that "never, never and never again shall it be that this beautiful land will again experience the oppression of one by another ."[9] In the treatment of migrants within its borders, South Africa has a long way to go to make this promise a reality.

Migration to South Africa Today

Estimating the total number of migrants currently residing in South Africa is a difficult task. Recent estimates have shown a distinct upwards trend, as Professor Jonathan Crush explains in a recent study:

> The numbers involved are a source of considerable controversy within South Africa, with wildly variable estimates being thrown around. Before 1994, most estimates of the total number of undocumented aliens were below two million (although even the basis of that figure is unclear). By late 1994, police were citing figures of eight million in total and 700,000 Mozambicans. This was hardly surprising; since those seeking more resources for policing were always likely to exaggerate the figures. More alarming was the pseudo-scientific justification for these kind of numbers. The Human Sciences Research Council (HSRC) conducted a methodologically suspect survey in 1994-95 and concluded that there were 9.5 million non-South Africans (not necessarily all undocumented) in the country.... In their latest unpublished report, the HSRC raises their estimate to as many as twelve million. These kinds of figures are waved around by the press, certain politicians and some commentators. Mathias Brunk has critically reviewed the figures and rightly concludes that "we have too little knowledge to justify any precise estimates or assumptions."[10]

Despite the unreliability of the popular estimates of the number of undocumented migrants in South Africa, certain public officials continue to invoke the highest estimates in order to suggest a state of crisis with regard to the presence of migrants into South Africa. For example, in his first introductory speech to Parliament,

---

[9]Nelson Mandela, "Inauguration Speech," Pretoria Union Buildings, May 10, 1994.

[10]Jonathan Crush, "Covert Operations: Clandestine Migration, Temporary Work and Immigration Policy in South Africa," *South African Migration Project, Migration Policy Series, No. 1* (Cape Town: South African Migration Project, 1997), p. 18.

Minister of Home Affairs Mangosutho Buthelezi stated that "if we as South Africans are going to compete for scarce resources with millions of aliens who are pouring into South Africa, then we can bid goodbye to our Reconstruction and Development Programme."[11]

Most likely, the total number of undocumented or "illegal" migrants is significantly smaller than the alarmist numbers being tossed around by politicians and the media in South Africa. The lack of reliable data makes it impossible to put a precise figure on the number of undocumented migrants in South Africa, since by definition they are not officially recorded, but an educated guess would place the number somewhere between 500,000 and 1.5 million, significantly lower than the figures commonly quoted by the media and politicians.[12] Refugees and asylum-seekers are more easy to count, as most of them have approached the Department of Home Affairs for documentation. In January 1998, South Africa had received 38,143 asylum applications.[13]

It is clear, however, that South Africa is deporting a much larger number of undocumented migrants today than ever before. The number of deportations has steadily grown from 44,225 in 1988, to 96,600 in 1993, to 180,713 in 1996.[14] The vast majority of these repatriations, 99.5 percent in 1995, were of citizens of the neighboring Southern African Development Community countries. In 1995, Mozambicans alone accounted for 131,689 of the 157,084 persons repatriated, and Zimbabweans were the second largest group, with 17,548 deportations. Other countries with a significant number of repatriations in 1995 were Lesotho (4,073), Malawi (1,154), Swaziland (837), and Tanzania (836). Although figures for 1997 show a slight decline in numbers deported, they remain high: South Africa

---

[11]National Assembly, "Minister of Home Affairs: Introductory Speech, Budgetary Appropriation," August 9, 1994.

[12]Jonathan Crush, "Exaggerated Figures Are Creating a Xenophobic Atmosphere," *Business Day*, June 30, 1997.

[13]Department of Home Affairs fax to Human Rights Watch, dated January 27, 1998.

[14]Crush, "Covert Operations," p.21.

deported 176,351 persons in 1997, including 146,285 Mozambicans and 21,673 Zimbabweans.[15]

It is unclear whether this quadrupling of deportations in less than a decade is a result of a stepped-up campaign to identify, arrest, and deport migrants, or instead reflects a similar absolute rise in the total number of undocumented migrants in South Africa. Some of the deportees interviewed by Human Rights Watch felt that there had been a definite increase in the efforts to trace, arrest, and deport undocumented migrants from South Africa. When asked if Mozambicans were also deported by the previous government, one recent Mozambican deportee responded:

> They were, but not the way it is happening now. Before, you could work for a year without having these problems. Now things are difficult. They arrest many people. You can't work for three weeks without getting arrested. If you have bad luck, you won't complete two days. Sometimes, they come and arrest you the day before pay-day, and you lose your money.[16]

Many migrants who are deported, especially those deported to neighboring countries, return almost immediately to South Africa. For some undocumented workers from these countries, arrest and deportation is a relatively routine, albeit unpleasant, part of working and residing in South Africa. Police and army officials repeatedly told Human Rights Watch about migrants whom they had arrested and deported dozens of times, and many of the persons interviewed by us had been previously deported—and frequently told us that they would return again to South Africa. Thus, deportation statistics are not a reliable method to estimate the total population of undocumented migrants in South Africa, since the same person is often counted multiple times. The creation of fourteen Internal Tracing Units within the South African Police Service since 1994, and the increasingly visible role of the South African Defence National Force in migrants control suggests that

---

[15]Department of Home Affairs, "Repatriation of Illegal Aliens," statistics supplied to Human Rights Watch via fax dated January 27, 1998.

[16]Nicola Johnston and Caetano Simbine, "The Usual Victims: The Aliens Control Act and the Voices of Mozambicans," in Jonathan Crush (ed.), *Beyond Control: Immigration Policy in a Democratic South Africa* (Cape Town, South African Migration Project, 1998).

the rise in repatriations is at least partly related to a rise in aggressive enforcement of immigration control laws.

Brief History of Migration to South Africa

Labor Migration to South Africa
South Africa has for well over a century been the center of an extensive system of labor migration in the southern African region.   Foreign mine workers have traditionally made up at least forty percent of the South African mine labor force, and in the 1960s foreigners represented eighty percent of mine workers.[17] Mozambique, Botswana, Lesotho, and Swaziland have historically provided the bulk of the mine labor, with Zimbabwe and Malawi providing smaller numbers. Work on the mines is one of the most important employment opportunities available to citizens of the main source countries, and these countries depend heavily on the income produced which returns to the home country through a system of mandatory remittances.   For example, a 1995 World Bank study commented on the importance of mine work to Lesotho's economy:

> Most important is Lesotho's export of human capital to South Africa, hence, its reputation as a labor pool for South Africa's mines. The 1986 census found that nearly half of Lesotho's adult male workers were employed in South Africa.   In the 1980s, remittances from Basotho laborers working in South Africa accounted for about half of country's gross national product (GNP), and equaled 100% of its gross domestic product (GDP). Today, about 40 % of the Basotho male labor force is employed in South Africa, and remittances account for a third of GNP.[18]

Historically, this migration system was regulated through a highly formalized system of bilateral contracts with neighboring countries for the purpose of supplying labor to the mines and for the large farms. These bilateral

---

[17]Jonathan Crush, "Contract Migration to South Africa: Past, Present and Future," Research Paper prepared for the Green Paper on International Migration, 1997. Available at http://www.polity.org.za:80/govdocs/green_papers/migration/crush.html (last visited February 10, 1998).

[18]Sechaba Consultants, "Riding the Tiger: Lesotho Miners and Permanent Residence in South Africa," *South Africa Migration Project Migration Policy Series No. 2* (Cape Town: South African Migration Project, 1997), p. 1.

intergovernmental treaties regulated the terms of employment and conditions of access to the South African labor market, including recruitment procedures, wages, mandatory remittance procedures, and the appointment of labor officials to oversee and protect the interests of the foreign workers.[19]   The entire process was implemented by the privately run Employment Bureau of Africa (TEBA) which has historically monopolized mine recruitment in Southern Africa.

The post-apartheid government inherited a series of bilateral labor agreements with the governments of Mozambique, Lesotho, Botswana, Swaziland, and Malawi.[20]   Foreign mine workers continue to be a large component of mine labor—currently estimated at about 200,000 persons or 50 percent of all mine workers—but the South African transition is having a major impact on the bilateral treaty system. The South African Department of Labor has proposed abolishing the bilateral labor agreement system, arguing that the treaties "do not conform in many respects to ILO norms and standards, that they are not uniform and that they are outmoded."[21] The South African government announced an amnesty in 1995 aimed at offering permanent residence status to foreign mine workers who had been in the country since 1986 and a significant number of foreign mine workers accepted this offer. An increasing number of foreign miners are being recruited through a sub-contracting system, a process that classifies them as temporary workers and exempts them from union wage agreements, death and benefit schemes, and retirement saving schemes.[22] Sub-contracting takes place both through the TEBA-administered system and through the direct recruitment of undocumented workers within South Africa. Improved working conditions on the mines have attracted an increasing number of South Africans to the industry, while at the same time the overall number of jobs available on the mines has declined, leading to heightened tensions between local and foreign miners and contributing to the outbreak of violence on some mines.

---

[19]Crush, "Covert Operations," p. 12.

[20]Ibid., p.10.

[21]Ibid, footnote 34, citing Guy Standing, John Sender and John Weeks, *Restructuring the Labour Market: The South African Challenge* (Geneva: International Labor Office, 1996), p. 177.

[22]Crush, "Contract Migration," p. 6. The National Union of Mineworkers (NUM) has described the subcontracting scheme as representing a "new path to poverty and oppression."

South Africa has had similar arrangements in place to regulate the employment of undocumented workers on South African farms. In the case of Mozambique, a labor office in Nelspruit and a recruitment office in Ressano Garcia aid South African farmers to obtain the required documents from the Department of Home Affairs for the recruitment of Mozambican labor. However, the ready availability of undocumented migrant farm workers prompts many farmers to flout the official recruitment procedures. Officially, a farmer is supposed to apply for a permit from the Department of Home Affairs which allows him legally to recruit a number of foreign farm workers, after a determination by the Department of Home Affairs that he cannot find adequate local labor. The undocumented migrants—most often, the farmer just recruits among the undocumented migrants already present in the region—then receive temporary work permits that legalize their status. In reality, many farmers never apply for the permit, partly because of the complex and time-consuming process and partly because an illegal worker is unlikely to approach the authorities about abuse because of fear of deportation. Even where a farmer has legalized his workers, the employee rarely benefits. In many cases, the farmer will keep the documents conferring legal status from the employee, thereby effectively forcing the employee to stay on the grounds of the farm because he could otherwise be apprehended and deported.

The Destabilization of the Frontline States[23] by the Apartheid Regime

One of the main causes of migration between the Southern African Development Community (SADC) states and South Africa is the high level of economic disparity in the region. For example, South Africa's per capita GNP is thirty-five times greater than that of neighboring Mozambique.[24] For some citizens of poor neighboring states, labor migration to South Africa is the most promising means of overcoming economic deprivation and ensuring the continued survival of the household in Mozambique. Army officials told us how Mozambican children would sometimes cross the border solely to beg for food from the soldiers. The importance of this economic disparity in fueling migration is demonstrated by the comparatively low level of migration to South Africa from its neighbor

---

[23]The term "frontline states" refers to the southern African countries who suffered the brunt of South Africa's destabilization efforts in the region. These states later came together to form the Southern African Development and Co-ordination Conference (SADCC, now SADC), and included Angola, Botswana, Malawi, Mozambique, Namibia, Swaziland, Tanzania, Zambia, and Zimbabwe.

[24]"Southern Africa Dreams of Unity," *The Economist*, September 2, 1995, p. 35.

Botswana, a country which has per capita income levels comparable to those of South Africa.

The causes of Southern Africa's economic stagnation are complex, and are at least partly caused by economic mismanagement and the pursuit of misguided economic policies in the region. The apartheid state's campaign to destabilize its neighbors is also an important contributing factor. As neighboring states became independent in the 1960s and 1970s, they became increasingly vocal in their opposition to apartheid policies in South Africa and assisted anti-apartheid organizations within their borders. In response, the increasingly militaristic government in South Africa, led by then-State President P. W. Botha, announced in 1978 that it would pursue a "total strategy" against the "total onslaught" of its opponents.[25] Over the next decade, South Africa launched a major campaign aimed at destabilizing its critics in the region.

A complete reckoning of the impact of the destabilization campaign launched by the apartheid state is beyond the subject area of the current report. South Africa occupied Namibia until 1990, in the face of international condemnation by the U.N. General Assembly, the U.N. Security Council, and the International Court of Justice. South Africa backed the rebel groups National Union for the Total Liberation of Angola (*União Nacional para a Independência Total de Angola*, UNITA) in Angola and Mozambique National Resistance (*Resistência Nacional Moçambicana*, RENAMO) in Mozambique. When UNITA came close to defeat, the South African Defence Force (SADF, now renamed the South African National Defence Force, SANDF) repeatedly intervened directly in Angola, as for example in 1981 when an estimated 10,000 SADF troops invaded Cunene Province of Angola. Decades of South African-sponsored conflict in Angola and Mozambique led to an almost complete destruction of transportation systems, educational institutions, agricultural production, safe water facilities, and the entire economic base of these countries. In 1982, South African forces invaded the Lesotho capital of Maseru in search of anti-apartheid guerrillas, killing twelve Basotho and thirty South Africans in the process. A similar attack in Gaborone, Botswana, in June 1985 left twelve people dead.[26]

---

[25]Joseph Hanlon, *Beggar Your Neighbours: Apartheid Power in Southern Africa* (Bloomington, Ind.: Indiana University Press, 1986); Phyllis Johnson and David Martin, *Apartheid Terrorism: The Destabilization Report* (London: Commonwealth Secretariat and James Currey, 1989).

[26]Asmal et al., *Reconciliation through Truth*, pp.175-76.

    South Africa played an extensive role in supporting the rebel group
RENAMO, thereby fueling armed conflict in Mozambique, source of the majority
of undocumented migrants currently in South Africa.   RENAMO received
extensive support from the apartheid state. As Zimbabwe gained independence on
April 18, 1980, the rear bases of RENAMO were transferred from Zimbabwe to
new bases in the South African lowveld, especially Phalaborwa in the Northern
Transvaal.[27] As discussed in an earlier report by Human Rights Watch on human
rights abuses in Mozambique:

> The transfer marked a turning point in the war, which, instead of dying
> down, soon began to escalate. The South African government used
> RENAMO as a tool for destabilizing Mozambique and as a bargaining
> counter against [President] Machel's support for the African National
> Congress (ANC); its aims were disabling Mozambique's infrastructure,
> bringing FRELIMO [*Frente de Libertação de Moçambique*, Front for the
> Liberation of Mozambique, the ruling party] to the bargaining table, and
> ultimately overthrowing FRELIMO and replacing it with a more amenable
> government.[28]

RENAMO's tactics soon earned the rebel movement a well-deserved reputation for
savagery. RENAMO rebels often targeted civilian populations and were feared for
their policy of mutilating civilians, including children, by "cutting off ears, noses,
lips, and sexual organs."[29] In addition, RENAMO destroyed almost the entire
infrastructure of Mozambique, in a calculated campaign targeting transport links,
health clinics, and schools. Between 1980 and 1988, RENAMO destroyed an
estimated 1,800 schools, 720 health clinics, and 1,300 buses and trucks.[30] Roy A.

---

[27]Alex Vines, *RENAMO: From Terrorism to Democracy in Mozambique?*
(London: James Currey, 1991), pp. 18-19.

[28]Africa Watch (now the Africa Division of Human Rights Watch), *Conspicuous
Destruction: War, Famine & The Reform Process in Mozambique* (New York: Human
Rights Watch, 1992), pp. 26-27.

[29]Ibid.

[30]Ibid. RENAMO's campaign against civilians was documented by a U.S.
Department of State commissioned report which led to a significant decrease in U.S. support
for the RENAMO movement, which had received some U.S. support by portraying itself as

Stacey, a U.S. Deputy Assistant of State for African Affairs, responded to reports of RENAMO abuses in unequivocal tones which are worth repeating when assessing South Africa's responsibility for RENAMO abuses:

> What has emerged in Mozambique is one of the most brutal holocausts against ordinary human beings since World War II.... The supporters of RENAMO, wherever they may be, cannot wash the blood from their hands unless all support for the unconscionable violence is halted immediately.... RENAMO is waging a war of terror against innocent Mozambican civilians through forced labor, starvation, physical abuse and wanton killings.[31]

The destruction of Angola's infrastructure followed similar lines. However, instead of relying solely on support for the rebel group UNITA, South Africa also conducted an extensive direct military campaign in Angola, involving thousands of troops. As described in an earlier Human Rights Watch report, "Through this war and extensive economic sabotage and widespread guerrilla warfare, UNITA and South Africa continue to devastate the country even further. Physical damages were estimated by the United Nations Security Council Commission as U.S. $ 17.6 billion between 1975 and 1985, the first ten years of independence."[32]

As post-apartheid revelations are making increasingly clear, the apartheid state carried out many more such destructive acts, overtly and covertly, in the region in order to bring its opponents into submission. One of its strongest tools was the economic embargo, especially against the landlocked states of Swaziland, Lesotho, and Botswana, which were heavily dependent on South African transport routes. One of the favorite targets of the destabilization campaign were the transport

---

an anti-Marxist movement. See Robert Gersony, *Summary of Mozambican Refugee Accounts of Principally Conflict-Related Experience in Mozambique: Report Submitted to Ambassador Moore and Dr. Chester A. Crocker* (Washington: Department of State Bureau for Refugee Programs, 1988). While the Gersony report focused exclusively on RENAMO abuses, all parties to the conflict in Mozambique committed serious human rights abuses, as documented in the reports of Human Rights Watch and other human rights organizations.

[31]James Brooke, "Visiting State Department Official Condemns Mozambique's Rebels," *New York Times*, April 27, 1988.

[32]Africa Watch (now the Africa Division of Human Rights Watch), *Angola: Violations of the Laws of War by Both Sides* (New York: Human Rights Watch, 1989), p. 8. See also, Africa Watch, *Land Mines in Angola* (New York: Human Rights Watch, 1993), pp. 4-11.

routes and oil supply lines in the region, which effectively disrupted any economic activity in the SADC states. A 1989 United Nations Children's Fund (UNICEF) report estimated that the South African destabilization campaign claimed 1.3 million lives and resulted in an economic loss to the SADC states estimated at U.S. $60 billion,[33] an estimate echoed by President Nelson Mandela who has put the loss of life at 2 million and the economic cost to the region at U.S. $62 billion.[34]

Although the past destabilization campaign features little in the public debate on migration today, some politicians have referred to this history and the questions of equity it raises, arguing that South Africa has a duty to redress the suffering it caused in the region with its past policies. Minister of Water Affairs Kader Asmal expressed such sentiments in a recent book:

> The front line states, which became the flashpoint of the civilised world's revulsion against apartheid, bore an involuntarily large share of the costs of the global resistance. It is something we must not forget in current debates over regional cooperation—and when faced with xenophobic calls for the expulsion or demonisation of "illegal aliens" from next door. The culpability of the old South Africa, its continuing responsibility for ongoing suffering on our cross-border door step, cannot be so easily evaded.[35]

Mpumalanga premier Matthews Phosa has expressed similar sentiments, urging a regional approach to the migration issue which takes into account the negative impact of apartheid on the region.[36]

---

[33]United Nations Children's Fund, "Children on the Frontline—1989 Update," (New York: United Nations, 1989), pp. 11, 38. See also Southern African Development Coordination Conference (SADCC), "The Cost of Destabilization: Memorandum Presented by SADCC to the 1985 Summit of the OAU" (1985); United Nations Economic Commission for Africa, "South African Destabilization: The Economic Cost of Frontline Resistance to Apartheid," (New York: United Nations, 1989).

[34]Nelson Mandela, "South Africa's Future Foreign Policy," *Foreign Affairs* 72 (5) (1993), p. 93.

[35]Asmal et al., *Reconciliation Through Truth*, p. 175.

[36]"Apartheid Created Southern Africa Refugee Crisis—Phosa," South African Press Association (SAPA), June 12, 1997.

The Repatriation of Mozambican Refugees

As the South-African sponsored RENAMO-FRELIMO conflict in Mozambique began to escalate in 1984, significant numbers of Mozambicans fled the fierce fighting and sought refuge in the Gazankulu and KaNgwane homelands of South Africa. To make it to relative safety in South Africa, Mozambican refugees had to pass through an electric fence capable of carrying lethal voltages, and often spent four or five days walking across the Kruger Park, a huge game reserve along the Mozambican border, avoiding dangerous animals as well as border patrols. Many people died while attempting to cross the fence between 1986 and 1990, when the border fence carried a lethal current of 3,300 volts and 1,000 amps.[37] The refugees were never formally recognized by South Africa. Although the government did reach an agreement with the Gazankulu and KaNgwane homelands to house the refugees, this agreement restricted the refugees to the homelands.[38] By 1990, it was estimated that as many as 350,000 Mozambican refugees were living in the nominally independent homelands.[39]

The refusal of the South African government to recognize the Mozambicans as refugees prevented international agencies such as UNHCR from providing urgently needed services to them and exacerbated bad living conditions and lack of employment opportunities.[40] The refugees were not issued any identification documents by the South African government and were frequently arrested if they moved outside designated areas. Their uncertain status, the lack of government

---

[37]Anthony Minnaar and Mike Hough, *Who Goes There?: Perspectives on Clandestine Migration and Illegal Aliens in Southern Africa* (Pretoria: Human Sciences Research Council, 1996) (estimating that 94 persons were electrocuted at the fence between 1986 and 1989).

[38]Chris Dolan and Vusi Nkuna, "'Refugees', 'Illegal Aliens', and the Labor Market—The Case for a Rights Based Approach to Labor Movement in South Africa" (Acornhoek: University of Witwatersrand Rural Facility, undated), p. 3. The apartheid government's refusal to recognize the Mozambican refugees stands in sharp contrast to its earlier welcome of white Mozambican and Rhodesian settlers who decided to leave their countries after the overthrow of colonial regimes in these states, again showing the racial bias in immigration practices of the apartheid government.

[39]Chris Dolan, "Policy Choices for the New South Africa," in Richard De Villiers and Maxine Reitzes (eds.), *Southern African Migration: Domestic and Regional Policy Implications* (Johannesburg: Centre for Policy Studies, 1995), pp. 53-8.

[40]Crush, "Covert Operations," p. 17.

protection, and the lack of relief efforts made the desperate refugees easy targets for economic exploitation by farmers in the region.[41] The lack of documentation, in particular, still causes problems today.

The office of the United Nations High Commissioner for Refugees (UNHCR) had attempted to reach an agreement with the South African government about the status of the Mozambican refugees since as early as 1985, but was repeatedly rebuffed by the apartheid government.[42] Following the peace accord between RENAMO and FRELIMO in Rome in 1992, the South African government signed a Basic Agreement with UNHCR on September 6, 1993, followed by a Tripartite Agreement between South Africa, Mozambique, and UNHCR on September 15, 1993, under which the South African government belatedly granted "group refugee status" to the Mozambican population. Even then, identity documents were never issued to the refugees, so that their freedom of movement and to seek employment continued to be restricted to the homeland areas, even after they were formally abolished in 1994.[43]

Following the Tripartite Agreement, UNHCR began the implementation of a voluntary repatriation program for Mozambican refugees, aiming to resettle 240,000 Mozambican refugees over the following two years.[44] Judged by its initial goals, the voluntary repatriation program was a failure:

By the end of the repatriation in April 1995 the total number of people returned under the organised repatriation was 31,589, while the total returns to Mozambique from South Africa stood at 67,060 in December 1995, suggesting that UNHCR/IOM [International Organization for Migration] assisted less than half of those who wished to repatriate from South Africa. By contrast, an astonishing 80,926 Mozambicans were forcibly deported by the South African National Defence Forces and South

---

[41]Ibid.

[42]Dolan and Nkuna, "'Refugees'," p. 3.

[43]Ibid. This practice continues to some extent today, as Human Rights Watch learned: Mozambican communities in the Bushbuckridge area, a former homeland, are relatively free from police harassment unless they try to move to urban areas.

[44]Chris Dolan, "The Changing Status of Mozambicans in South Africa and the Impact of This on Repatriation to and Re-integration in Mozambique," (Final Report to Norwegian Refugee Council, February 1997), p. 2.

African Police in 1993 alone, followed by 71,279 in 1994, despite the fact that the Government's official position was that "The voluntary character of the repatriation operation would be adhered to until the Cessation clause was invoked, after which the residual caseload would be dealt with in terms of the Aliens Control Act."[45]

In May 1996, a meeting of the Tripartite commission between the governments of Mozambique and South Africa and the UNHCR resolved that: "In view of the peace and stability which have returned to Mozambique and the fundamental and sustained change that has taken place, Mozambican refugees will not have refugee status after 31 December 1996. ... The status of Mozambicans who elect to remain in South Africa after 31 December 1996 will be determined according to accepted international principles and the applicable South African laws."[46]

The SADC Amnesty

In early 1996, the South African cabinet agreed to grant a limited amnesty to nationals of Southern African Development Community (SADC) countries. According to the conditions announced by Minister of Home Affairs Mangosuthu Buthelezi on June 4, 1996 and additional conditions contained in internal Department of Home Affairs guidelines, citizens of the SADC countries would be granted permanent residence if they could prove they had continuously lived in South Africa since at least July 1, 1991, had no criminal record, and were either economically active or married to a South African, or had dependent children who were born or were residing lawfully in South Africa.

The Department of Home Affairs had originally stated that out of an estimated two to four million undocumented migrants, they expected "about one million of them to qualify for permanent residence in terms of the recent cabinet decision in this regard."[47] Minister Buthelezi stressed later that the amnesty should not be seen as a relaxing of immigration controls:

---

[45]Ibid, p. 3.

[46]Joint Communique by the Deputy Minister of Home Affairs, South Africa, the Vice Minister of Foreign Affairs and Cooperation of Mozambique, and the United Nations High Commissioner for Refugees, dated June 3, 1996.

[47]"Millions could get residence in SA," *The Citizen*, June 25, 1996.

South Africa has extended a gesture of goodwill to its neighbouring countries by granting these exemptions. This gesture should not be construed as a softening of our approach to illegal immigrants. To the contrary, it provides the moral high ground, after a period of discrimination, to deal with the problem stricter according to the Aliens Control Act.[48]

In light of the expectations of the cabinet and the Department of Home Affairs, the SADC amnesty proved a failure. Only 124,073 persons were granted permanent residence, out of a total of 201,602 applications, while 77,108 persons were rejected.[49] Another 50,692 migrant workers were granted permanent residence under a separate amnesty previously announced by the Department of Home Affairs after discussions with the National Union of Mineworkers, bringing the total to about 175,000, still far short of the expected one million.[50]

The reasons for the low take-up of the SADC amnesty are complex, but include a general lack of access to information among the target population due to poverty and illiteracy, costs associated with applications, fear of detection, as well as corruption within the application process. Many Mozambicans live in rural areas and illiteracy rates are high, so news of the amnesty only reached many eligible persons during its final weeks. Others were afraid that the information obtained by the Department of Home Affairs would be used to deport them if their application was turned down, a fear which seems to have been justified. Human Rights Watch interviewed three rejected applicants who received instead seven-day permits and

---

[48]Minister of Home Affairs Mangosuthu Buthelezi, "Parliamentary Media Briefing," February 13, 1997. The Minister continued: "I would, therefore, appeal to the various service departments such as welfare, education, housing, etc, as well as Provincial Governments as well as private employers, to request the identity documents or passports of all foreigners requesting services subsidized by the government and in this way ensure that they do not gain access to services in short supply to our own people."

[49]Department of Home Affairs, "SADC Exemption Statistics: Grand total for the whole of South Africa," fax from the Department of Home Affairs to Human Rights Watch, dated January 27, 1998; "More than 100,000 SADC immigrants given citizenship," *Star*, April 11, 1997; "174,000 aliens to stay," *Pretoria News*, September 11, 1997.

[50]"174,000 aliens to stay," *Pretoria News*, September 11, 1997.

were told they had to leave the country within this period.[51] Repeated visits—first to apply, then to check criminal records, again to bring supporting documents and to check on the progress of the application—to often far-away Home Affairs offices also placed the process beyond the reach of many families, who found the cost of taxi fare and loss of work hours too expensive.

One of the major impediments to an effective amnesty process was the petty corruption that accompanied it.   According to Refugee Research Project coordinator Nicola Johnston,

> It was too expensive for many to travel to the local Home Affairs office to make the applications. There were also hidden costs of corruption, which made it difficult for them. Headmen, for example, were charging about nineteen rands [U.S. $ 3.80] for a referral letter stating how long the person had been in the country, clerks were demanding six rands [U.S. $ 1.20] to take fingerprints, and people were having to pay twenty rands [U.S. $ 4.00] to clerks to speed up their applications.[52]

Tribal authorities were often called upon to write a referral letter to prove the applicant's length of stay in the area, and used this opportunity to ask for a "fee," sometimes referred to as "chief's money," ranging between ten and ninety rands [U.S. $ 2-18]. One applicant stated that "the Tribal Authority refers us to the chief to fetch a referral letter, and the referral letter costs ninety rands [U.S. $ 18]."[53] Another applicant told of a similar experience, stating that,

> we knew about the amnesty, it has been broadcast over the radio. The problem is that the Tribal Office wants a sum of twenty rands [U.S. $ 4], to give you a referral letter, proving that you are a resident of New Forest.

---

[51]Human Rights Watch interviewed two such persons at the Department of Home Affairs offices on Harrison Street, Johannesburg, on July 1, 1996, and a third person at the same location on July 2, 1996.

[52]Marion Edmunds, "Another Amnesty offer after poor results," *Mail & Guardian*, April 25, 1997.

[53]Nicola Johnston, "Permanent Residency Exemption for SADC Citizens: South Africa Welcoming its Neighbours or Monitoring 'Outsiders'?, The Case of Mozambicans in the rural Eastern border region of South Africa (Cape Town: Southern Africa Migration Project, 1997).

So you are supposed to take that letter to Thulamahashe to apply for amnesty. So the money we are spending for amnesty is thirty-five rands [U.S. $ 7], because at Thulamahashe we are supposed to pay fifteen rands [U.S. $ 3] for photos.[54]

Women in particular had a difficult time applying for the amnesty, especially in rural areas. The application model envisioned a principal applicant filling out the form for an entire family, but this was complicated by the fact that many eligible women live in remote rural areas while their husbands work in urban areas. In the traditional culture, men are regarded as the head of the household and wives have to seek permission from their husbands before taking a significant step such as applying for amnesty. In the words of one Mozambican woman, "I am married and could not do anything without the permission of my husband."[55] This strong male bias was reinforced by Home Affairs officials, who often told unaccompanied women applicants to return and apply with their husbands if married:

On my first day, they told me to come with a letter from the tribal office, and I did as I was told. Then the following day I came with that letter, and they said to me that I must come with my husband. I don't know where to find him, because he is not here. He is at his work place. He left here a long time ago. He has been away for more than a year now, and I have not heard from him. So how am I supposed to go there with him, when I don't know where he is? This is really frustrating. When we heard that we must go and apply for ID books, we thought that everybody was encouraged to do so, only to find that it is really difficult for women.... I have already lost courage of getting there again. I will not go there anymore. Maybe if my husband was here, I would have applied already.[56]

Amnesty applicants who were denied were told they could appeal these decisions within thirty days but were often not furnished with reasons for their denial, making it very difficult to offer an effective appeal against a negative

---

[54]Ibid.

[55]Ibid.; see Human Rights Watch, *Violence Against Women in South Africa: The State Response to Domestic Violence and Rape* (New York: Human Rights Watch, 1995) for a discussion of the law relating to women in South Africa.

[56]Johnston, "Permanent Residency Exemption for SADC Citizens."

decision. Because of these and other problems, many eligible candidates for permanent residence status did not apply for the SADC amnesty and continue to live in South Africa while classified as "illegal." This is particularly unfortunate as the SADC amnesty was seen as a rectification of the injustices of the apartheid period, when black immigrants simply were ineligible for permanent residence status due to racist legislation.

According to the Department of Home Affairs and the Chair of the Parliamentary Portfolio Committee on Home Affairs, Desmond Lockey M.P., the cabinet has approved an additional amnesty which will focus exclusively on former Mozambican refugees still living in South Africa.[57] This additional amnesty grows out of the Tripartite Agreement between South Africa, Mozambique, and UNHCR on the repatriation of the Mozambican refugees, which resolved that "The Status of Mozambicans who elect to remain in South Africa after 31 December 1996, will be determined according to accepted international principles and applicable South African laws."[58] It presumably represents a recognition that many "Mozambicans" who fled their country during its civil war have in fact been in South Africa for a decade or more, or have grown up in South Africa, and have never had their status satisfactorily regularized, despite the Tripartite Agreement between the South African and Mozambican governments and UNHCR. Although this decision was taken by the cabinet in the middle of 1997, the Department of Home Affairs is continuing to work out the actual procedure that will be followed to determine the status of applicants. According to Mr. Schravesande of the Department of Home Affairs, the procedure is complicated by the fact that South Africa never recognized the status of the refugees, and the refugees were thus never registered or issued with documents which could now be used to prove their past status. Human Rights Watch hopes that some of the deficiencies of the previous amnesty process will be addressed and remedied by the Mozambican refugee amnesty process.

---

[57]Human Rights Watch interview with Mr. Desmond Lockey M.P., Chair, Parliamentary Portfolio Committee on Home Affairs, New Parliament Buildings, Cape Town, December 9, 1997; Human Rights Watch interview with Mr. Claude Schravesande, Director, Admissions and Aliens Control, Department of Home Affairs, Pretoria, December 3, 1997.

[58]Joint Communique by the Deputy Minister of Home Affairs, South Africa, the Vice Minister of Foreign Affairs and Cooperation of Mozambique, and the United Nations High Commissioner for Refugees, dated June 3, 1996.

IV. THE TREATMENT OF UNDOCUMENTED MIGRANTS
IN SOUTH AFRICA

Labor Exploitation

Undocumented migrants are employed in a variety of sectors of the South African economy, and form one of the most exploited and vulnerable groups of workers in the country. Because of their illegal status, undocumented migrants are compelled to "accept employment whatever the payment, risk, physical demand or working hours involved."[59] Undocumented migrants from Mozambique and Zimbabwe are especially prevalent in the farm sector in Mpumalanga and Northern provinces, and also in the construction sector in Johannesburg.

The undocumented and thus "illegal" status of many Mozambicans prevents them from approaching the authorities for redress of grievances and gives employers tremendous power over their workers. Human Rights Watch discovered several cases in which employers laid off workers at the end of a work period without paying them their earned wage. In one case, workers at a farm near Pretoria were told to "take a day off" two days before the end of their first work month, only to find the gate locked when they returned and a new team of illegal workers employed in their place. They were told to leave the premises or face arrest. According to the gate-keeper at the compound, the newly hired workers faced the same fate at the end of their first month.[60] In the wealthy Parktown suburb of Johannesburg, a Mozambican gardener who complained to his white employer about not having been paid for the past two months promptly found himself reported to the police, arrested, and deported.[61]

Abuses committed by white farmers and their foremen against undocumented migrants appear to be especially common and severe. Undocumented migrants working as farm workers are among the lowest paid workers in the country, earning on average as little as five to ten rands [U.S. $ 1-2] per day. For example, Sylvester Langa, a farm worker interviewed while awaiting deportation at Komatipoort police station, told us he earned 250 rands [U.S. $ 50] per month

---

[59]Maxine Reitzes, "Alien Issues," *Indicator SA* 12(1), 1994, pp. 7-11.

[60]Human Rights Watch interview with gate keeper, Pretoria, August 1995.

[61]Human Rights Watch interview with gardener who had returned to South Africa after his deportation, Parktown, March 1996.

working on a farm.[62] Local farm workers, although also subject to many abuses, earn significantly more, about 800 to 1,000 rands [U.S. $ 160-200] per month.[63] Similar abuses exist in other trades as well, especially in the building trade. Lodric Ndlovu, who was earning twenty rands [U.S. $ 4] per day working in the construction industry, told Human Rights Watch that at his previous job, he was paid eight rands [U.S. $ 1.60] per completed structure, a task which often took longer than one week.[64] Undocumented migrants are forced to work very long hours and are abused by foremen and security personnel. Mr. Ngobeni, a Mozambican farm worker who told us he earned five rands [U.S. $ 1] per day, complained that he and other workers were often beaten to make them work harder: "We must always run when we work, even when carrying boxes of bananas. The foremen slapped me hard because they said I wasn't working hard enough."[65] In the words of Captain Liebenberg, Superintendent of Komatipoort police station,

> This poor guy from Mozambique, he will do anything just to get those few bucks to get on with life. He will take any abuse. The salaries on the farms are very low—a lorry driver gets fifteen rands [U.S. $ 3] a day, but normally the workers get between five rands [U.S. $ 1] and ten rands [U.S. $ 2] a day. And 95 percent are Mozambican.[66]

---

[62]Human Rights Watch interview with Sylvester Langa, Mozambican citizen, Komatipoort police station, December 2, 1997.

[63]The range of wages is based on interviews with former farm workers currently involved in informal businesses in Soweto, recent deportees in Mozambique, street vendors in Johannesburg, and farm workers awaiting deportation.

[64]Human Rights Watch interview with Lodric Ndlovu, New Forest settlement, Bushbuckridge, November 30, 1997.

[65]Human Rights Watch interview with Z. Ngobeni, Mozambican citizen, Komatipoort Police Station, December 2, 1997.

[66]Human Rights Watch interview with Captain Liebenberg, Superintendent of Komatipoort police station, December 2, 1997.

Captain Chilembe, head of the Internal Tracing Unit at Nelspruit, also described physical abuse of farm workers by farmers as "common."[67]

Many of the illegal immigrants working in the rural areas adjoining the Mozambican border are children, some as young as ten years old. Human Rights Watch interviewed a group of farm workers near Chongwe, Mpumalanga, including children as young as fourteen, but was forced to cut the interview short when a security guard approached us and asked us to leave.[68] An investigation into child labor by the *Mail & Guardian* newspaper found similar instances of child labor, including two boys, aged fifteen and sixteen, who were working twelve hours per day for a primary school teacher, earning only 150 rands [U.S. $ 30] per month.[69]

Although the Aliens Control Act provides for a mechanism to prosecute and fine employers in the amount of 20,000 rands [U.S. $ 4,000] per "illegal alien," Human Rights Watch found evidence of very few such prosecutions. According to one source,

> Very few farmers employing illegal aliens have been brought to court in the Mpumalanga province. In the last four years only six employers have been charged in the courts at Nelspruit, while only two received fines. One of the problems in prosecuting them has been the difficulty of proving that an illegal alien is employed on the farm, since a farmer's books merely show a cash entry under "wages."[70]

During our three-week investigation, Human Rights Watch was told of only a single prosecution of an employer of undocumented migrants, involving a contractor and his recruitment agent for employing about forty-five undocumented migrants on a building site. The undocumented workers from Mozambique were

---

[67]Human Rights Watch interview with Captain Chilembe, Head, Nelspruit Internal Tracing Unit, South African Police Service, Nelspruit, December 1, 1997.

[68]Human Rights Watch interview with farm workers aged 14, 16, 15, and 14 years, near Shongwe, December 1, 1997.

[69]Mukoni T. Ratshitanga, "Slave Labor in Northern Province," *Mail & Guardian*, November 14-20, 1997.

[70]Minnaar and Hough, *Who Goes There?*, p. 118.

kept in detention for two months at Pollsmoor prison in order to be available to testify at the trial.

During the early 1990s, it was a common practice of South African farmers to hire a group of undocumented migrants, make them work for a certain period of time (normally one or two months), and then call the local police station to have the farm workers deported without pay. Local police stations often were complicit in these practices, and rarely asked any questions of farmers who reported undocumented migrants for deportation. Although the practice appears less common today, our interviews suggest that such collaboration between local police stations and farmers continues in some areas. One farm worker who had opted to remain in Mozambique after suffering abuses on South African farms told us that at one farm he worked on, "at the end of the month, they sent a truck to pick us all up, and our wages were kept by the boss."[71]

Captain Chilembe, head of the Internal Tracing Unit in Nelspruit, in the heart of the South African farming area, ensured Human Rights Watch that police stations had been instructed to investigate farmers who reported undocumented migrants in order to ensure that the farmer was not trying to avoid paying his workers by having them deported.[72] However, when we visited the Komatipoort police station, we interviewed three young Mozambicans, aged between sixteen and eighteen years, who were being deported without the police questioning the farmer who had reported them, and who told us about abuse on the farm were they worked. Eighteen-year-old Albin Mashaba spoke for the three, describing their experience since coming to South Africa:

> We were arrested last night on the farm. The boss foreman took us to the gate of the farm and called the police. We worked collecting bananas, earning five rands [U.S. $ 1] per day. We worked from 6 a.m to 8 p.m. The foreman's name was Ngoma. We had no accommodation, so would sleep outside in the open. We received only a little food, not enough. At

---

[71]Human Rights Watch interview with Armando Ubisse, Matangomane, Mozambique, April 25, 1996.

[72]Human Rights Watch interview with Captain Chilembe, Head, Nelspruit Internal Tracing Unit, South African Police Services, Nelspruit, December 1, 1997. Captain Andre Nel, Superintendent of the Malelane Police Station, confirmed a similar practice: "If a farmer brings Mozambicans to the police station, we tell him he must pay the person before deportation. We started this practice in 1991." Human Rights Watch interview with Captain Andre Nel, Superintendent, Malelane Police Station, Malelane, December 1, 1997.

lunch we had to provide for ourselves. We only got half an hour for lunch and had to cook and eat very fast. There was never enough time to eat. There were different foremen, but they all beat us. They always wanted us to work faster. They beat us with the handle of a knife, and with baton sticks.

We don't know why we were arrested. The foreman said we were trying to run away. We couldn't leave, we were forced to stay on the farm. The farmer had paid us for the last two weeks, but the foreman took the ninety rands [U.S. $ 18] and called the police to have us deported. Now we have nothing. The policemen asked the foreman no questions, they just took us away. It is all very wrong. We were the ones working, and the foremen were the thieves.[73]

When Human Rights Watch tried to discuss the case of these three young men with the police officers on duty after the men had been deported, a disturbing problem came to light. It became clear that no paperwork had been prepared by the arresting officer, so the three didn't exist in the files of the Komatipoort police station. A sergeant on duty told us that he had just told the three young men to get on the bus, which was picking up the other detainees awaiting repatriation, and "go home."[74] When we discussed the treatment of the boys on the farm with the sergeant, he told us that he sees lots of beatings and even dog bites, but that the undocumented Mozambicans rarely want to press charges: They prefer to be deported rather than spend a long time in detention while the case drags on.[75] Captain Nel, superintendent of the Malelane Police Station, told us about similar problems with prosecuting farmers:

It is a big problem to prosecute farmers because the Mozambican has to serve as a witness, and so we have to keep the Mozambican in custody. Then we have to go to the Attorney-General to get permission to keep them

---

[73]Human Rights Watch interview with Albin Mashaba, 18-year-old Mozambican, Komatipoort Police Station, December 2, 1997. The other two farm workers arrested with him were Ernest, aged sixteen, and Domingo Jeshmeine, aged eighteen years.

[74]Human Rights Watch interview with Sergeant Mathebula, Komatipoort Police Station, December 2, 1997.

[75]Ibid.

in the cells. So the farmers just ask for extensions, and the poor farm worker stays in jail the whole time.[76]

A high-ranking police official who spoke on condition of anonymity claimed that political interference made it difficult to arrest and prosecute farmers for hiring undocumented migrants or abusing their workers: "We started prosecuting the farmers, but it's a big fight. It's a political issue. If we charge the farmers, they turn against the government. So higher up, they don't want us to charge the farmer."[77]

The almost complete lack of accountability for abuses committed against undocumented farm workers has led to some horrific instances of violence against undocumented migrants. According to one newspaper account, a Northern province farmer allegedly tested his rifle by shooting at the leg of one of his farm workers, who as a result had to have his foot amputated. At the time of the article, the farmer had not been prosecuted, and no compensation had been paid to the victim.[78]

The case of Florentino Edmundo Amade is equally disturbing. Amade was working for a crocodile farmer on a farm called Gravelotte, when he had a disagreement in June, 1993, with the farmer, Mr. Torre. The farmer denied him food for three days. After three days, Amade was caught by the farmer trying to eat a piece of the meat he was supposed to feed to the crocodiles. Amade claims he was beaten by the farmer, and later again by white police officers called by the farmer, who arrived in two police vans with dogs. At the end of the beating, Amade had a broken left arm and had several dog bites from police dogs.

Torre allegedly forced Amade to remain on the farm for several days without access to medical treatment, out of fear of being prosecuted for the beating. After three days, Torre took Amade to a doctor in town in the back of a pick-up truck used for transporting the meat for the crocodiles. The doctor refused to treat Amade, arguing that he should have been brought earlier. Amade walked himself to the nearby "black" Tintswalo Hospital, where he remained for two months to recover from his injuries. A legal case was opened by Amade against Torre, but

---

[76]Human Rights Watch interview with Captain Andre Nel, Malelane, December 1, 1997.

[77]Human Rights Watch interview, name of interviewee, place and date of interview on record.

[78]*Sowetan*, April 4, 1996.

it was dismissed after Torre allegedly lied to the court, saying that Amade had returned to Mozambique. Human Rights Watch last met with Amade in October 1997 and noted that his left arm remained virtually unusable and that Amade was unable to find employment because most physical work caused his arm to become painfully swollen. The farmer was never prosecuted, and no compensation was paid to Amade.[79]

Even when the police take action against abuses, it is often to the detriment of the undocumented migrant who has been victimized. According to press reports, five young undocumented migrants from Zimbabwe were languishing in Louis Trichardt prison for more than five months after being attacked with pick-ax handles, shocked with a cattle prod, and thrown off a moving pick-up truck by five men in the town of Vivo on the night of September 28, 1996.[80] According to the investigative officer, Sergeant Seckle, the five victims were being kept in custody out of fear that they might otherwise skip the country, and the case against the perpetrators would have to be withdrawn.[81] In another case, two Mozambicans who went to the police to report the theft of firewood which had taken them six weeks to collect found themselves arrested and deported instead.[82]

Self-employed immigrants involved in informal business such as vehicle and electrical repairs, vegetable selling, clothes repair, and shoe mending, are also vulnerable to exploitation. Sometimes, South Africans engage the services of such persons, but later collect their goods without paying. If the undocumented migrant dares to complain, he or she is in danger of being assaulted or reported to the police and deported. Human Rights Watch interviewed a Mozambican electrical engineer in Soweto who had a "smoking" car brought to him for repairs by a policeman in civilian clothes. When the work was completed, the officer returned in uniform to collect both the repaired car and the hapless engineer, who was driven to the police station and forced to pay a 500 rands [U.S. $ 100] bribe to the police officers

---

[79]Human Rights Watch interview with Florentino Edmundo Amade, Acornhoek, August 18, 1997, and October 23 and 24, 1997.

[80]Khathu Mamaila, "Five still locked up after assault: Complainants are still held behind bars while the accused are free," *Sowetan*, April 2, 1997.

[81]Ibid.

[82]The firewood had been stolen by the man whom they had asked to transport the firewood. Human Rights Watch interview with the mother of the two men, Champagne farms, Chochocho, February 1997.

before being released. Needless to say, he was never paid by the police officer for his repair work on the car.[83] Another self-employed undocumented Mozambican supplied a police officer with seat covers for his car but was never paid for the service.[84]

Reports have repeatedly surfaced about Mozambican women and children being sold into forced servitude or sexual bondage in South Africa by Mozambican smugglers. In 1990, a reporter from the *Mail & Guardian* wrote about purchasing two young Mozambican women, aged 14 and 17, and claimed that many more women were being offered to South African men as "wives."[85] Anti-Slavery International documented several similar cases of women being sold to South African men as "wives" in a 1992 report.[86] The clandestine nature of border crossings between South Africa and Mozambique and the rural remoteness of the South Africa border region make it difficult to monitor such abuses, and it is likely that they continue on some unknown scale. The significant rise in open prostitution in South Africa since liberalization of morality laws in the 1990s also raises concerns about the trafficking of women into South Africa for purposes of forced sexual labor.

Abuses During the Arrest Process

The Agencies Involved in the Detection of Undocumented Migrants

A number of agencies in South Africa play an important role in the detection and arrest of undocumented migrants, including different branches of the South African Police Service (SAPS), the Department of Home Affairs, and the South African National Defence Force (SANDF). In addition to these formal structures,

---

[83]Human Rights Watch interview with the electrical engineer, Mozambican citizen, Soweto, September 12, 1996.

[84]Human Rights Watch interview with RM, New Forest refugee camp, Mpumalanga, November 12, 1996.

[85]Eddie Koch & Phliip Molefe, "Exiles Sold As Slaves in South Africa," *Guardian* (London), November 16, 1990; see also Alex Vines, "Mozambique: Slaves and the Snake of Fire," *Anti-Slavery Reporter Vol. 13, No. 7,* 1991.

[86]Sally McKibbin, "Mozambican Victims of Slave Trade in South Africa" (London: Anti-Slavery International, 1992)

informal community structures are in existence to "aid" these agencies in tracking down and arresting undocumented migrants.

Most South African police stations play at least a contributory role in tracking down and arresting undocumented migrants during their ordinary duties. In urban centers with large numbers of undocumented migrants, such as Johannesburg, arrest records suggest that tracking down undocumented migrants is one of the major occupations of many police officers. Frequently, undocumented migrants are arrested in order to boost arrest figures. For example, when the Johannesburg police announced in June 1997 that they had arrested 11,916 suspects in recent crime sweeps as part of a high-density crime operation, a closer reading revealed that 5,776 of those arrested were undocumented immigrants.[87] Another Johannesburg crime prevention sweep over two days in September 1997 yielded about 1,400 arrests, of which 736 were undocumented migrants.[88] Because undocumented migrants are probably easier to track down and arrest than hardened criminals, including them in crime sweep arrest figures may improve the image of the police, but it also increases the perception among South Africans that there is a strong link between crime and undocumented migration.

The South African Police Service (SAPS) has also established a number of Internal Tracing Units (ITU), some formerly known informally as the "Maputo squads," which focus exclusively on the tracking down, identifying, and arrest of undocumented migrants. By the time of our investigation, at least fourteen such ITUs were operating in South Africa, mostly in major urban areas and in areas with high concentrations of undocumented migrants such as the border area with Mozambique. In addition to the ITUs, there exists a national Aliens Investigation Unit which concentrates on the organized inflow of undocumented migrants into South Africa and certain wide-spread fraudulent practices associated with the issuing of false documents.[89]

The Department of Home Affairs also identifies and arrests undocumented migrants, although it focuses mostly on processing the suspected undocumented

---

[87]"Johannesburg Police Arrest 11,916 Suspects in Crime Prevention Operations," *SAPA*, June 25, 1997.

[88]"Johannesburg Police Arrest 1,400 People in Crime-prevention Operation," *SAPA*, September 18, 1997.

[89]Anthony Minnaar and Mike Hough, "Illegal in South Africa: Scope, Extent and Impact," Paper presented at the International Organization for Migration (IOM) Conference in Pretoria, August 25, 1996, p. 7.

migrants detained by the police and army. Human Rights Watch interviewed a number of persons who had been arrested on the street by officials from the Department of Home Affairs, while police officials at Johannesburg Central police station confirmed that persons are detained directly by the Department of Home Affairs at their offices at 15 Market Street in Johannesburg.   The director of admissions and migrants control confirmed that the Department of Home Affairs itself traces and arrests suspected undocumented migrants.[90]

The South African National Defence Force (SANDF) plays an important role in the detection and arrest of suspected undocumented migrants. One company, comprising an estimated 200 soldiers, is constantly deployed on the Mozambican border. The army also uses mobile vehicle control points as well as road blocks to inspect vehicles and intercept undocumented migrants as they make their way to urban centers.[91] Undocumented migrants apprehended while attempting to cross the border are briefly detained at the substations near the border, where they are questioned before being transferred to the Macadamia army base.[92] From the Macadamia base, the detainees are transferred to the custody of the police at Komatipoort police station on the border with Mozambique.[93] Major Visser, the commanding officer of the company deployed at the border at the time of our visit, estimated that on average about thirty-five persons per day are detained by his troops at the border.[94] A road block easily nets more than 250 undocumented migrants.[95] Throughout South Africa, an estimated 6,490 soldiers are deployed each month to help combat crime, and these soldiers arrested 38,902 undocumented

---

[90]Human Rights Watch interview with Mr. Claude Schravesande, Director, Admissions and Aliens Control, Department of Home Affairs, Pretoria, December 3, 1997.

[91]Human Rights Watch interview with Major Olivier, Company Commander, Group 33, South African National Defence Forces, Komatipoort, December 1, 1997. Vehicle control points involve a single vehicle or helicopter which is deployed to quickly establish a control point which operates for only a few hours before being moved to a new location, while road blocks involve a more extensive deployment and usually remain in one location for a longer time.

[92]Ibid.

[93]Ibid.

[94]Ibid.

[95]Ibid.

migrants, compared to 5,075 criminal suspects between January and December 15, 1997.[96]

For its interception operations at the Mozambican border, the SANDF relies extensively on the 3,300-volt electric fence that separates South Africa from Maputo province in Mozambique. The fence runs for sixty-three kilometers between the Swaziland border and the South African border town of Komatipoort. Constructed in 1986 and turned on in August 1987, the fence was ostensibly created to prevent anti-apartheid guerrillas from the ANC and other liberation movements from infiltrating South Africa via Mozambique. The fence consists of six coils of ten-foot-high razor wire and ten electrified cables, each capable of carrying 3,300 volts. The fence itself is divided into eleven sections, with each section serviced by a substation and a generator to boost the current. Current levels can be set at two levels: lethal and non-lethal. It is estimated that more than one hundred people were killed from electrocution by the fence between its turn-on date and February 1990, when the South African authorities reported that the current on the fence was turned down to non-lethal levels and that the current was switched off from time to time.[97]

The use of a lower, non-lethal, current brings its own problems, with people "sticking" to the fence on occasion. Maria Macamo lives in Machava, outside Mozambique's capital city Maputo. She told Human Rights Watch in February 1997 that she had attempted to cross the electric fence south of Ressano Garcia in March 1996. She threw wet mud at the fence, and when she did not see any sparks, she assumed that it would be safe to cross through a passage dug underneath the fence by border jumpers. However, while attempting to pass underneath the fence, she accidentally touched some of the wires and got stuck to the fence, unable to move from the fence until a fellow Mozambican pulled her off. Her left arm was badly scarred, and she told us that she had lost most of the strength in that arm.

---

[96]These were the figures given by Minister of Defence Joe Modise in response to a parliamentary question from Colonel Nyambeni Ramaremisa (NP). "SANDF Operations Net 38,902 Illegal Immigrants," *SAPA*, December 15, 1997.

[97]Alex Vines, "Mozambique: Slaves and the Snake of Fire," *Anti-Slavery Reporter*, Series VII, 1991 vol.13, no.17, pp.41-43. The current was apparently turned off during periods of heavy fighting on the Mozambican side of the fence, in order to allow local persons to seek refuge in South Africa. Apparently, the South African authorities created a number of gates in the fence in order to facilitate the temporary movement into South Africa of Mozambicans fleeing heavy fighting. Minnaar and Hough, *Who Goes There?*, pp. 141-43.

Unable to perform many forms of physical labor, she now tries to eke out a living selling cashew nuts in Maputo.[98] She said she heard of many other Mozambicans who have been injured at the fence. Maputo's Central Hospital confirms that it receives a number of cases each year of people injured by the border fence, but it does not keep records.[99]

In addition to these formal structures, an increasing number of informal structures are also playing a role in tracing and arresting undocumented migrants. This development follows an August 1994 speech by Minister of Home Affairs Buthelezi in which he called upon the South African public to help his department curb the influx of foreigners by reporting suspected undocumented migrants.[100] Police officials have encouraged participation of the public by advertising toll-free "crime stop" numbers which persons can call to report undocumented migrants and by offering reward money for reporting undocumented migrants. According to a resident of Soweto, the Department of Home Affairs has similarly attempted to get the public involved in tracking down undocumented migrants:

> There has been a document issued by the Department of Home Affairs urging the locals to report any Mozambican to the police. It was sort of an underhanded activity, and they were not up-front about it since it was not an official document. But I know it was a police number you had to dial to. There was an unclear Home Affairs seal, and it indicated the reward was fifty rands [U.S. $ 10] per illegal alien.[101]

Senior police officials at Yeoville and Hillbrow confirmed that the public is encouraged to call "crime stop" numbers to report undocumented migrants, and

---

[98]Human Rights Watch interview with Maria Macamo, Maputo, February 11, 1997.

[99]Human Rights Watch interview with João Save, Maputo Central Hospital, Maputo, February 12, 1997.

[100]Minnaar and Hough, *Who Goes There?*, p. 184.

[101]Human Rights Watch interview with informant, Orlando West neighborhood of Soweto, August 17, 1996.

that they regularly trace undocumented migrants this way.[102] Colonel Raymond Dowd of the Western Cape Police Services has told the press that almost ten thousand rands [U.S. $ 2,000] had been paid out in reward money to the public for reporting undocumented migrants, and encouraged increased public participation "to enable the ITUs to fulfill their functions."[103]   Jurie de Wet, chief immigration officer for the Western Cape, recently wrote that his office had "already had discussions with the editor of the Khayelitsha News to ask the public for their co-operation in the detection of illegal aliens and it is our intention to eventually reach every township in the Western Cape in this manner."[104] The use of citizens to locate and arrest undocumented migrants presents troubling potential areas of abuse. Desmond Lockey M.P., the chair of the Parliamentary Portfolio Committee on Home Affairs, told Human Rights Watch how local persons in his own district of Winterveld near Pretoria had in the past colluded with the police to get migrants deported so they could loot the property of the migrants afterwards.[105]

In addition to general involvement of the public, anti-immigrant community structures are also playing an increasingly active role in the detection of undocumented migrants. For example, the African Chamber of Hawkers and Independent Businessmen (ACHIB), one of the hawker organizations involved in organizing violent protests against foreign hawkers, has established structures to prevent undocumented migrants from hawking. ACHIB has divided Johannesburg into hawking blocks, and has appointed "block committees" in each hawking block to identify undocumented migrants, place them under "community arrest," and hand them over to the police. At a March 26, 1997, meeting attended by a Human Rights Watch representative, the Gauteng Member of the Executive Council (MEC) for Safety and Security, Jesse Duarte and ACHIB representatives agreed to establish a joint committee to meet regularly to coordinate cooperation between

---

[102]Human Rights Watch interview with Captain Botes, Yeoville police station, March 16, 1997, and with Captain Du Pisanie, Hillbrow police station, March 17, 1997.

[103]*Citizen*, June 29, 1995.

[104]Jurie De Wet, Chief, Immigration Services for the Western Cape, Department of Home Affairs, in communication discussing the Draft Green Paper on International Migration, dated August 7, 1997.

[105]Human Rights Watch interview with Desmond Lockey M.P., chair, Parliamentary Portfolio Committee on Home Affairs, New Parliament Building, Cape Town, December 9, 1997.

ACHIB and the South African Police Services.[106] Human Rights Watch fears that such close cooperation between the police and a group linked to vigilante violence against foreigners may lead to an increase in abuses against migrants

Abuses Committed During Detection and Arrest

Arbitrary Identification Procedures

All structures involved in the detection, tracing and arrest of undocumented migrants were accused of abuse by the persons interviewed by Human Rights Watch. One of the most common complaints was the arbitrary mechanisms used to identify suspected undocumented migrants for arrest. The tactics used by the Internal Tracing Units were described in one study:

> The internal tracing units of the [South African Police Service] have become adept at spotting an illegal ... In trying to establish whether a suspect is an illegal (sic) or not, members of the internal tracing units focus on a number of aspects. One of these is language: accent, the pronouncement of certain words. Some are asked what nationality they are and if they reply "Sud" African this is a dead give-away for a Mozambican, while Malawians tend to pronounce the letter "r" as "errow." In Durban many claim to be Zulu but speak very little. Some of those arrested as undocumented migrants are found with home-made phrase books in their pockets. Often they are unable to answer simple questions in Zulu or are caught out if asked who the Zulu king is. Often the reply is "Mandela."... Appearance is another factor in trying to establish whether a suspect is illegal—hairstyle, type of clothing worn as well as actual physical appearance. In the case of Mozambicans a dead give-away is the vaccination mark on the lower left forearm. Some Mozambicans, knowing this, have taken to either self-mutilation (cutting out the vaccination mark), having a tattoo put over it, only wearing long-sleeved shirts and never rolling up the sleeves, or wearing a watch halfway up the arm to cover the mark.[107]

---

[106]Meeting attended by Human Rights Watch representative Busani Selabe, Johannesburg, March 26, 1997.

[107]Anthony Minnaar and Michael Hough, "Causes, Extent and Impact of Clandestine Immigration in Selected Southern African Countries with Specific Reference to South Africa" (Pretoria: Human Sciences Research Council, 1995), pp. 90-91.

Despite an appearance of objectivity, the indicators used are in fact arbitrary and based upon overly generalized stereotypes. The reliance on these indicators results in the wrongful identification and arrest of a large number of South African citizens as undocumented migrants. Equally troubling is the fact that the identification strategies focus exclusively on black persons, although there are a large number of non-black persons who overstay their visas in South Africa. In fact, during our entire investigation, all persons we saw in detention were black (including Indian and Pakistani detainees).

Human Rights Watch interviewed a significant number of persons who were in detention after being wrongfully identified as undocumented migrants. Benneth Mabaso, awaiting deportation at Komatipoort police station, related to us how he had lived in South Africa his entire life, but had received a Mozambican inoculation mark during a visit to Mozambique with his Mozambican father. A week before our visit, soldiers had destroyed his ID document because he had an inoculation mark:

> The soldiers destroyed my ID document a week before. They looked at my inoculation mark and told me my ID was false and ripped it up. They said I couldn't be South African with a mark.[108]

Mr. Mabaso was traveling to a South African town near the Mozambican border to arrange the funeral for his sister who had recently died, but instead found himself being deported to Mozambique.[109]

Zephaniah Mabaso (unrelated to Benneth Mabaso) was awaiting deportation at Komatipoort police station. He claimed to be a South African citizen, and showed us a copy of his ID, claiming he kept the original at home out of fear that it would be destroyed by officials. He had received an inoculation during a visit to Mozambique with his mother, and now "wherever I go, I get arrested."[110] Dumisa Mavimbela was in detention at the Witbank police station. He told Human Rights Watch how he had been detained because he had a Swaziland inoculation mark, even though he had an ID book on his person. He explained that he had

---

[108]Human Rights Watch interview with Benneth Mabaso, Komatipoort police station, December 2, 1997.

[109]Ibid.

[110]Human Rights Watch interview with Zephaniah Mabaso, Komatipoort police station, December 2, 1997.

grown up near the Mozambican border and had been inoculated on a visit to relatives in Swaziland.[111]

Ethnic groups in border areas can often be found on both sides of the border: Shangaans live in both South Africa and Mozambique, and Swazis live in both South Africa and Swaziland. Cross-border traffic is frequent, and special procedures even exist to facilitate border crossings for people living in border areas.[112] One official interviewed by Human Rights Watch compared the Swazi border to the Berlin Wall, because of its artificial separation of a contiguous Swazi community found on both sides of the border. Under these circumstances, procedures that rely heavily on identifying marks such as inoculation scars often victimize local populations.

The standards used for identifying undocumented migrants are often absurd. A newspaper report relates the story of a man who was arrested because, according to the arresting officer, "he walked like a foreigner."[113] Another person claimed that the police had destroyed his South African ID without checking its authenticity because they felt he was "too black" to qualify for a South African ID.[114] The South African Human Rights Commission, a state-funded but independent body under the constitution, has taken up the case of a South African man who had his ID documents destroyed and came close to being deported because he had a foreign surname, Banda.

Despite this enormous margin of error, police and the Department of Home Affairs continue to use arbitrary identification marks when arresting suspected illegal immigrants. A "foreign" appearance can mean frequent harassment by police officers. A recent newspaper account described the experience of a Zimbabwean woman legally in South Africa who was arrested three times within

---

[111]Human Rights Watch interview with Dumisa Mavimbela, Witbank police station, November 29, 1997.

[112]Major Olivier of the SANDF explained how at the Swazi border, people can get permission from the Induna (chief) to cross the border for a day trip at designated informal border crossings manned by citizen force personnel. Human Rights Watch interview with Major Olivier, Komatipoort border area, December 1, 1997.

[113]Eddie Koch, "The Pass Laws keep on Prowling," *Mail & Guardian*, July 15, 1994.

[114]Human Rights Watch interviews with students, University of the Witwatersrand, April 18 and 26, 1995.

an hour in the city center of Johannesburg.[115] Another newspaper account relates the story of Handsome Siwela, whose legitimate ID documents had not "deterred police from accusing him of being an illegal immigrant" from Zimbabwe and arresting him three times within seven months.[116]

The magnitude of the problem of mistaken identification is perhaps best told by the statistics obtained by Human Rights Watch at the Lindela private detention camp and discussed in greater detail in the Lindela section of this report. Our calculations based on the data obtained suggest that as many as one of out five persons detained by the police on suspicion of being an undocumented migrant is later released after proving his or her identity as a South African citizen or a lawful resident. Detainees in the Gauteng area are brought to the Lindela detention facility by officials from the Department of Home Affairs as well as by police officials. Lindela has permission from the Department of Home Affairs to pick up suspected migrants being detained at certain police stations, such as the Sophiatown Police Station (formerly Newlands Police Station).[117] Our investigation discovered that a disturbingly large number of South African citizens as well as lawful residents in South Africa end up being brought to Lindela, and that a large number of these persons are actually detained at Lindela for a period of time.

According to Lindela officials, a large number of detainees brought to the facility by police officials are released prior to intake into Lindela because they were able to satisfy the Department of Home Affairs officials at Lindela that they were South African citizens or were lawfully residing in South Africa.[118] Human Rights Watch, with the assistance of Lindela officials, did a count of the number of persons so released within one month (October 1997) and came up with a rough

---

[115]Mukoni Ratshitanga, "Visiting SA an alien experience," *Mail & Guardian*, August 1-7, 1997.

[116]*The Star*, June 3, 1996.

[117]Human Rights Watch interview with Sergeant Singer, Sophiatown Police Station, November 28, 1997. Sergeant Singer told us that "a bus from Lindela comes to pick them [the suspected undocumented migrants] up. I will call to arrange it. A Mr. van der Lith at Lindela is the one I make arrangements with." Officials at Lindela confirmed that they were authorized to transfer suspected undocumented migrants from certain police stations to Lindela. Human Rights Watch interviews with Judas and Dave, Lindela staff, at Lindela, December 4, 1997.

[118]Human Rights Watch interview with Mr. Frans Le Grange, Lindela official, at Lindela, November 24, 1997.

estimate of about 10 percent of all detainees brought to Lindela being so released.[119] This would suggest that approximately 8,000 South Africans and lawful residents held in police detention were released prior to intake at Lindela between August 1996 and October 1997.[120]

Human Rights Watch witnessed the release of one such person, Robert Mhlambi, during our November 24, 1997, visit to Lindela. Mr. Mhlambi, aged twenty-nine, was traveling in a van with other construction workers to his job site when the van was stopped by police officers from Booysen Police Station.[121] He recounted to us what happened next:

> They [the police] just collected us. Then someone failed to produce papers. Then as I produced my paper, they said, "no, you are going to meet Home Affairs to prove your papers are correct." They took all of us.... They didn't even bother to look at the ID book; they put it into their pocket.... This is my first time. I have only small money for my return. I do not know the way back to where I am staying in Soweto.[122]

Mr. Mhlambi was released a few hours after his arrival at Lindela after convincing the Department of Home Affairs officials that his documents were genuine. However, he was not provided with transportation and was forced to find his own way home from Lindela, which is located quite far from Soweto.

In addition to the many persons released prior to intake into Lindela, an equally significant number of persons are released after intake at Lindela after being able to prove their South African citizenship or lawful residence within South Africa. According to Lindela statistics, 11,037 persons were released on such a warrant of release between August 1996 and October 1997, out of a total of 79,378 persons

---

[119]In our company, a Lindela official counted the total number of persons released prior to intake and divided the number by the total number of persons brought to Lindela during October 1997. His calculations suggested an 11 percent release rate prior to intake.

[120]As said before, the total number of persons admitted into Lindela during this period was 79,378. 8,000 persons would represent slightly more than 10 percent of this figure.

[121]Human Rights Watch interview with Robert Mhlambi, Lindela, November 24, 1997.

[122]Ibid.

detained at Lindela. This represents approximately 14 percent of all persons detained at Lindela. Taken together, our research suggests that approximately one fifth of all people detained on suspicion of being undocumented migrants are ultimately released after proving South African citizenship or lawful, often after spending considerable time in detention at Lindela or in police cells. During their October 18, 1997, visit to Lindela, the South African Human Rights Commission interviewed a number of detainees who claimed to be South African citizens, at least one of whom was later released from Lindela after proving his South African citizenship.[123] Again, it should be stressed that persons detained on suspicion of being undocumented migrants are almost universally black, despite the fact that Department of Home Affairs statistics illustrate a high number of visa-overstays from other parts of the world, such as Europe. This racial disparity in the implementation of South Africa's migrants control system also raises troubling issues of racial discrimination in an officially non-racial society.

The Destruction of Documents

Persons interviewed by Human Rights Watch frequently claimed that police and army officers destroyed their identification documents after reaching a conclusion that they were undocumented migrants with fraudulent documents. Phineas Mugwambe, awaiting deportation at Lindela, claimed that the South African police had destroyed the documents he had received under the recent SADC amnesty:

My main worry is that South Africa gave me amnesty but the police don't respect our documents. My documents were destroyed by the police at Diepkloof Zone 5 on the 26th of November. Now I have no more documents. I was never even given the chance to tell the police or Home Affairs about my documents. I'm afraid to get beaten.[124]

When a person fails to produce a required document on the spot, but claims to have the document elsewhere, he or she should be given the opportunity to collect the document in the company of an official. In practice, many suspected migrants are immediately taken to jail, prison, or a detention center without being given the

---

[123]South African Human Rights Commission, "Report on a Visit to Lindela Repatriation Centre," October 28, 1997, pp. 4-5.

[124]Human Rights Watch interview with Phineas Mugwambe, Lindela, December 4, 1997.

opportunity to prove their legal status. A Mozambican interviewed by Human Rights Watch at Pretoria Central Police Station had been picked up on his way to the Department of Home Affairs to collect his documents:

> The police found me at Kempton Park station waiting for a taxi to the Home Affairs office. They asked me what my nationality was, and since I have nothing to hide, I told them I am a Mozambican going to collect my ID from the Home Affairs office. They then said, "Do not worry, you will get your ID in Mozambique," and at the same time they both picked me up and put me into the police van and brought me here.[125]

At the time of our interview, he was still in possession of the home affairs document indicating his name, date of application and the possible date of collection. A Congolese person told Human Rights Watch how he went to the Hillbrow police station to report the theft of his wallet, which had held his temporary residence permit, and was promptly arrested and brought to Lindela.[126]

Bribery, Extortion and Theft during the Arrest Process

Being arrested without documents does not automatically translate into deportation: in most cases, it appears that the arrested person will be able to bribe his or her way out of the arrest if he or she has sufficient money available. From the testimonies gathered by Human Rights Watch and press reports, such bribery seems pervasive. On occasion, police officers have even offered to drive suspected persons without papers to a bank automated teller machine (ATM) to withdraw the necessary funds for the bribe.[127] Another case described to Human Rights Watch concerned two men who had been arrested while crossing the Kruger National Park in an attempt to re-enter South Africa after having been deported. The two men were arrested and brought to the Skukuza rest camp, were they were told that a 400 rands [U.S. $ 80] bribe would obtain their release. The men did not have that

---

[125]Human Rights Watch interview with detainee, Pretoria Central Police Station, October 11, 1996.

[126]Human Rights Watch interview with Mouapotho Stanislas Yvon Fabrice, People's Republic of Congo citizen, Lindela, December 4, 1997.

[127]Human Rights Watch interview with victim of such practice, Parktown suburb of Johannesburg, September 29, 1996.

amount of money, but the arresting officers contacted a brother of the men residing in South Africa, who paid the bribe. The men were then released.[128]

A street trader in Yeoville explained to Human Rights Watch how two policemen would extract bribes from foreigners every weekend at the Shoprite store across the street from his stand:

> The policemen wait in front of Shoprite every Friday and Saturday. They wait for foreigners and ask them for papers. If you have no papers, they take you to the back. But the police station is up the street, in the other direction. Then they ask you for "special money"—normally fifty rands [U.S. $ 10]. If you don't have the money, they arrest you and take you to Hillbrow police station.[129]

Two security guards working as night-watchmen at the Nedbank building in Johannesburg told Human Rights Watch how they had offered a bribe to police officers after being arrested while waiting outside their work office. The police van pulled over at a liquor store, and the security guards were told to "fill the table" with beers, which they did. After drinking a large amount of beer and questioning the security guards about why they had come to South Africa, the police officers talked among themselves, before one of them said, "anyway, it is too late to take them to Lindela." The security guards were then asked by the police officers to "give us some extra money for beer." After paying the officers 480 rands [U.S. $ 96] "extra money," the two security guards were told that they were free to go.[130]

Fernando Ntive, now living in Mozambique, was arrested in South Africa in late 1995. He described how he was asked for a bribe almost as soon as he identified himself as a Mozambican: "Then a black policeman came, and asked for drink money, twenty rands [U.S. $ 4]. I asked him, why do I need to pay this money. He insisted I give him drink money. I said I wouldn't give it, and if he

---

[128]Human Rights Watch interview with PK, New Forest refugee settlement, Mpumalanga, November 12, 1996.

[129]Human Rights Watch interview with hawker M (full name withheld on request), Yeoville, October 28, 1997.

[130]Human Rights Watch interview with security guards, Nedbank Building, Braamfontein, August 9, 1997.

wanted to see my documents we could go to my house."[131] He was then taken to the police station, where "the officer who was searching us demanded ten rands [U.S. $ 2], so I could leave."[132] He again refused to pay a bribe, and spent several days in detention before being deported. Another former deportee, Manuel Ubisse, told of how he was asked for a bribe after being arrested at Protea Glen: "They asked if we had 300 rands [U.S. $ 60] "bail" each to give them before they took us to the police station, because once we were there the bail amount was going to be very high."[133] The amount of bribes varies significantly, according to one source:

In most cases, especially here at Protea North police station, people used to pay up to 300 rands [U.S. $ 60]. But if those policemen are bankrupt, they even take a mere twenty rands [U.S. $ 4]. The problem with them is that if they know you are selling something like vegetables, they keep coming to you, particularly at the end of the month. They come and threaten you with deportation knowing that you are going to give them money. During these times, they usually demand up to 500 rands [U.S. $ 100].[134]

The conduct of police and immigration officials in some cases suggests that arrests are sometimes made for the primary purpose of extracting bribes. In one case documented by Lawyers for Human Rights, a twenty-six-year-old Mauritian citizen had a serious heart condition and was required to return to South Africa every six months for treatment. During March 1997, his temporary resident permit lapsed, partly because he was bedridden and too sick to have the permit renewed. On March 14, 1997, a group of men in civilian clothing came to the house he was staying in and arrested the ailing Mauritian as a prohibited person. The men never identified themselves. While driving around Pretoria, the men told him that if he gave them 2,000 rands [U.S. $ 400], they could "do something" for him. When he

---

[131]Interview by Refugee Research Program with Fernando Ntive, aged 33, at Muine, Mozambique, March 3, 1996.

[132]Ibid.

[133]Interview by Refugee Research Project with Manuel Ubisse, Soweto, April 1995.

[134]Interview by Refugee Research Project with Boaventura Ndlovu, Soweto, February 1995.

said he did not carry that sort of money on him, he was taken to the Pretoria police station. At the police station, the Mauritian asked for a doctor and a lawyer after being forced to sign a paper listing his constitutional rights, but was told, "You are an illegal immigrant and this [i.e. the constitutional rights] doesn't apply to you. There will be no court case and you will be deported on the first flight." During his detention, the Mauritian's medical condition started deteriorating rapidly, as his limbs became swollen and he collapsed repeatedly. When he was finally taken to the hospital, he was immediately rushed to the intensive care unit where he remained for two weeks (under police guard) with a serious heart condition. He was never charged with any crime, and upon his release his extension of stay application was granted.[135]

Two fruit sellers in the Protea North area of Soweto told Human Rights Watch how they had been arrested by police officers and forced to pay bribes of 500 and 700 rands [U.S. $ 100-140] to secure their release. Since their original arrests, the arresting officers visited the vendors on a regular basis, demanding fruit and vegetables in return for "no longer arresting us."[136] Human Rights Watch also received complaints from some undocumented hawkers that officials would arrest them in the street, leaving their stands to be looted. Cliff Mucheka, a Malawian curio seller, told us he was arrested in Cape Town by an immigration officer while trading in Darling Street, and that his "curios were left in the street."[137]

Police officers are not the only officials routinely accused of such bribery and extortion attempts during the arrest process. In our brief visit to the border, we found similar abuses committed by army troops. Benneth Mabaso, for example, told us how army personnel had taken 100 rands [U.S. $ 20] from him and a friend after arresting them at a railroad station, in a case described in greater detail below.

Human Rights Watch also found significant evidence of corrupt practices by officials in the Department of Home Affairs. One of the most disturbing

---

[135]Lawyers for Human Rights, "Alleged Abuse of a Non Citizen's Constitutional Rights," Communication to the South African Human Rights Commission, dated May 29, 1997.

[136]Human Rights Watch interview with two fruit vendors, Protea North, Soweto, September 1996.

[137]Human Rights Watch interview with Cliff Mucheka, Malawian citizen, at Pollsmoor prison, Cape Town, December 10, 1997.

allegations made against Home Affairs officials working at Lindela[138] is that they require people to pay bribes to be released even after proving their citizenship or legal status. A reporter of the *City Press* newspaper who had come to Lindela to seek the release of his girlfriend told Human Rights Watch that he was glad we were present because he would not be required to pay a bribe to get his girlfriend released. The reporter related how he had come to Lindela on a previous occasion to seek the release of a South African friend and was forced to pay a bribe of 360 rands [U.S. $ 72] before the person was released.[139] Other detainees at Lindela told of similar experiences, suggesting that even when a person detained at Lindela is legally entitled to be released, he or she may be required to pay a bribe to be able to enforce this right.

During our inspection of Lindela, we received numerous allegations of corruption, mostly leveled against officials of the Department of Home Affairs working at Lindela. Some detainees alleged that officials from the Department of Home Affairs would manipulate their departure dates in order to extract bribes:

When people want to go home, they don't let you be deported until you pay them money. Home Affairs wants you to pay 100 to 400 rands [U.S. $ 20-80], whatever you've got. Otherwise, you just stay here. They let people go without ID, just give them some money.[140]

During their visit, officials from the South African Human Rights Commission interviewed Mr. Solomon Mashaba, who claimed that he was asked to pay five rands [U.S. $ 1] to have his deportation delayed.[141] Mr. Fabion Ndlovu, one of the persons who alleged he was beaten by Lindela guards, also claimed that he had

---

[138]The Department of Home Affairs maintains an office at Lindela with several staff persons, responsible for processing the detainees at Lindela. According to Lindela officials, detainees cannot be released from Lindela without the approval of the Department of Home Affairs.

[139]Statements of City Press reporter to Human Rights Watch, Lindela, December 4, 1997.

[140]Human Rights Watch interview with Mr. Manthla, Swaziland citizen, at Lindela, December 4, 1997.

[141]South African Human Rights Commission, "Report on a Visit to Lindela Repatriation Centre," October 28, 1997, p. 4.

paid a 100 rands [U.S. $ 20] bribe to a black Home Affairs official who promised to get him released, although the promise was not kept.[142] Another man who appeared to be in his fifties and claimed to be a South African citizen spoke to us on condition of anonymity:

> I have been three weeks at Lindela. I was arrested at Roodepoort in the Transvaal. I did not have my details [identity documents]. It is 200 rands [U.S. $ 40] to get out without your details. Sometimes it is more. There have been many, many South Africans who have given the money in this way. More than fifteen. But I am without money.

> If you complain, they [the guards] will beat you and tell you you are complaining to the white people. I tried to solve my problem. I approached a white man who took me to the Department of Home Affairs in the offices. After the white man left, they hit me. They asked me, "How much have I got?" I replied, "Nothing." After that they refused to let me out. When I kept talking to them, they said they would hit me and that I am a problem, so I decided to leave the matter. Now I will wait to see what they do, or until they force me to another country.[143]

A Zimbabwean named Dennis, who had obtained South African identity papers by claiming to be from Bophuthatswana during the 1994 reintegration of the homelands into South Africa, told Human Rights Watch that he believed he would have to pay a 100 rand [U.S. $ 20] bribe to be released from Lindela, despite the fact that he had South African identity documents: "I have been arrested three times, and have paid twice.... Here, everybody knows that to get out, you need to bribe. Everybody knows that. So many guys have gotten out of here by paying money."[144]

In response to the allegations of corruption that have been reported in the media, Lindela posted a 1,000 rand [U.S. $ 200] reward notice near the intake counter for information about corruption or abuse by guards. During our

---

[142]Human Rights Watch interview with Fabion Ndlovu, Lindela, December 4, 1997.

[143]Human Rights Watch interview with anonymous man, Lindela, December 4, 1997.

[144]Human Rights Watch interview with Dennis, Lindela, December 4, 1997.

November 24, 1997, visit, Lindela management claimed that it investigated allegations of abuse and corruption, but that up to that time no disciplinary proceedings against guards had been instituted because no allegations had ever been substantiated. Lindela management claimed that three Department of Home Affairs officials had been caught taking bribes in a sting operation, but they were not prosecuted because the sting money had disappeared.[145] According to the chief immigration officer for Cape Town, corruption has been such a serious problem at Lindela that the Cape Town Home Affairs office was forced to institute its own system of checks to ensure that persons it sent to Lindela were not released without its permission.[146]

Physical Abuse During the Arrest Process

At the Lindela detention facility, we were shown a logbook by Lindela officials in which they entered any allegations made by incoming detainees about police beatings or other forms of abuse. The logbook, which, judging from the entry dates, appeared to have been in use for only a few days in October 1997, included a number of accounts of beatings by police. Accompanying photographs of the detainees showed the physical marks left by the beatings, and often suggested the seriousness of the beatings. The alleged assaults included the following: Bongani Tshuma, allegedly assaulted by police officers at the Booysen police station; Nelson Biyela, allegedly assaulted by police officers at Hillbrow police station; and Manuel Mlungu, allegedly beaten by police officers at the Florida police station. Given that these alleged beatings took place within a period of only a few days, it appears that police abuse, especially police abuse against migrants, remains disturbingly common in South Africa, partly because of xenophobic hostility towards migrants.

Public and police hostility against Nigerians is especially high, because of a wide-spread belief that Nigerians are extensively involved in the drug trade and other illicit operations. According to two Nigerians interviewed by Human Rights Watch, the police accompanied by local South Africans raided their Hillbrow

---

[145]Human Rights Watch interview with Mr. Frans Le Grange, Lindela, November 24, 1997.

[146]Human Rights Watch interview with Mr. Jurie de Wet, Chief Immigration Officer, Department of Home Affairs, Cape Town, December 9, 1997.

apartment on the evening of November 21, 1996.[147] The eight Nigerian and six Ghanaian occupants of the apartment—sharing the apartment to minimize cost and to protect themselves against attacks by locals—were forced down the corridor, marched down to a police van and taken to the Hillbrow police station. The Nigerians claimed that they had been severely assaulted at the police station and had been threatened with shooting.[148] The two Nigerians interviewed by Human Rights Watch had a number of serious injuries, including gashes on their heads and legs. One of the two Nigerians, a medical doctor, claimed that the police had taken about "half of the nairas and dollars" while searching their apartment, luggage, and dressing tables.[149] While Human Rights Watch was conducting the interview, one of the Nigerians went to make a phone call to his family in Nigeria and was attacked by a group of six youth, who stole the money he was carrying. Needless to say, he did not consider going to the police station to report the incident as a realistic option.

Human Rights Watch also uncovered evidence of physical abuse of undocumented migrants at the hands of members of the armed forces. Benneth Mabaso, awaiting deportation at Komatipoort police station, told us how soldiers had assaulted him after he had alleged that they had stolen money from him:

> They stopped the van and took us out to cross-question us. They were wearing camouflage uniforms. We insisted that they had taken our money, and they then beat us badly. When we were on the ground, they jumped on us with their heavy boots. My ribs were very sore. After that, the soldiers took us to the hospital.[150]

Mr. Mabaso showed signs of a recent beating and showed us the medication the hospital had given him for his injuries. Human Rights Watch brought this incident to the attention of police officials, who appeared unaware of the incident at the time. Superintendent Liebenberg commented that he frequently received

---

[147]Human Rights Watch interview with two Nigerians, corner of Twist and Essellen Streets, Hillbrow neighborhood of Johannesburg, November 22, 1996.

[148]Ibid.

[149]Ibid.

[150]Human Rights Watch interview with Benneth Mabaso, Mozambican citizen, at Komatipoort police station, December 2, 1997.

complaints about theft and abuse against army personnel, "but when we try to open a case, they say that they just want to go back to Mozambique."[151] According to a December 2, 1997, fax from the Komatipoort police station to Human Rights Watch, this is exactly what happened in one of the cases we had requested the police to investigate: the victims reiterated their charges to the police, but said that they didn't want to press charges because they wanted to go home.[152] Superintendent Liebenberg told Human Rights Watch about a current court case where the victim had pressed charges, in which a woman attempting to cross the border illegally had been raped on March 19, 1997, by a military person.[153] However, in this case the woman was not kept in custody, and lived with her father in Thembisa, near Johannesburg. Military personnel often patrol the border in groups as small as two persons, which may increase incidents of abuse as there is little direct oversight of their activities while on patrol.

Our investigation suggests that the fear of long-term detention while charges of abuse or theft are being investigated is one of the main reasons why undocumented migrants do not bring formal complaints. Time and time again we were told by police officials that investigations into abuses were closed because the undocumented migrant had withdrawn the charges, opting to "go home." Considering the substandard conditions of detention faced by undocumented migrants (discussed below) and the fact that many undocumented migrants are important (if not the only) breadwinners for their families, this reluctance to remain in detention for a period of months is not surprising. In addition many migrants expressed doubt about their chances of obtaining justice in South Africa, a doubt certainly bolstered by the fact that they had allegedly been assaulted by representatives of the state in the first place.

As illustrated by the case of Benneth Mabaso, who reported being beaten by army personnel after complaining about the fact that they had stolen money from him, complaining about abuses often results in further abuse, not recourse to justice. In addition, the high level of decentralization in the migrants control system, the lack of a coherent oversight authority because of the confusion of

---

[151]Human Rights Watch interview with Captain Liebenberg, Superintendent, Komatipoort Police Station, Komatipoort Police Station, December 2, 1997.

[152]Fax from the South African Police Service to Human Rights Watch, dated December 2, 1997.

[153]Human Rights Watch interview with Captain Liebenberg, Superintendent, Komatipoort Police Station, Komatipoort Police Station, December 2, 1997.

agencies involved, and the speed with which some migrants (albeit by no means all) are deported allow abuses to take place without their being brought to light, and thus foster a culture of impunity and a disturbing lack of accountability for abuses. In other words, under the current system it is entirely possible that an undocumented person will be abused at a police station and deported soon thereafter without any outside knowledge of the abuse.

In the opinion of Human Rights Watch, the climate of xenophobia in South Africa and the common inflammatory remarks of politicians against migrants, foster the official abuses described in this report. Migrants are erroneously perceived as responsible for rising crime and as a serious threat to South Africa's socio-economic well-being.[154] Our interviews suggest that some police, army, and Home Affairs officials feel that they are serving their country's interests by abusing undocumented migrants, as this is likely to guarantee that the migrants will not return anytime soon to South Africa. The verbal insults thrown at undocumented migrants during abuse, and the common attitude of police officials that "you came to this country and brought this abuse upon yourself," lend credence to this interpretation.

Threats to Academic and Journalistic Freedom

Human Rights Watch is particularly concerned about a number of press reports which suggest that officials from the Department of Home Affairs are using their extensive powers under the Aliens Control Act to harass and deport critics of the current government, especially foreign academics and journalists.

In August 1997, officials from the Department of Home Affairs burst in on a lecture by American lecturer Aaron Amaral, teaching a class on Marxist philosophy at the University of the Western Cape. The lecturer was arrested in front of his class. Amaral is an outspoken Marxist, and was intimately involved in an organizing effort at the university by the Socialist Students' Action Committee, a student organization that was challenging the ruling ANC-aligned South African Students' Congress.[155] Ten days prior to the arrest, Amaral had received another visit from the same two immigration officials. According to Amaral, the officials

---

[154]Some studies have noted that migrants make important contributions to the South African economy. See, for example, C. M. Rogerson, "International Migration, Immigrant Entrepreneurs and South Africa's Small Enterprise Economy," *Southern Africa Migration Project Migration Policy Series No. 3* (Cape Town: IDASA, 1997).

[155]Marion Edmunds, "State Arrests UWC Marxist," *Mail & Guardian*, August 29 to September 4, 1997.

told him that they were acting on orders from Pretoria (i.e., the headquarters of the Department of Home Affairs), but seemed entirely unclear of their assignment: "What was obvious about the intervention was that they wanted to get me off campus."[156] The head of UWC's philosophy department, Professor Andrew Nash, agreed with this assessment of the motivation of the officers: "These officers arrived with no knowledge of whether he was illegal or legal. All they knew was that they wanted him off campus. The whole thing smacks of victimization."[157]

Sixty-six academics signed a letter of protest in response, concluding that "the Department of Home Affairs has no business policing ideas on university campuses."[158] Human Rights Watch is concerned that the actions of the Department of Home Affairs will have a chilling effect on academic discourse in South Africa. South Africa has a significant number of foreign academics, lecturers, and teachers employed at its educational institutions and should aim to foster an environment of free inquiry, rational discourse, and open exchange of ideas. In the case of Amaral, it was alleged that home affairs officials described Amaral's work as "confusing our people."[159] The alleged victimization of Amaral is inconsistent with the internationally recognized—and constitutionally protected—freedom to seek, receive, and impart information and ideas of all kind.

The deportation proceedings commenced in February 1998 against Newton Kanhema, a leading Zimbabwean journalist working in South Africa, also raise the troubling specter that immigration proceedings are being used to limit freedom of the press in South Africa. Kanhema, a reporter with the *Sunday Independent* in Johannesburg, was the author of a number of muckracking articles critical of the ANC government. Kanhema exposed a controversial £1 billion (U.S. $ 1.65 billion) arms contract between South Africa and Saudi Arabia, which called into question South Africa's commitment to a new "moral" arms exporting policy.[160] In addition, he conducted a highly controversial interview with Winnie Madikizela-

---

[156]Ibid.

[157]Ibid.

[158]Letters, "Home Affairs Must Offer Some Answers," *Mail & Guardian*, October 1 to 7, 1997.

[159]Edmunds, "State Arrests UWC Marxist."

[160]Alec Russell, "Reporter who criticized ANC faces Deportation," *Sunday Telegraph*, February 8, 1998.

Mandela a few days before the ANC's 1997 Party Congress, in which she detailed her troubles with the ANC's leadership and criticized the government.[161] His journalistic activities had been repeatedly criticized by top ANC leaders, including by President Mandela's speech writers who approached the *Sunday Independent* and "questioned the advisability" of employing a foreign journalist as a senior political writer.[162]

In February 1998, Kanhema's wife was presented with a deportation order while her husband was abroad in the United States on a four-month Freedom Forum sabbatical at Emory University. The deportation notice was dated January 14 and gave the Kanhemas twenty-one days to leave the country.[163] Ostensibly, the deportation order is based on the ground that Kanhema misrepresented himself on his application for permanent residence under the amnesty for SADC citizens, but many observers are of the opinion that the real reason for the deportation proceedings are political in nature. The director of the journalism program at Emory University wrote a letter of protest to South African ambassador Franklin Sonn, commenting that "One could say Kanhema has stepped on government toes and they decided to withdraw his permanent residence permit on far-fetched grounds of technicality."[164] According to Sam Sole, president of the South African Union of Journalists:

> While a direct link between the politicians and the officials has yet to be proved, we have no doubt about the political motive. Threats were made to Newton to watch out and be careful. He was told he is a foreigner and should not meddle in our politics.[165]

---

[161]Ibid.

[162]Ibid. Carl Niehaus, a member of Parliament and of the ANC's National Executive Committee, also singled out Kanhema for criticism in a published November 1996 letter to the *Star* newspaper. President Mandela's attack on the "intrusion of this self-same media within our ranks ... to encourage our own destruction" during his political report at the ANC's 1997 Party Congress was also widely perceived as a direct reference to Kanhema's controversial interview with Winnie Mandela.

[163]Joan Mower, "South Africa deports journalist," *Freedom Forum Online*, February 4, 1998.

[164]Ibid.

[165]Russell, "Reporter who criticized ANC faces Deportation."

Conditions of Detention

Once an individual has been arrested as a suspected undocumented migrant, he or she will spend some time in detention awaiting determination of status and, where appropriate, deportation. The time spent in detention varies widely, from a few days for uncomplicated cases from some neighboring countries, to several months or even over a year for complicated cases. Usually, the person will first be held in a police cell for a few days, and later transferred to a prison or a specially designated detention facility where he or she will stay until his or her status has been determined, arrangements have been made with the home country through the national embassy, and transport has been arranged.

For example, in the greater Johannesburg/Pretoria area (Gauteng Province), the Department of Home Affairs has contracted a private detention center, the Lindela Detention Center in Krugersdorp, to serve as a centralized detention facility for the detention of migrants awaiting determination of their status and/or deportation. Most police stations and the Department of Home Affairs offices in the greater Gauteng area bring suspected undocumented migrants to the facility on a regular basis, either daily or several times per week. Thus, most police stations and Home Affairs offices only serve as temporary holding facilities, and the prison system is not extensively used in this area to detain undocumented migrants (although the prisons do detain foreigners who are awaiting trial on criminal charges or have been sentenced). By contrast, in Cape Town most migrants are detained either at local police stations such as Seapoint police station, or at prisons such as Pollsmoor prison.[166] Migrants are also detained in police cells in more remote areas, such as the Komatipoort police station near the Mozambican border.

In the case of Mozambican and Zimbabwean undocumented migrants, who comprise the vast majority of deported persons, the procedures are standardized. The Mozambican government has authorized the South African authorities to determine the nationality of Mozambicans, and thus no individual approval is needed from the Mozambican authorities prior to deportation.[167] Zimbabwean

---

[166]The Department of Home Affairs in Cape Town and Durban also send undocumented Mozambicans and Zimbabweans to Lindela after they have been cleared for deportation, as this allows them to take advantage of the regularly scheduled deportation trains which leave from Lindela.

[167]Human Rights Watch interview with Mr. Claude Schravesande, Director, Admissions and Aliens Control, Department of Home Affairs, Pretoria, December 3, 1997. In a few cases, the Mozambican border authorities have refused to accept an individual deportee, on the grounds that they are not satisfied that the person is a Mozambican national.

authorities visit the Lindela detention facility on a regular basis, and thus facilitate the repatriation process for Zimbabweans.[168] For other nationals, the process can be much more cumbersome. If the country has a diplomatic mission in South Africa, the mission will be contacted by the Department of Home Affairs to approve the repatriation; in some cases, where no mission exists, approval for repatriation must be sought via mail.[169] Human Rights Watch interviewed a number of people who had remained in detention for lengthy periods of time because of a lack of cooperation from their embassies. This included both people from neighboring countries such as Namibia and Tanzania, as well as people from more distant countries such as Mexico. According to the governing regulations, detention more than thirty days must be authorized by a judge of the High Court. Our investigation suggests that more often than not this does not happen.

Detainees awaiting deportation in police cells are the responsibility of the South African Police Service, rather than the Department of Home Affairs. The facilities in the police cells are designed to accommodate detainees for a period of forty-eight hours at a time, or at a maximum for a weekend, pending appearance in court. Conditions in the cells are regulated by the South African Police Service Act No. 68 of 1995.

Detainees held in prisons fall under the authority of the Department of Correctional Services; conditions in prisons are governed by the Correctional Services Act of 1959 and regulations under the act.[170] The prisons most used for the detention of undocumented migrants include Diepkloof (Johannesburg Central), Modderbee, Pretoria Central, Barberton, and Leeuwkop. Pietersburg prison in the Northern Province is also used for the same purpose.

As described above, the Department of Home Affairs has recently contracted out to a private company, the Dyambu Trust, the operation of a specialized detention center for undocumented migrants awaiting deportation. There is only one center of this kind, situated in Krugersdorp outside Johannesburg, the Lindela

---

It appears that non-Mozambicans sometimes claim Mozambican nationality in order to be deported to Mozambique, because it is relatively easy to re-enter South Africa from the Mozambican border.

[168]Ibid.

[169]Ibid.

[170]See Human Rights Watch, *Prison Conditions in South Africa* (New York: Human Rights Watch, 1993).

Detention Center. According to Home Affairs officials, "there are no similar centres in other provinces, nor are there any plans to create such centres. The reason for the establishment of such a centre in Gauteng was that the police and prison cells in that region are more overcrowded than detention centres elsewhere. This does not mean that all the other provinces should bring illegal aliens to this centre. Instead they should make use of the police and prison cells."[171]

Human Rights Watch visited a number of prison and police cells where individuals are held awaiting deportation, including at least one example of each type of facility. In addition we interviewed former detainees about their experiences and spoke to lawyers and others involved in refugee advocacy about detention conditions at various facilities. We visited the Dyambu-Lindela detention facility on three occasions. We also visited the Modderbee, Johannesburg (Diepkloof) and Pollsmoor prisons, and a number of police cells, including the Sophiatown (formerly Newlands), Johannesburg Central (formerly John Vorster), Witbank, Nelspruit, Komatipoort, Malelane, Hillbrow, Highpoint Satellite, and Pretoria Central police stations.

Lindela Facility

The Lindela detention facility is a privately owned and operated detention facility for migrants awaiting deportation. Lindela was formerly used as a compound to house migrant workers. The facility consists of an administrative block and two housing units, one for adult males and a second for women and children under sixteen years of age. It is located in Krugersdorp, about thirty minutes from Johannesburg, and serves as a centralized detention facility for Gauteng province. The facility was opened on August 19, 1996, in order to alleviate the chronic overcrowding of police and prison cells in the Gauteng region.[172] With an average daily population that fluctuates between 1,200 and 1,800 persons,[173] Lindela is the largest detention facility for undocumented migrants in the country, and the only facility specifically designated for that

---

[171]Claude Schravesande, Director, Admissions and Aliens Control, Department of Home Affairs, in a letter to Human Rights Watch, headed "Legal Aspects for the Detention of Illegal Aliens," Ref. 21/5/1, June 5, 1997.

[172]Letter of Director of Aliens Control Mr. C. Schravesande, Department of Home Affairs, dated June 5, 1997.

[173]These averages are calculated on a monthly basis, and it is likely that the maximum population at Lindela has been well in excess of 1,800 persons.

purpose. Most police stations and home affairs offices now bring suspected undocumented migrants to Lindela on a daily basis, or at least every few days.

The Department of Home Affairs pays the Dyambu Trust nineteen rands ninety-five cents [U.S. $ 4] per detainee per day to house and feed the detainee.[174] According to Lindela officials, this is substantially lower than the cost of housing a person in the prison system.

The decision by the Department of Home Affairs to use Lindela for the detention of undocumented migrants awaiting deportation was a matter of controversy. Dyambu Trust was created by several prominent members of the ANC's Women's League, including the present deputy minister of home affairs Lindiwe Sisulu, who resigned from the trust upon her appointment.[175] The Democratic Party has called for an investigation into whether or not appropriate tendering procedures were followed in awarding the contract to the Dyambu Trust.[176]

From its inception in August 1996 until the end of October 1997, Lindela detained 79,378 persons at its facility.[177] Of these, 67,186 were repatriated, while another 11,037 were released.[178] Mozambicans made up an estimated 64 percent of the total, with Zimbabweans accounting for another 27 percent. Human Rights Watch also spoke with people from many other African countries at the facility, as well as people from Mexico, Brazil, Pakistan, and India. Human Rights Watch visited the facility on three different occasions: on October 8, 1996, six weeks after the facility opened, on November 24, 1997, and on December 4, 1997. The facility has also been inspected twice by the South African Human Rights Commission, and Human Rights Watch was briefed by Commissioner Jody Kollapen on the findings of his October 28, 1997, inspection of Lindela.

---

[174]Human Rights Watch interview with Mr. Frans Le Grange, Lindela official, at Lindela detention facility, November 24, 1997.

[175]Hein Marais, "Deporting for Cash," *Mail & Guardian*, February 7 to 13, 1997, p. 2.

[176]Statement by Dene Smuts, Democratic Party Spokesperson on Home Affairs, dated February 8, 1997.

[177]Lindela Centre for Illegal Immigrants, Statistics, October 1997.

[178]Ibid. The remaining 1,155 persons were carried over to the next month.

Dormitory room in the male compound at Lindela with broken beds on the right, December 1997

The Intake and Processing of Detainees

Lindela's administrative area consists of several offices for Home Affairs and Lindela personnel, a sick bay with five beds, and a number of rooms used for the registration and processing of detainees. The detainees are registered on arrival, and then taken to an adjacent room where they are photographed, fingerprinted, and registered in an electronic database called Unisys. In a second room, detainees receive an identity card bearing their name, date of arrival, and the country to which they are likely to be deported. Both rooms are bare, except for cement benches on which the inmates sit. Detainees are often processed in large groups, which causes long waiting periods in uncomfortable circumstances. Throughout our visits, Human Rights Watch observed people sitting or standing in long lines, often for almost the entire day. The attitude of officials is often unfriendly, and our own observations support those of the South African Human Rights Commission:

> The officials' attitude is very aggressive and hostile. The inmates' names were shouted out at them and they are expected to act in concert with the commands from the officials. The situation is reminiscent of the old pass law offices or some military barracks. Although it is common cause that the inmates are of foreign origin, the officials use Zulu as a language of instruction and this leads to some confusion.[179]

Accommodation

After completing the intake process, detainees are brought into the general population. The male compound consists of thirty-two separate dormitory rooms, with an average of thirty-two beds each, facing a central courtyard. Beds are metal frame bunks with mattresses, and some lockers are placed in the rooms. There are screened open-air urinals and a shower building are found in the middle of the courtyard. At the end of the courtyard, there are a number of toilets in a building with a very bad smell with pools of dirty water on the floor. The women's compound is essentially similar, albeit smaller. There are thirteen rooms in the women's compound, with five in active use and the others being used for storage purposes.

---

[179]South African Human Rights Commission, Report on a visit to Lindela, dated October 28, 1997 (SAHRC Report).

Lindela officials claimed that the facility had a carrying capacity of 2,500 persons.[180] After receiving several complaints from male detainees that they were forced to sleep two persons to a single bed, we decided to conduct a bed count for the entire compound. Our count found 1,010 functioning beds in the male compound, and a total of 115 functioning beds in the female compound.[181] Our inspection of the log book in the front office revealed numerous days when the population was greatly in excess of the number of available beds, rising above 1,700 on some days; statistics supplied by Lindela reveal that the *average* number of inmates in June and July 1997 was 1,647 and 1,516 respectively.[182] Thus, it is clear that the population of Lindela often exceeds the number of available beds, especially in the male compound which accommodates the majority of the Lindela population. Such conditions are incompatible with the United Nations Standard Minimum Rules for the Treatment of Prisoners, which require that "[e]very prisoner shall, in accordance with local or national standards, be provided with a separate bed."[183]

Food
Detainees at Lindela receive two meals per day, at 6 a.m. and at 3 p.m., a meal pattern similar to that of many South African prisons.[184] The first meal consists of

---

[180]Human Rights Watch interview with Mr. Frans Le Grange, Lindela official, at Lindela, November 24, 1997. This same figure was given to the South African Human Rights Commission. SAHRC report, p. 2.

[181]The following number of beds were counted in the thirty-two rooms in the male compound. Figures in parenthesis indicate the number of broken beds in that room: 34; 34; 36; 34; 32; 36; 24 (10); 35 (1); 16 (18); 29 (5); 31 (2); 29 (5); 30 (2); 31 (6); 31 (1); 34; 34; 34; 34; 30 (4); 34; 34; 34; 33 (1); 25 (9); 33 (5); 26 (4). This adds up to a total of 1,010 functioning beds, and 81 broken beds. In the women's compound, rooms 33 to 39 were locked and used for storage, although they did contain a number of beds, 175 functioning beds in total. The rooms in use in the women's compound contained the following number of beds, with broken beds in parenthesis: 19 (5); 26 (2); 24; 22; 24 (2). This adds up to 115 functioning beds in the rooms in use.

[182]Lindela Centre for Illegal Immigrants, Statistics, October 1997.

[183]Standard Minimum Rules for the Treatment of Prisoners, Rule 19.

[184]Human Rights Watch interview with Mr. Frans Le Grange, Lindela official, at Lindela, November 24, 1997

pap (cornmeal porridge, a staple food) and five or six slices of bread, while the second meal consists of pap and soup containing some meat. Meals are taken in a communal dining hall which appeared spacious enough. Complaints about the quality of the food were one of the most common concerns raised by inmates with Human Rights Watch. One Somali detainee told Human Rights Watch that the "soup is bad. It's for the pigs, I don't eat it."[185] A young Zimbabwean detainee told Human Rights Watch: "The food is very bad. Many of us are sick with stomach problems. I eat the food and get sick. They are poisoning us."[186] Detainees also complained that the meat in the soup sometimes appeared spoiled, and that this made the food difficult to swallow. There is a small shop inside the male compound which sells basic supplies, including bread. However, since many undocumented migrants are often arrested on the streets and not allowed to fetch their belongings, many detainees told Human Rights Watch that they did not have sufficient money to purchase things at the shop. During our December 4, 1997, visit, several detainees told us that the guards had denied them food privileges in retaliation for a recent protest by inmates.[187]

Telephone Access

Lindela officials claimed that each detainee is allowed one free phone call during his or her stay at Lindela, and has to pay for additional calls at the rate of five rands [U.S. $ 1] per call.[188] However, many people told Human Rights Watch that they were never allowed to make the free call. During our visits, we were often asked to call family members or friends to inform them about their detention at Lindela. For example, Michael Mululu, a Namibian who had been detained at Lindela since October 7, 1997, told us that his repeated requests to make a phone

---

[185]Human Rights Watch interview with Somali detainee, Lindela, November 24, 1997.

[186]Human Rights Watch interview with young Zimbabwean detainee, Lindela, November 24, 1997.

[187]Human Rights Watch interview with John Lobo, Mozambican, Lindela, December 4, 1997. The detainees made similar statements to the Krugersdorp police sergeant called to investigate beating allegations. Statement of Thomas Sithole to Krugersdorp police sergeant, December 4, 1997. The incident is discussed in greater length when discussing guard abuse of detainees below.

[188]Human Rights Watch interview with Mr. Frans Le Grange, Lindela official, at Lindela, November 24, 1997.

call had been denied. He told us that he had never been informed of his right to one free phone call.[189] Four other Namibians told us that they were required to pay five rands [U.S. $ 1] to security personnel or office personnel to make outgoing calls, and that incoming calls were cut off after one minute.[190] Dennis, a Zimbabwean, told Human Rights Watch: "They say you are allowed one free call, but there isn't. You have to pay five rands [U.S. $ 1] to the security. Then they say it is busy. It is busy. So sometimes even if you pay you can't have the call."[191]

Similar allegations that persons are denied access to a free phone were made to reporters of the *Star* newspaper when they visited Lindela during October 1997. Danny Mansell, operations manager for Dyambu, reportedly responded to the *Star* reporters that the right to a phone call applied only to South Africans, and that the persons at Lindela were not South Africans.[192]

Abuse of Inmates by Guards

Detainees often complained about the rude behavior of the security guards working at the facility. In the words of a thirty-six year old Liberian detainee who asked to remain anonymous:

> The guards are very rude. When I ask them something, they just walk away. And they yell at us and we are supposed to run to obey their orders. You know, I am not a criminal and should not be treated as one. I am an honest businessman.[193]

A former Somali inmate at Lindela, now a recognized refugee living in Johannesburg, related a similar experience with the guards at Lindela:

---

[189]Human Rights Watch interview with Michael Mululu, Namibian, Lindela, November 24, 1997.

[190]Human Rights Watch interview with four Namibians, Lindela, December 4, 1997.

[191]Human Rights Watch interview with Dennis, Lindela, December 4, 1997.

[192]Gill Gifford, "'Ill Treatment' of Inmates at Repatriation Camp," *Star*, October 15, 1997.

[193]Human Rights Watch interview with anonymous Liberian detainee, 36 years old, Lindela, November 24, 1997.

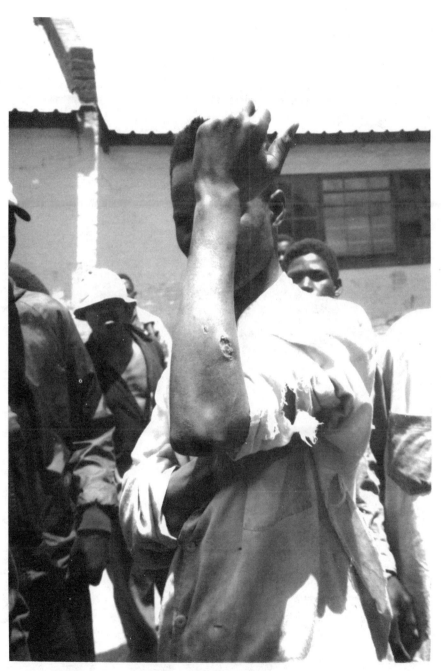

A detainee at Lindela, showing the untreated and infected dog bites which he received following a failed escape attempt, December 1997.

In Lindela, the food was a problem. Pap two times a day and very bad soup with bad taste. Second problem was the security guards who used to beat the people badly. I saw them beat the people, especially the Mozambicans. At night you can't sleep because of the loudspeakers on the roof. They drink at night and then assault the people. If you refuse an order, you are taken care of, beaten.[194]

During our first inspection of Lindela, Human Rights Watch was approached by one detainee who complained of having lost some teeth and sustaining other injuries after being assaulted by a Lindela guard for complaining about the extremely hot conditions in his dormitory room. We observed that the complainant did have several teeth missing, with the gums still bleeding, which would suggest a recent incident. The allegation was supported by three other detainees who claimed to have witnessed the incident. The witnesses claimed that the same guard had assaulted them a few days earlier after they inquired about their deportation date.[195]

During our December 4, 1997, visit, Human Rights Watch uncovered troubling evidence of a series of three severe beating incidents involving Lindela personnel which had taken place over the previous few days. A twenty-three year old Lesotho man, Qoane Francis Motlomelo, visibly in pain and walking slowly, was brought to us by a few of his friends soon after we entered the men's compound. He related in detail how he had been beaten a few days before:

I was locked into a room by myself, room twenty-three. Yesterday, three men entered the room. I was handcuffed and my leg was tied to a bed. One man started beating me. He punched me in the face and kicked me to the bladder. Later, I was urinating blood. My jaw is very swollen. After beating me up, they left me handcuffed. I was released by a night shift worker. They beat me from 10 a.m. and they beat me until 5 p.m., changing the people who beat me. That is when they left me. The next shift released me at 8 or 9 p.m.

They were wearing the very same uniform as the guys walking around here now. [He pointed to a Lindela security guard walking around outside. All

---

[194]Human Rights Watch interview with D. Omar, Becker Street, Johannesburg, November 27, 1997.

[195]Human Rights Watch interviews at Lindela, October 8, 1996.

Lindela staff wear the same outfit with a medium-dark blue shirt and a reddish tie with the Dyambu trust symbol.] I was taken to the doctor last night for treatment, around 10 p.m. I couldn't speak last night, my teeth are very sore. I couldn't walk or go to the bathroom. I am nearly naked now because my clothes are full of blood. They told me if I tell the police they will kill me. I am afraid.[196]

Mr. Motlomelo gave an essentially similar statement to the Krugersdorp police officers who were called at the request of Human Rights Watch to investigate the allegations.[197] A Lindela security guard, speaking on condition of anonymity, confirmed that the beating had taken place and that the screams of Mr. Motlomelo were audible throughout the Lindela compound.[198] Mr. Motlomelo's version of events was corroborated by four other Basotho detainees. One of the men, John Lefosa, told Human Rights Watch how he and some other men were waiting to collect their Lindela ID cards when a Lindela security guard entered the room with Mr. Motlomelo and started beating him. Two other security guards came and joined in the beating of Mr. Motlomelo in the waiting room, before taking him to room twenty-three. Mr. Motlomelo exited the room several hours later in the company of a security guard, disfigured and looking much worse. He was then taken to the Lindela doctor by Mr. Lefosa.[199]

Human Rights Watch discussed the incident with the Lindela doctor, Dr. Khota, who confirmed that Mr. Motlomelo had been examined by him. His short examination report, obtained by Human Rights Watch, noted that Mr. Motlomelo has a swollen jaw on the right side, a tender abdomen, and a possible bladder injury. The report further noted that Mr. Motlomelo had alleged that the injuries were a result of assault, and the doctor concluded that the patient should remain

---

[196]Human Rights Watch interview with Mr Qoane Francis Motlomelo, Lindela, December 4, 1997.

[197]Statement under oath of Qoane Francis Motlomelo, Krugersdorp Police Station, December 4, 1997.

[198]Human Rights Watch interview with Lindela security guard, Lindela, December 4, 1997.

[199]Human Rights Watch interview with Mr. John Lefosa, Lindela, December 4, 1997.

under observation and be sent to a hospital if his situation deteriorated further.[200] Lindela officials ultimately took action against two persons involved in this incident, who worked at a neighboring Dyambu Trust-owned hostel, not the Lindela detention facility.[201]

A second serious beating allegation was made by Fabion Ndlovu, an eighteen-year-old Zimbabwean detainee. According to Mr. Ndlovu, a black male official of the Department of Home Affairs had called him and another Zimbabwean by the name of Taylor to the office on Friday, November 28, 1997. The official demanded that they pay a 100 rands [U.S. $ 20] bribe, or 50 rands [U.S. $ 10] each, and promised to get them released from Lindela. Mr. Ndlovu paid the bribe, but never heard again from the Home Affairs official. The next day, Saturday, Mr. Ndlovu and fourteen other inmates residing in dormitory room eight at Lindela managed to escape, but Mr. Ndlovu and another inmate were caught at 2 a.m. on Sunday. According to the sworn statement given by Mr. Ndlovu to the Krugersdorp police station,

The security officer at Lindela called us and started assaulting us with baton sticks all over the body. They then took us to the office and let the dogs free to bite us. They continued to hit us and kicked us with boots. They then thereafter took us to room eight where they hit other inmates who were there. They again they took us to room one where they let the inmates hit us. One of the security officers demanded that I give him my car keys as I had told him the place where I parked it. I did not give him the car keys.

After hitting and assaulting us they took us to room thirty-four where they locked us up until Wednesday without giving us food and water and not allowing us to go to the toilet.[202]

---

[200]Medical report of Dr. Khota, dated December 3, 1997.

[201]Fax of Danny Mansell to Human Rights Watch, dated December 23, 1997. The fax stated in relevant part: "Regarding the case of the Lesotho man, we unfortunately could not press the charge of assault legally as he elected to withdraw his case in order to go home. We have however, taken disciplinary action against the two persons involved. One was dismissed and the other reprimanded."

[202]Statement under oath of Fabion Ndlovu, Krugersdorp Police Station, December 4, 1997.

Human Rights Watch observed that Mr. Ndlovu had untreated and infected dog bites on his left forearm.[203] His clothes were torn, especially around the arms, suggesting that they were shredded by the dog bites as Mr. Ndlovu was trying to fend off the attack.

The third beating incident had taken place the day before our December 4, 1997, visit. Apparently, the usual weekly train used to deport persons to Mozambique had not arrived on December 3, 1997, and Mozambican detainees grew concerned about the length of time that they would have to spend in detention at Lindela. Thomas Sithole, a Mozambican detainee, related what happened next:

> I was fetched from my room with the other seven who were from Mozambique. The four security officers who fetched us claimed that we were planning a strike when we asked them, "When are we going home?" Then they started taking our ID cards while beating us with baton-sticks and clenched fists. We could therefore not go into the kitchen for our card were taken away. One by one these officers assaulted each one of us while we stood and watched.[204]

Our own observations and the perfunctory medical examination conducted by Dr. Khota confirm that the Mozambican inmates had been assaulted. For example, Dr. Khota noted the following during his examination of Samuel Sithole, one of the Mozambican detainees who claimed to have been assaulted: "Bruising and linear marks; Buttock with haematoma."[205]   The linear bruises and haematomas on the buttocks of the alleged beating victims suggest a punitive beating incident in which the victims were bent over and whipped on the buttocks, consistent with their own testimony about the incident.

One detainee, David Nkuna, was taken to the hospital on the evening of December 4, 1997, because of internal injuries. He was rolling around on his bed and seemed in serious pain. He was bleeding from the nose and crying, and Dr. Khota said he was feverish and suspected internal bleeding. Before being taken to the hospital, Mr. Nkuna told Human Rights Watch: "The security took 100 rands [U.S. $ 20] from me while they were beating me. They turned me upside down and

---

[203]The infected dog bites were also noted in Dr. Khota's medical report.

[204]Statement under oath of Thomas Sithole, Krugersdorp Police Station, December 4, 1997.

[205]Medical Report of Dr. Khota, Lindela, December 4, 1997.

the money fell out of my pocket. They let me pick up the coins but took the 100 rand [U.S. $ 20] note."[206]

This third beating incident was confirmed by many inmates at Lindela. John Khambune, a Mozambican detainee who arrived at Lindela on the day of the alleged beating, told Human Rights Watch that "[y]esterday, they went from cell to cell beating people. Yesterday, they woke us at night, beating us. This place is bad."[207] Another detainee from Zimbabwe, Dennis, told us,

> The problem is that we are not treated like human beings. Yesterday, guys were beaten severely. One guy was thirteen years old. He was beaten severely with a baton stick. And kickings. Very bad. These guys from Maputo [Mozambique] were complaining that they wanted to go home. So for this, they were beaten severely.[208]

The press reported that Lindela's operations manager Danny Mansell had confirmed that an incident had taken place at Lindela the day before our visit. He claimed that the incident started when 600 Mozambican detainees, impatient to go home, stormed the Lindela gate and hurled bottles and other projectiles at guards. Guards retaliated with dogs and batons. He reportedly acknowledged that guards were accused of beating detainees hours after the confrontation and admitted that detainees had identified four guards involved in the post-incident beating from a line-up.[209]

Mr. Mansell also told the press that the detainees later dropped the charges because they were desperate to go home, but that Lindela was continuing its investigation of the four guards. A later fax from Mr. Mansell informed us that no disciplinary action had been taken with regard to this incident.[210] None of the

---

[206]Human Rights Watch interview with David Nkuna, Lindela, December 4, 1997.

[207]Human Rights Watch interview with John Khambune, Lindela, December 4, 1997.

[208]Human Rights Watch interview with Dennis, Zimbabwean, Lindela, December 4, 1997.

[209]Andy Duffy, "Riot on the Eve of Detention-camp Probe," *Mail & Guardian*, December 12 to 18, 1997.

[210]Fax of Danny Mansell to Human Rights Watch, dated December 23, 1997.

detainees interviewed by Human Rights Watch about the incident mentioned a riot-like situation. Moreover, the testimonies gathered by Human Rights Watch and the injuries inflicted strongly suggest that the beatings took place while security guards were in full control of the situation. Thus, the evidence suggests that the beatings were punitive in nature and were not a proportionate use of force to re-establish control over unruly detainees.

International standards provide certain guidelines for the imposition of disciplinary and punitive measures. The U.N. Standard Minimum Rules for the Treatment of Prisoners require that conduct constituting a disciplinary offense, the types and duration of possible punishments and disciplinary actions, and the authority competent to impose such disciplinary measures must all be defined in the regulations of the institution or determined by law.[211] When asked if Lindela had such a disciplinary code prior to when the above-described allegations came to light, a Lindela official replied that they never had disciplinary problems at the institution and that, if a fight or something would occur, they just placed the offenders in room one, so the guards could "keep an eye on them."[212] Human Rights Watch did not find a coherent system to inform Lindela detainees of their rights and duties, and there appeared to be no rules or standard disciplinary procedures in place.[213] The Standard Minimum Rules also expressly prohibit the kind of physical punishment that was meted out to the detainees in these cases:

---

[211]U.N. Standard Minimum Rules for the Treatment of Prisoners, Rule 29.

[212]Human Rights Watch interview with Frans Le Grange, Lindela official, at Lindela, November 24, 1997. Room 1 is the room closest to the compound gate, and there is always a guard on duty at this location.

[213]Lindela claims it provides each detainee with a sheet of paper listing certain "rights" which Lindela will guarantee to detainees. Some of these rights, such as the right to one free phone call, do not appear to be enforced. The list of rights is only available in English, and most of the detainees Human Rights Watch interviewed did not speak or read English. The detainees interviewed by Human Rights Watch did not seem to be aware of the existence of this document, let alone its content. The Standard Minimum Rules require that each prisoner be provided with written information about "the regulations governing the treatment of prisoners of his category, the disciplinary requirements of the institution, the authorized methods of seeking information and making complaints, and all such other matters as are necessary to enable him to understand both his rights and his obligations and to adapt himself to the life of the institution." Rule 35(1). They also require that the information be conveyed orally if the prisoner is illiterate. Rule 35(2).

Corporal punishment, punishment by placing in a dark cell, and all cruel, inhuman and degrading punishments shall be completely prohibited as punishments for disciplinary offences.[214]

At the time of our visit, it did not appear that any investigation into these three incidents had been initiated. At the request of the victims, Human Rights Watch brought the incidents to the attention of the Lindela management and requested that the police be contacted to conduct an independent investigation. The Krugersdorp police officers arrived approximately seven hours after having been initially contacted about the beatings and seemed reluctant to get involved. It took some insistence by Human Rights Watch to get the officers to take statements and open an investigation of these serious allegations. During the day, the ten detainees told Human Rights Watch that a security officer came into the room where they were waiting for the police and threatened them with retribution later that night. Concerned about the safety of the ten detainees in light of this alleged threat, Human Rights Watch suggested that the detainees be removed from Lindela and taken into police custody. However, an official of the Department of Home Affairs, refused to authorize the required body receipt—a document necessary to authorize the transfer of a detainee from the authority of the Department of Home Affairs to the authority of the police.

Human Rights Watch believes that this incident illustrates a serious lack of accountability at Lindela. It would appear that no investigation into these allegations would have taken place in the absence of the intervention by Human Rights Watch. Although management was aware of the escape attempt and the incident involving the Mozambicans, and the doctor had examined Mr Motlomelo and had included the allegation of beating in his report, no internal investigation had commenced by the time Human Rights Watch brought these incidents to the attention of management. Even with the intervention of Human Rights Watch, the ensuing investigation by the Krugersdorp Police Station was flawed and marked by a lack of serious concern for the safety of the alleged victims, even after they claimed to have been threatened with further harm by a Lindela guard. It took an insistent phone call from Human Rights Watch to the superintendent of the Krugersdorp police station to convince the police to investigate the allegations, and even then the conduct of the police remained extremely reluctant.

The fact that most detainees only remain at Lindela for an average of five days before being deported severely limits the time available for the investigation of abuse claims. In the cases investigated by Human Rights Watch, detainees seemed

---

[214]U.N. Standard Minimum Rules for the treatment of prisoners, Art. 31.

to have a complete lack of confidence in the ability of Lindela to investigate claims of abuse, and most detainees did not even attempt to bring abuse to the attention of management. The fact that detainees would have to remain in custody at Lindela for several months in order to allow for an investigation and prosecution further hampers detainees from pursuing complaints of abuse against Lindela. Time and time again, Human Rights Watch spoke with people who were reluctant to pursue their cases because, in the words of Lindela manager Danny Mansell, they were just "desperate to go home."

In the case of the beating allegations discussed above, the detainees ultimately withdrew all charges against Lindela security personnel. According to two of the original complainants, Thomas Sithole and Armando Nyashale, the complainants were approached by Lindela security guards and told that they would have to remain in detention at Lindela "until next December"—an entire year—if they pursued their case.[215] Armando Nyashale told us, "This was imprisonment, so we decided to withdraw. The others stopped the suit, only I and Thomas were left, thus it was futile."[216] Despite promises to Human Rights Watch by the Lindela operations manager that the complainants would not be physically threatened or otherwise pressured into withdrawing their complaints to the police, the two complainants interviewed by Human Rights Watch after the withdrawal of the complaint said that they had been intimidated into withdrawing their complaints. They claimed they were brought into a room in pairs where they were questioned by a white, out-of-uniform person, whom they believed to be a Lindela staff member, and a translator.[217] When these allegations were raised with Lindela management, they replied that these meetings were part of an internal investigation into the abuse allegations and not an attempt to interfere with the police investigation.

We engaged in some limited discussions with Lindela about remedying some of the problems discovered during our inspection of the facility. One of the improvements suggested by operations manager Danny Mansell was the placement

---

[215]Human Rights Watch interview with Thomas Sithole and Armando Nyashale, Lindela, December 11, 1997.

[216]Human Rights Watch interview with Armando Nyashale, Lindela, December 11, 1997.

[217]Ibid. According to Thomas Sithole, the other alleged beating victims did not want to talk to Human Rights Watch during our December 11, 1997, follow-up visit out of fear of retribution from Lindela staff.

of an independent ombudsperson at Lindela, to which detainees could direct complaints. Human Rights Watch agrees that the placement of an independent ombudsperson would help provide some of the necessary oversight of the Lindela facility which is currently lacking and may help limit incidents of abuse at Lindela. In order to be effective, such an ombudsperson should be truly independent and adequately trained, and preferably from the South African Human Rights Commission or another similarly independent body (or a human rights nongovernmental organization) in order to prevent conflicts of interest. Because of the short period of time many undocumented migrants spend at Lindela, it is essential that the ombudsperson is present at the facility on a frequent and regular basis, at least for one day per week. The ombudsperson should have the power to investigate a wide variety of complaints, including conditions of detention, complaints of physical abuse, and claims of bribery and corruption.

Claude Schravesande, Department of Home Affairs Director of Admission and Aliens Control, told Human Rights Watch that it is possible that Lindela may cease being used as a detention facility in 1998 because no funds are available to continue the contract.[218] At the time of our visit, negotiations between the Department of Home Affairs and the parliament to obtain funding for Lindela were continuing. A fax sent to Human Rights Watch by Lindela management informed us that the contract has been extended until March 1998.[219]

Despite the many serious problems at Lindela, many commentators and officials consider the use of a centralized facility preferable to a return to a decentralized system where persons are detained in police cells and prison facilities only. Police cells and prison facilities are already severely overcrowded, and detaining migrants awaiting determination of status or deportation in these facilities presents equally serious problems. Police and prison officials were uniformly apprehensive about housing a large number of undocumented migrants at their facilities. When we asked Superintendent Du Pisanie of the Hillbrow police station about the possibility of Lindela shutting down, he told us:

I hope Lindela does not shut down. That would create problems. A few years ago, we had fifty to sixty foreigners here over Christmas. Home Affairs shut down, and we were left with the problems. There was a

---

[218]Human Rights Watch interview with Mr. Claude Schravesande, Director, Admissions and Aliens Control, Department of Home Affairs, December 3, 1997.

[219]Fax from Mr. Danny Mansell to Human Rights Watch, dated December 23, 1997.

hunger strike and all sorts of demands. These people are not criminals and should not take up our cell space.[220]

Human Rights Watch agrees with some of these concerns about a return to a system of detention of undocumented migrants which relies primarily on police cells and prisons. As documented in this report, undocumented migrants in detention are in danger of being assaulted and robbed by criminal suspects in unsegregated environments.[221] Detaining undocumented migrants in police cells also creates problems of adequate oversight and complicates the status determination process since Department of Home Affairs officials must then travel to a greater number of detention facilities to interview and determine the status of detainees. In our opinion, these envisioned complications are serious enough to recommend the continued use of a specialized detention facility for undocumented migrants.[222]

However, the conditions of detention of such a detention facility must be in compliance with internationally recognized minimum standards and must meet the requirements set forth in the South African constitution and relevant legislation.

---

[220]Human Rights Watch interview with Superintendent Du Pisanie, Hillbrow Police Station, December 19, 1997.

[221]It was such concerns which led the European Committee for the Prevention of Torture and Inhuman or Degrading Treatment or Punishment (CPT), which considered the question of detention of foreign nationals in a 1997 report, to recommend that prison not be used for the detention of immigration detainees in prisons: "Even if the actual conditions of detention for these persons in the establishments concerned are adequate—which has not always been the case—the CPT considers such an approach to be fundamentally flawed. A prison is by definition not a suitable place in which to detain someone who is neither convicted nor suspected of a criminal offence." European Committee for the Prevention of Torture and Inhuman and Degrading Treatment or Punishment, *7th General Report on the CPT's activities covering the period 1 January to 31 December 1996* (Strasbourg: Council of Europe, 1997), p. 12

[222]This is also the general position of the European Committee for the Prevention of Torture and Inhuman or Degrading Treatment or Punishment (CPT):

> In the view of the CPT, in those cases where it is deemed necessary to deprive persons of their liberty for an extended period under aliens legislation, they should be accommodated in **centres specifically designed for that purpose**, offering material conditions and a regime appropriate to their legal situation and staffed by suitably qualified personnel.

Ibid. (emphasis in original).

Our investigation establishes that the current detention conditions at Lindela do not meet these minimum requirements in a number of important areas. The Department of Home Affairs, as the government agency under whose authority undocumented migrants are detained at Lindela, has the primary responsibility to ensure compliance with these standards. It cannot abdicate this responsibility by contracting with the Dyambu Trust for the detention of undocumented migrants.

Prison Facilities

Human Rights Watch visited Modderbee (near Johannesburg), Johannesburg (Diepkloof) and Pollsmoor (Cape Town) prisons during our investigation. The number of undocumented migrants detained within the prison system varies greatly from day to day, and it appears that other prisons in addition to the ones visited, including Barberton prison near the Mozambican border, are occasionally used for the detention of undocumented migrants. As the policy regarding detention of undocumented migrants is in great flux, it is possible that prisons may play a greater role in the future in the detention of undocumented migrants. According to the Director of Admissions and Aliens Control, the Department of Home Affairs was at the time of our interview negotiating with the Department of Corrections about the use of prisons to detain undocumented migrants, partly in anticipation of the possible closure of the Lindela detention facility.[223] In his opinion, the Department of Corrections was required to house undocumented migrants brought to their facilities, as this was part of its statutory duties.[224]

In general, prison facilities appeared to be physically inferior to the Lindela facilities and much more restrictive of movement. Conditions of detention in the South African prison system remained similar to those found by Human Rights Watch during our earlier (1992-93) investigation, reported in *Prison Conditions in South Africa,*[225] although overcrowding had led to a further deterioration of standards in some cases. According to Home Affairs officials, the South African prison system is currently running at an average occupancy rate of over 200 percent

---

[223]Human Rights Watch interview with Mr. Claude Schravesande, Director, Admissions and Aliens Control, Department of Home Affairs, Pretoria, December 3, 1997.

[224]Ibid.

[225]Human Rights Watch, *Prison Conditions in South Africa* (New York: Human Rights Watch, 1994).

and is suffering from a severe staff shortage.[226] According to officials at both Modderbee and Pollsmoor prisons, all prisons are currently approved to operate at a 175 percent occupancy level because of the severe overcrowding problems, and many prisons have occupancy rates in excess of this. Complaints about lack of access to showers, dirty blankets, and other unsanitary conditions, as well as the quality of the food, were more frequent during our prison interviews than at Lindela. On the other hand, complaints about guard abuse were less frequent, although detainees did complain about abuse at the hands of South African inmates.

Pretoria Central Prison

Human Rights Watch visited Pretoria Central prison on October 11, 1996. Prison officials refused us access to the cells and denied us the opportunity to select detainees for interviews, claiming that such access would be dangerous because they were understaffed and it would be difficult for them to guarantee our safety. According to officials, there were about fifty undocumented migrants in the facility at the time of our visit, including five women. A less than satisfactory compromise was reached, whereby the prison authorities selected a few of the detainees to come and talk to us in the office of one of the prison officials.

Mr. Mafwala, one of the two persons interviewed at Pretoria prison by Human Rights Watch, described the conditions in the prison to us, since we had been refused an opportunity to inspect the facilities ourselves. He told us that all of a group of persons arrested at a protest at the Union Buildings against the standards used for refugee status determination (discussed below) stayed in one communal cell. There was a single toilet in the cell, but it was often blocked, including at the time of our visit. There was also a shower and a sink in the room, but the water in these was not working at the time. They had told the guards about the lack of water, but nothing was done about this. He continued, "We have bunk beds and mattresses, but they are dirty. The blankets are not washed and most people are complaining of skin problems. We found the blankets dirty on our arrival, infested with fleas and lice. We are provided only with soap, toilet paper, and toothpaste, and wash our clothes ourselves when there is water."[227] Two meals a day were served, one at 7 a.m. consisting of pap (porridge) and the second at midday when the detainees get pap again, with meat on Mondays and Fridays and with eggs on

---

[226]Human Rights Watch interview with Mr. Claude Schravesande, Director, Admissions and Aliens Control, Department of Home Affairs, Pretoria, December 3, 1997.

[227]Ibid.

Saturdays. The meal schedule means an up to nineteen-hour wait between the midday meal and the next morning meal, a common and persistent problem in South African prisons.

The second person we interviewed, Goma Nsika, told us that although the cell lighting was good, the windows were placed so high that they could not see outside the cell. During their long detention, the detainees arrested following the Union Buildings protest had only been allowed outside the cell once, on the Sunday before our visit. The detainees had requested to be able to use the sport facilities, but this was denied on the grounds that they were only temporary detainees. Mr. Nkisa also told us that the detainees had been using the same sheets for the last month and a half, and that their blankets had not been washed in forty-one days. He said many people were complaining about bed-sores, and described the cell as a "chicken-house."

Johannesburg (Diepkloof) Prison

Human Rights Watch visited Johannesburg (Diepkloof) Prison on May 20, 1997. Diepkloof is a medium security prison, designed for prisoners serving sentences of five years or more. The prison is divided into several sectors, called Mediums A, B, and C, and a female section. Medium A is reserved mainly for unsentenced prisoners, although there are a number of sentenced prisoners who work in cooking and cleaning. Medium B is strictly for sentenced prisoners, as is Medium C which is reserved for inmates serving longer sentences. The female section holds sentenced as well as unsentenced prisoners in segregated cells. Each cell block includes large communal cells as well as individual cells.

At the time of our visit, we were informed that since early 1997, undocumented migrants awaiting deportation were no longer kept in the prison. However, during our later visit to Modderbee Prison, an official from the Department of Correctional Services informed us that approximately 500 female undocumented migrants awaiting deportation were in the process of being transferred to Diepkloof Prison.[228] Thus, it appears that Diepkloof continues to be used on at least an occasional basis for the detention of undocumented migrants awaiting deportation. Sources indicated to Human Rights Watch that it was likely that Lindela would be turned into an all-male institution, and that Diepkloof Prison would become the preferred detention facility for female detainees awaiting deportation.

---

[228]Human Rights Watch interview with Mr. Rudi Potgieter, Liaison Officer for Gauteng Province, Department of Correctional Services, Modderbee Prison, December 5, 1997.

Conditions at Diepkloof appeared similar to those at other prisons. Due to overcrowding, the usual schedule of three meals per day had been reduced to two meals, with breakfast served at about 8 a.m. and a second meal served between noon and 2 p.m. When Diepkloof was used more extensively as a detention center for undocumented migrants in 1996, the undocumented migrants were kept in communal cells in Medium B, which tended to get overcrowded following police raids in which undocumented migrants were arrested. There were no recreational opportunities, so detainees spent most of their time either cleaning their cells, kitchen, and dining hall or sitting around in an enclosed and guarded area adjoining their cells. According to the Diepkloof internal security supervisor, it is difficult to organize any activities for persons awaiting deportation because they can be released or deported at any time.

Human Rights Watch interviewed two former detainees from Diepkloof about conditions at the facility. A Zimbabwean former detainee told us that he had been arrested at Rosebank, Johannesburg, on May 15, 1996. He told us he was kept at Hillbrow police station for about two weeks before being transferred to Diepkloof where he spent an additional three weeks before being deported to Beit Bridge at the Zimbabwean border on June 14, 1996.[229] He claimed that when he was deported, the prison authorities kept his belongings, telling him and his fellow deportees that "anyway, you are coming back soon."[230] A second former detainee told us that the prison officials would occasionally deny food to detainees as a form of punishment for refusing to do cleaning work and other such petty reasons. At other times, the detainees were given only porridge for food, without any meat or soup. The former detainee also described a beating incident that occurred during his stay at the prison in 1995, in which he claimed detainees were beaten, kicked, and slapped with the aim of "discouraging us from coming back to South Africa," and said that other detainees from Mozambique were ill-treated and told by guards that they must "get used to their country," implying that such abuse is routine in Mozambique.[231]

---

[229]Interview with former Johannesburg (Diepkloof) Prison detainee from Zimbabwe, originally deported in June 1996, now a security guard for Callguard Security in Parktown, in Johannesburg, July 28, 1997.

[230]Ibid.

[231]Interview with former Johannesburg (Diepkloof) Prison detainee from Zimbabwe, originally deported in July 1995, now a security guard for Grey Security, in Johannesburg, July 27, 1997.

Pollsmoor Prison

At the time of our December 10, 1997, visit, there were 6,195 persons detained at Pollsmoor Prison, comprising 2,904 unsentenced persons and 3,291 persons serving sentences. The occupancy level for which Pollsmoor was designed is 3,261 persons. Considering that there are always a number of un-usable cells in a prison this size, and taking into account the requirement to segregate certain classes of inmates, it is clear that the prison was operating at a severe level of overcrowding, conservatively estimated at 200 percent occupancy.

Approximately forty-five Mozambicans were about to be deported on the day of our visit to Pollsmoor. These men had all been arrested at a building site in Cape Town on October 10, 1997, and had been kept in custody for two months while the Department of Home Affairs prosecuted their employer and the recruiting officer for violations of the Aliens Control Act's prohibitions on hiring undocumented migrants.[232] The Mozambican workers were not prosecuted, but had to remain in custody for the two-month period in order to testify against their employer and recruiter. One worker told us he had been attacked by South African gang members—gang violence is a major problem in South African prisons[233] and on the Cape Peninsula—when the Mozambican workers were initially kept in a large communal cell with prisoners awaiting trial, and he showed us a scar on his chin.[234] He claimed that other attacks by gangsters and thefts had taken place when they were being transported to the court in Cape Town and while awaiting the court hearings in the cells at the court.

Later, Human Rights Watch interviewed other migrants from Uganda, Tanzania, and Malawi who told similar stories about abuse at the hands of prisoners awaiting trial. Joseph Mugisha, a Ugandan, explained how he had been robbed upon arrival at Pollsmoor:

---

[232]Human Rights Watch interview with Isaac Pondik, Mozambican citizen, Pollsmoor prison, December 10, 1997.

[233]Human Rights Watch, *Prison Conditions in South Africa*, pp. 43-48.

[234]Human Rights Watch interview with Isaac Pondik, Mozambican citizen, Pollsmoor prison, December 10, 1997.

I came to Pollsmoor on December 5. We were put here with hardcore criminals in a communal cell. The criminals took my watch and my shirt. I was in a communal cell on Friday, Saturday, and Sunday, three days.[235]

Luggy Lianda, a Tanzanian detainee, told us that "[a]t first, I was put together in a cell with criminals. The other inmates stole my money, shoes, and trousers."[236] Another Tanzanian, Aridi Omali, told us how he was kept in a communal cell for three weeks with prisoners awaiting trial:

When we arrived, we were mixed with the criminals, and they took my money, 300 rands [U.S. $ 60], and my trousers and shoes. I was mixed with them for three weeks. They didn't hurt me because I just allowed them to take my stuff. After that, I sneaked into the cells with the Mozambicans. The chiefs [i.e. guards] slapped me in the face because I was not supposed to be in this cell. After that, the Mozambicans complained to the chiefs saying that I was a foreigner like them and should be allowed to stay with them. Then the chiefs let me stay.[237]

Cliff Mucheka, a Malawian citizen, was similarly robbed by prisoners awaiting trial and complained to the guards. According to him, the guards told him: "Why did you come to this country? It is your own fault."[238] When Human Rights Watch discussed these abuses informally with prison officials at the end of our visit, they acknowledged that suspected undocumented migrants were kept together with inmates awaiting trial during the intake process. According to them, all prisoners brought to Pollsmoor on a certain day are kept in a large communal cell until time can be found to process and intake them. Depending on the number of persons needing to be processed, detainees can spend several days in this communal cell,

---

[235]Human Rights Watch interview with Joseph Mugisha, Ugandan citizen, Pollsmoor Prison, December 10, 1997.

[236]Human Rights Watch interview with Luggy Lianda, Tanzanian citizen, Pollsmoor Prison, December 10, 1997.

[237]Human Rights Watch interview with Aridi Omali, Tanzanian citizen, Pollsmoor Prison, December 10, 1997.

[238]Human Rights Watch interview with Cliff Mucheka, Malawian citizen, Pollsmoor Prison, December 10, 1997.

especially over weekends when staff levels are reduced. However, this explanation does not address the additional allegations made by some detainees that they were kept in communal cells for several weeks with prisoners awaiting trial.

The practice of keeping detainees awaiting determination of status or deportation in the same cells as criminal suspects is in contravention of the U.N. Standard Minimum Rules for the Treatment of Prisoners. The Standard Minimum Rules require the segregation of different categories of prisoners, including segregation on the basis of "the legal reason for their detention."[239] Particularly, the Standard Minimum Rules require the segregation of civil detainees from persons imprisoned by reason of a criminal offense.[240]

Living conditions at Pollsmoor were similar to other prisons inspected. The building housing undocumented migrants is a very large cell block, and the noise level is deafening, with constant yelling down the corridors. During our visit, a group of inmates was busy polishing the floor to the point of a dangerous slickness, while dancing, stamping, and loudly singing down the corridors in an impressive display. We inspected one large communal room which had just been vacated by the Mozambican worker group that had spent almost two months in the cell, and was in the process of being cleaned. It measured about 5.5 meters by thirteen meters and had a pile of mats on one side. There was a toilet and a shower in the room and a series of lockers to store possessions, although without locks.

Most of the remaining detainees were found in groups of three in individual cells. The tiny cells, measuring about two meters by 2.5 meters, contained only a single bed (a few cells had bunk beds) and a small sink. The cells appeared very crowded when occupied by three persons, and the detainees explained that they sleep with two persons in the single bed, while the third person sleeps on a mat on the floor. Mr. Mucheka told us that "conditions at Pollsmoor are tough. There are lice, and the toilets are dirty and unsanitary. We have to eat in the cells but they are not conducive to eating because of the bad smell."[241] Aridi Omali complained that "the lice bite me. The blankets are dirty, like they haven't been washed in a year. It causes sickness."[242]

---

[239]Standard Minimum Rules for the Treatment of Prisoners, Rule 8.

[240]Ibid, Rule 8(c).

[241]Ibid.

[242]Human Rights Watch interview with Aridi Omali, Pollsmoor Prison, December 10, 1997.

Sanitary conditions were deplorable, and washing facilities were often unavailable. Mr. Mugisha told us: "There are no baths so we can't wash our bodies. I asked to go wash today, but they said the showers don't work. Even the sink in our cell is broken."[243] Some of the detainees claimed that they had never been able to wash their bodies while at Pollsmoor. Even when there were washing facilities available, the severe overcrowding made it difficult to keep a sanitary environment. In the communal cell, "there were a lot of people, about fifty-five, so you have to wash quickly because there are many people waiting and there is only a bit of hot water. There was only one toilet which we all had to use."[244] Detainees also complained that the bright lights in the room, which were constantly turned on, even at night, hurt their eyes. One detainee told us that he had repeatedly requested medical attention for a painful toothache for almost two months, but had not received any medical attention or medication.[245]

Detainees at Pollsmoor receive two meals per day. At about 8 a.m., they receive a breakfast of porridge, two pieces of bread, and coffee with sugar. The second and final meal of the day, served around noon, consists of boiled corn, some chicken or pork, four slices of bread, and a drink that detainees make from water mixed with a powder. For the twenty hours between the noon meal and the next breakfast, no food is served. In the words of one detainee, "by 8 p.m., you are very hungry."[246] The U.N. Standard Minimum Rules for the Treatment of Prisoners require that "Every prisoner shall be provided by the administration at the usual hours with food of nutritional value adequate for health and strength, of wholesome quality and well prepared and served."[247] The meal schedule adhered to at Pollsmoor and other prisons is inconsistent with this international standard.

---

[243]Human Rights Watch interview with Joseph Mugisha, Pollsmoor Prison, December 10, 1997.

[244]Human Rights Watch interview with Aridi Omali, Pollsmoor Prison, December 10, 1997.

[245]Human Rights Watch interview with Luggy Lianda, Pollsmoor Prison, December 10, 1997.

[246]Human Rights Watch interview with Joseph Mugisha, Pollsmoor Prison, December 10, 1997.

[247]U.N. Standard Minimum Rules for the Treatment of Prisoners, Rule 20(1).

In addition to the large group of Mozambicans who had spent almost two months at Pollsmoor, there were other undocumented migrants at Pollsmoor who were awaiting deportation who had been detained for similar periods of time. Luggy Lianda had spent about a week in detention at Sea Point police station before transferring to Pollsmoor, where he had spent close to two months at the time of our visit. Aridi Omali and Abdallah Lamazani both claimed to have spent about a month in detention at the time of our visit. Detainees spend almost their entire time locked down in the cells, except for when they get food. Joseph Mugisha, who had been at Pollsmoor for five days, claimed that he had only been allowed outside his cell once during this time. The U.N. Standard Minimum Rules for the Treatment of Prisoners require at least one hour of outdoor exercise per day.[248]

Police Cells

Police cells in South Africa are mainly designed for the temporary detention of criminal suspects and do not have the necessary infrastructure for long-term detention, whether of undocumented migrants awaiting deportation or of others (during the course of our visits, we interviewed a number of criminal convicts who were serving sentences of a number of months in police cells). Human Rights Watch visited a number of police stations, including Sophiatown (formerly Newlands), Johannesburg Central (formerly John Vorster Square), Witbank, Nelspruit, Komatipoort, Malelane, Hillbrow, Highpoint Satellite, and Pretoria Central police stations. Detention conditions at most of the police stations were quite similar. Living conditions are very cramped, in dark, damp, smelly and overcrowded cells. Washing facilities are often limited, and recreation is non-existent.

The cells at most police stations were of two standard types: a ten-person cell and a larger twenty-five-person cell. The standard ten-person cell measured about four meters by four meters, while the standard twenty-five-person cell measured about four meters by eight meters. Even when used at their suggested capacity, the cells were extremely crowded, with mattresses covering the entire floor and almost no space to move around in the cell. At Witbank, a detainee complained, "We are very overcrowded. It is bad because we can get diseases."[249] In most cells we

---

[248]Ibid., Rule 21(1): "Every prisoner who is not employed in outdoor work shall have at least one hour of suitable exercise in the open air daily if the weather permits."

[249]Human Rights Watch interview with Dumisa Mavimbela, Witbank police station, November 29, 1997.

visited, detainees were just lying around on the floor, talking to each other. Detainees were often locked in their cells for entire days, and were not able to exercise or engage in physical or recreational activity.

The crowded conditions and inadequate access to sanitation caused many of the cells to have a sharp and unpleasant odor. At Pretoria Central police station,[250] the one available toilet adjoining the cell in which undocumented migrants were detained was blocked and filled to the brim with excrement. Dirty water had overflowed the toilet bowl and covered the floor. The smell, almost unbearable, was very strong inside the adjoining cell where the detainees were kept. The detainees in the cell claimed that the toilet had been blocked since before their arrival at the police cells.[251] The detainees had volunteered to clean the toilet themselves because of the smell and out of fear of getting sick, but they claimed that the police officials refused to provide them with the necessary cleaning materials.[252] At the Witbank police station, detainees in a large communal cell had covered the toilet inside their cell with blankets in order to try and contain the smell.[253]

Ventilation in many of the cells was inadequate, exacerbating unsanitary and unpleasant conditions. At Pretoria Central and other police stations, inmates were unable to control windows and thus ventilation. Inmates at Pretoria Central complained of the excessive heat in the cells during the summer, saying that they were continuously sweating and uncomfortable because of the heat.[254] During the night and in winter, thin cell walls and inadequate blankets often made the cells bitterly cold. One inmate at Bushbuckridge police station, Moses Matevula, complained to us about the cold: "We do not have adequate blankets, so it is cold

---

[250]Visited October 11, 1996.

[251]Human Rights Watch interview with detainees, Pretoria Central police station, October 11, 1996.

[252]Ibid.

[253]Visited by Human Rights Watch on November 29, 1997.

[254]Human Rights Watch interview with detainees, Pretoria Central police station, October 11, 1996.

at night."[255] As with the prisons we visited, blankets were dirty and often covered with lice. According to the South African Human Rights Commission, detainees at Alexandra police station "were held overnight in cells with no beds or bunks, very few blankets, a shortage of hot water, and often a shortage of food."[256]

Washing facilities were extremely limited. At Witbank police station, the sergeant showing us around the facility complained about the shoddy quality of construction of the facility: "Many cells are broken, and the toilets and showers often are not working. These buildings are not strong. Many cells are not working. Six are in good order, three don't work."[257] At Pretoria Central police station, the shower available to detainees was not working, allowing only the "earliest bird" to wash, "but only his face."[258] At Bushbuckridge, only cold water was available, and inmates were not given soap to wash with.[259] At Kameelsdrift police station, detainees had only a washbasin available.[260]

Because many police detention facilities were not designed for long-term detention, facilities for food preparation were often inadequate. Detainees at Kameelsdrift complained that they receive only bread and tea (without sugar) and a small amount of pap (porridge) and meat, but never vegetables.[261] At Bushbuckridge police station, detainees complained that "we always eat beans," describing both lunch and dinner as consisting of porridge and beans, sometimes

---

[255]Human Rights Watch interview with Moses Matevula, Bushbuckridge police station, November 11, 1997.

[256]"Holding Conditions at Alex police station Appalling—SAHRC," *SAPA*, July 28, 1997.

[257]Human Rights Watch interview with police official, Witbank police station, November 29, 1997.

[258]Human Rights Watch interview with detainees, Pretoria Central police station, October 11, 1996.

[259]Human Rights Watch interview with detainees in Cell 1, Bushbuckridge police station, November 11, 1997.

[260]Lawyers for Human Rights, letter to Minister Buthelezi, dated August 21, 1996.

[261]Ibid.

with cabbage or chicken.[262] A Pakistani detainee at Pretoria Central complained that food was often inadequate and described the soup as "water in which hundreds of people washed themselves until it becomes solid."[263]

Although most police stations provided three meals to inmates, sometimes only two meals were provided, ostensibly because of inadequate staff. Male detainees at Pretoria Central police station also complained of thirst and did not appear to have free access to drinking water, a direct violation of the Standard Minimum Rules which provide that "Drinking water shall be available to every prisoner whenever he needs it."[264] Further, detainees at Pretoria Central police station ate in their cells, despite the very strong odors emanating from the blocked toilet. Male inmates told us, and Human Rights Watch observed, that soup was brought to the cell in a communal container, with bread on the side, and that they all ate from the same container without being given spoons.

Although men and women were separately housed in all police cells visited by Human Rights Watch, juveniles were often housed with adults, and undocumented migrants awaiting deportation were often housed with prisoners awaiting trial. At Witbank, for example, there was a Swazi awaiting deportation who was housed alone in a cell with a large number of criminal suspects, while the cell with most of the undocumented migrants also contained a mentally disturbed criminal suspect. At Bushbuckridge police station, several juveniles were housed in cells with adults. Police officials at Johannesburg Central police station told us that the limited number of cells available to them due to renovation work forced them to mix criminal suspects with undocumented migrants awaiting deportation.[265]

We also received several complaints about the lack of access to health care. At Bushbuckridge, we were approached by two inmates in separate cells who had severely infected, septic wounds and who claimed that they had not had adequate access to a doctor. A third man showed us a serious rash and claimed that the police officials had refused to take him to a doctor. A Zimbabwean woman who

---

[262]Human Rights Watch interviews with detainees in cell 1, Bushbuckridge police station, November 30, 1997.

[263]Human Rights Watch interview with Pakistani detainee, Pretoria Central police station, October 11, 1996.

[264]Standard Minimum Rules for the Treatment of Prisoners, Rule 20 (2).

[265]Human Rights Watch interview with Inspector Kruger, Johannesburg Central Police Station, November 25, 1997.

was transferred to Lindela from Queenstown police station a few days before our visit complained about the lack of health care at both the police station and Lindela: "I have been sick for two weeks, but they give me no treatment, no injection, nothing. I haven't even seen a doctor, I don't even know if there is a doctor here."[266] Luggy Lianda, from Tanzania, was detained at Sea Point police station in Cape Town for a week and complained of a toothache: "I was ill with a toothache and told the police about this, but nothing was done about this."[267]

Despite these deplorable conditions, suspected undocumented migrants often spend significant amounts of time in police detention, either awaiting deportation or transfer to another detention facility. A Zimbabwean woman at Lindela recounted to Human Rights Watch how she and a group of Zimbabwean women had been detained at Queenstown police station for three weeks:

> We were arrested at Burgersdorp, near East London, all of us together, on the 13th of November.... Home Affairs took us to the police station, and the same day they took us to Queenstown police station. They put us in prison [sic] for three weeks. The food we were given was just bread and soup, the soup was just flour and carrots, and tea without sugar. Three times a day we were fed. We were mixed with criminals, sometimes there were more than twenty people in the one cell which was about four meters by four meters. We slept on mats on the floor. The Home Affairs people didn't even come to see us until the 1st of December. Then they took us here in a combi [a minivan], but they didn't give us any food during the trip which took the whole day.[268]

Other people interviewed by Human Rights Watch had also been in detention at police cells for several weeks, such as Dumisa Mavimbela who had been arrested on November 14 and was interviewed by us at Witbank police station on November 29. Lucas Morris, interviewed at Lindela, told us he had spent a month in detention at C.R. Swart police station in Durban prior to transfer to Lindela.

---

[266]Human Rights Watch interview with Martha Manyozo, Zimbabwean citizen, Lindela, December 4, 1997.

[267]Human Rights Watch interview with Luggy Lianda, Tanzanian citizen, Pollsmoor, December 10, 1997.

[268]Human Rights Watch interview with Martha Manyozo, Zimbabwean citizen, Lindela, December 4, 1997.

Military Detention

Although we were briefed by military personnel about the scope and nature of their operations at the Mozambican border, and we observed these operations during a night mission, Human Rights Watch did not inspect any military detention facilities. While our team was observing the military's border operations, a single Mozambican was caught while attempting to cross the border. He was brought to one of the substations adjoining the border fence and asked to sit on the curb where he remained until we left about four hours later. One of the soldiers offered the detainee some food, apparently out of his own personal rations.

According to military officials, undocumented migrants detained by the military are normally kept at the substation for a few hours while being questioned by military personnel to gather information about how they entered the country, and especially about organized smuggling groups.[269] Detainees are kept at the substation until these interviews are done, and until enough undocumented migrants have been apprehended to make a trip to the Macademia base worthwhile.[270] If persons are detained for more than four hours, they are given water and food. At the base, the platoon commander hands over the undocumented migrants together with an incident report and a body receipt. Detainees are kept at the base until they are brought to the Komatipoort police station, where they are handed over into the custody of the police. If undocumented migrants are found who seem to have valuable information about smuggling rings or other matters, they may be kept at the base for further interrogation.

Unlawful Long-term Detention of Undocumented Migrants

According to the legislation covering the detention of undocumented migrants, detainees must be informed of the reason for their detention after the first forty-eight hours in detention, and their detention must be reviewed after a period of thirty days by a judge of the High Court (as discussed in Appendix A to this report). Despite these statutory requirements, Human Rights Watch found all of the persons at Lindela who had been detained there for more than thirty days to have been detained without review, in some cases for several months. The case of Valentim Daimone Manheira seemed typical of these long-term detainees. Mr. Manheira, a gentle man in his fifties, told us about his experience at Lindela:

---

[269]Human Rights Watch interview with Major Olivier, Company Commander, Group 33, Komatipoort border, December 1, 1997.

[270]Ibid.

I came to South Africa in 1956, when I was a small boy. I lived in Pretoria West, Court Street Number 76. I am a panel beater [auto body repairer] by profession. I got arrested in Pretoria on June 25, 1997. The police man said 'we don't need people from other countries here.'...

The police just brought me to Lindela, and I have been here ever since. They say they must contact the Brazilian embassy, so I just wait. They don't care that I have been here so long. I don't know now if they will get me a permit or send me back to Brazil. I know nobody in Brazil, my parents died a long time ago when I was small.

I have never been to court to see a judge, just to the Brazil embassy in Pretoria. In three months, I have only talked to Home Affairs twice (sic). The first was when they gave me my [Lindela identification] card. The second was the 13th of October, when they took me to the embassy. On the 27th of November, we went again to the embassy.

I have no money left. My wife doesn't even know I am here. She lives in a remote part [of KwaZulu] and has no phone. I just follow the guards' orders and they leave me alone. But people do get beaten, I've seen it myself. They beat you very bad if you try to escape.

I only have one set of clothes and they are all broken. When I wash my clothes, I wear a blanket. All my possessions are at my home in Pretoria. I don't know if they have broken into the house by now, it has been so long.[271]

Mr. Manheira was not alone. According to data obtained at Lindela by Human Rights Watch, twenty-seven persons were detained for periods longer than thirty days at the time of our December 4, 1997, visit.[272] Mr. Babo Munelele, a suspected undocumented migrant from the United Kingdom, had been at Lindela since

---

[271]Human Rights Watch interview with Mr. Valentim Daimone Manheira, Lindela, December 4, 1997.

[272]Lindela detention facility, document entitled "Time Analysis," dated December 4, 1997, provided to Human Rights Watch by Lindela, December 4, 1997.

August 1, 1997, a period of four months.[273] Mr. William Tambo, a suspected undocumented migrant from Mexico, had been at Lindela since August 5, 1997.[274] There were also a Cameroonian, several Namibians and Angolans, a Botswanan, a Somali, a Malawian, as well as two Pakistanis and an Indian who had all been detained well in excess of thirty days at Lindela.

In addition, many of these individuals had spent additional time in police custody prior to transfer to Lindela. For example, David Petrus, a Namibian citizen, told us that he had been detained at Pollsmoor prison in Cape Town for three weeks from the time of his arrest on August 28, 1997, until his transfer to Lindela on September 18, 1997.[275] A Tanzanian detainee, Lucas Morris, told us,

> I was arrested in Durban in August. I have had piece jobs there for a year.
> I was kept in C.R. Swart police station for one month. Then I went to the
> Westville jail in Durban. Then here to Lindela. We were told that we must
> wait here until January.[276]

It does not appear that there is any working system in place to track the time undocumented migrants spend in detention and to ensure that their statutory rights are enforced. Lindela management had tried to implement a computer tracking system for detainees at its facility, but this system was not operating correctly at the time of our visit.[277] Especially in the case of detainees who are transferred from other institutions after spending significant amounts of time in detention at these prior institutions (most commonly police cells but also prisons), there is no system

---

[273]The ID numbers given to Lindela inmates allow for an accurate determination of intake dates, since they include the date of intake. Mr. Munelele's ID number was 199708010045, reflecting that he was brought to Lindela on August 1, 1997.

[274]As indicated by the "Time Analysis" document.

[275]Human Rights Watch interview with Mr. David Petrus, Namibian citizen, Lindela, December 4, 1997.

[276]Human Rights Watch interview with Mr. Lucas Morris, Tanzanian citizen, Lindela, December 4, 1997.

[277]In the opinion of Human Rights Watch, it is the responsibility of the Department of Home Affairs, as the government agency under whose authority people are detained at Lindela and elsewhere, to keep track of the time people spend in detention and to ensure that the statutory limits are enforced.

to calculate the time that detainees spend in detention prior to arrival at Lindela. Thus, the legal rights of detainees often go unenforced. In the particular case of the twenty-seven persons detained at Lindela for more than thirty days, Mr. Erasmus, the ranking Department of Home Affairs official at Lindela, agreed to release the twenty-seven detainees after the matter was brought to his attention by Human Rights Watch. He admitted that the correct legal procedures had not been followed in these cases and promised to remedy the situation. As with other detainees released from Lindela, the twenty-seven were released from the facility without any offer of transportation. It appeared to Human Rights Watch that most of the men were not in possession of any money, and their clothes were ragged after their long detention. Many of the men had to find their own way home under these trying conditions, often to locations as far away as Cape Town, more than 1,500 kilometers away.

As at Lindela, long-term detention of suspected undocumented migrants while their status is being determined by the Department of Home Affairs is a problem at Pollsmoor. One especially disturbing case is the fourteen-month detention of Eddie Johnson at Pollsmoor by the Department of Home Affairs. Eddie Johnson claims to have been born in South Africa in the 1970s, but to have moved to Zambia when he was about three years old.[278] He returned to South Africa in the early 1990s, successfully obtained South African identification documents, and voted in the historic 1994 elections. One early morning in August 1994, about ten immigration officers burst into his Cape Town home and arrested Eddie Johnson on four immigration-related criminal charges. On December 21, 1994, he was found not guilty on three of the charges and convicted on the fourth charge, and given a sentence which was totally suspended for five years. As he walked out of the court room, Eddie Johnson was again detained by immigration officials. On the basis of their suspicion that Mr. Johnson was lying about his origins, the Department of Home Affairs detained him at Pollsmoor for the remainder of 1994 and the entire year of 1995. But the Department of Home Affairs was unable to deport Eddie Johnson, because the Zambian and Tanzanian High Commissioners refused to recognize Mr. Johnson as a citizen of their respective countries. Eddie Johnson was ultimately released on January 16, 1996, after the University of Cape

---

[278]Human Rights Watch interview with Lee Anne de la Hunt, Director, University of Cape Town Law Clinic, Cape Town. December 8, 1997. The case of Eddie Johnson is discussed in Anton Katz, "Immigration and the Courts," *Southern African Migration Project Migration Policy Series No. 3* (1997). The case is also the subject of an unreported CPD High Court decision, *Eddie Johnson v. Minister of Home Affairs*, Case No. 1560/1995 (delivered August 14, 1996).

Town Law Clinic obtained a court order for his release on the basis that his constitutional rights had been violated.

Although it appears that the Department of Home Affairs in Cape Town does generally abide by the requirement to seek judicial approval for detentions in excess of thirty days, attorneys complained to Human Rights Watch about the general lack of scrutiny with which some judges approved such applications. One attorney told Human Rights Watch about the case of three Pakistani seamen whom he was able to get released in October 1997 after they had been detained for six months under the Aliens Control Act. Two different judges had approved extensions of detention, at first for a period of 120 days. It appeared from the file that the second judge had not been notified of the lengthy period for which the persons had already been detained and did not bother to ask. The form did not even have a space for the signature of the detainee, strongly suggesting that the detainees had never been notified of either the application or the decision of the court. The entire proceedings as described by the attorney suggest an unjustifiable lack of diligence by the courts in reviewing applications for the deprivation of liberty of persons.

The Deportation Process: The Train to Mozambique

After their status as deportable undocumented migrants has been determined and approval for repatriation has been obtained from their home countries, the Department of Home Affairs will repatriate people. The repatriation can take a number of forms, depending on the location of the home country. Repatriations to Mozambique and Zimbabwe—which account for the vast majority of repatriations—are mostly done by train and by cramped prisoner transfer vehicles. Repatriations to more distant countries such as Malawi are most often done by air.

Human Rights Watch interviewed a number of persons who had previously been deported by train to Mozambique. Although the former deportees were interviewed on separate occasions, they all told a remarkably similar tale about the abuses they faced on the train while being deported. The experience related by Jack Ballas was typical of these testimonials:

> I was deported via train to Mozambique three weeks ago. We are made to run to the train fast, so we don't see the station. We have to take off our belts and put them on top. The reason for this is to make it easy for the officials to see whether one has money. We are made to squat with our head between our legs. The police sjambok us on the train to make sure we keep our heads down. They ask us if we have money, and they beat us all the way to Ressano Garcia. It takes a long time, about ten hours. We have

Mozambican migrants awaiting processing and deportation at Lindela detention facility, December 1997.

The cramped vehicles used to deport migrants to Mozambique and Zimbabwe, a trip which may take as many as twelve hours. Trains are also used for deportation. December 1997. (Inside view of vehicle on opposite page)

to sit like that the whole time. It gets very painful and people get swollen. Many people are bleeding, many people become unconscious. The police just laugh. If you straighten your head, you have to pay fifty rands [U.S. $ 10], or you get beaten. If you pay the money, you can sit straight. We do get water, but only one person is allowed to fetch water for everyone.

In Ressano Garcia, we must jump while the train is moving. The train is very crowded and they close all the windows. It gets very hot and people are sweating. The police go through our luggage and take what they want.

We saw many people get off the train after paying a fee. They allow them to jump off when the train is moving. You have to pay 150 rands [U.S. $ 30] or whatever you have.[279]

The remarkable similarity between the accounts from people who were deported and interviewed at different times lend a high degree of credibility to them. Zitto Vilakazi, another Mozambican, told us his story:

I was arrested and deported to Mozambique in October 1997. We have to run to the train. Then we have to run all the way to the front of the coach. Then they tell us to squat with our heads between our legs. When we sit down, the officials start asking for money when we have our head down. If you have money, you can sit up. It cost 50 rands [U.S. $ 10], 100 rands [U.S. $ 20], it depends. If you can't pay, you must keep squatted. Then the beatings start. If you can't pay, they ask you "do you want to reach home or what?" It is a threat, and many then pay. If you try and keep your money, you won't reach home. Those who have money are released before reaching the station when the train slows down.

I did refuse because I had no money, and they didn't beat me. But I saw many getting beaten because the police knew they had money. Those who don't have money must suffer the chafkop system [the squatting position] before they are deported.

The journey took the whole night. We left Lindela at 6 p.m. and arrived at Ressano at 7 a.m. The police ask us to buy them cool drinks and beat us

---

[279]Human Rights Watch interview with Jack Ballas, Mozambican citizen, Lindela, December 3, 1997.

if we have no money. And the police insult us for being Shangaan from Mozambique. You can't even write the things they say, they speak about our mother's vaginas and things. We don't get water or food. The police will sell you things but if you have no money, you get nothing. This is not my own country, but we should be treated well. We suffer a great deal for being Mozambican.[280]

During an earlier investigative visit to the Mozambican border area during July 1996, we received similar testimonials from recent deportees. One person interviewed claimed that the police jumped on top of his toes and used iron implements to squeeze his fingers to extract bribes, and that the police officers had thrown one of his fellow Mozambicans from the train into the Komati River "for having tried to protect himself and his money. He had a lot of money since he had just been caught early that morning."[281] News reports have published similar accounts of the deportation process to Mozambique. An October 1997 newspaper article gave an account by Geoffrey Mabuna, a recent deportee, describing how the

---

[280]Human Rights Watch interview with Zitto Vilakazi, Mozambican citizen, Lindela, December 4, 1997. Phenias Mugwambe, another Mozambican citizen interviewed by Human Rights Watch, gave yet another similar account: "I was deported in March 1996. I never reached Mozambique because I have a lot of property in South Africa. We are taken to the backyard of Lindela to the station. We have to run while getting beaten by the officials. When we get to the train, we have to remove all of our clothes except for the trousers. We have to remove our belts. If your belt or shirt is nice, you never see it again. And we have to bend our heads. At the same time, they start beating us but you can't see who beats you because your head is down. They use the leather belts to beat us. If you want to straighten your neck you have to pay money. After you pay money, you are their friend. The amount varies, depending on the distance from Johannesburg. If you pay 20 to 50 rands [U.S. $ 4-10] , you can only straighten your neck. If you want off the train, the fee is 200 rands [U.S. $ 40]. If you are from Johannesburg and want to be released before Witbank, the fee is 150 rands [U.S. $ 30] and up. If you are near Komatipoort, the fee rises to 200 rands [U.S. $ 40]and above." Human Rights Watch interview with Phenias Mugwambe, Mozambican citizen, Lindela, December 4, 1997.

[281]Human Rights Watch interview with deportee, Matuba village of Chokwe, Gaza Province, Mozambique, July 19, 1996.

deportees were forced to sit in the chafkop position and how many deportees had bribed their way off the train.[282]

The Department of Home Affairs also deports persons directly by vehicle, and similar incidents of bribery and physical abuse involving Home Affairs officials have taken place. Captain Chilembe of the Nelspruit Internal Tracing Unit described a case to us in which the responsible officials were actually caught, prosecuted, and convicted:

> There was a case involving two Home Affairs officials who were transporting people to the border. They went to the border and had the deportation order stamped, but they came back with the people. We set a trap and they were caught and are now serving three years in jail. All of the illegals had to pay 100 rands [U.S. $ 20] each, and those who couldn't pay were assaulted. They testified in court because they were assaulted, staying in detention for three months to testify.[283]

Because of the systematic extortion and bribery on the train and at earlier stages in the deportation process, many of those deported reach Mozambique or Zimbabwe without any money or possessions except for the clothes they are wearing. Deportees are dropped just across the border, in the town of Ressano Garcia in the case of Mozambique and Beit Bridge for Zimbabwe. Without any financial means, the return trip home is often complicated. Deportees are often forced to sell their last possessions to make the trip home. A deportee interviewed by Human Rights Watch in Mozambique told of his and his friend's three-week attempt to make their way home:

> We spent three weeks at Gaxa trying to get money for the *Panthera Azul* bus to Maputo. My friend sold his leather jacket at the trade market and waited for me to sell my shirt so that we may go. My shirt was bought after three weeks. We then arrived at Maputo and stayed in the streets for two months trying to get money for the *Xibomba* [bus] to go to Chokwe.

---

[282]Lucas Ledwaba, "Slipped Bucks and Blind Eyes," *Sunday Times*, October 19, 1997.

[283]Human Rights Watch interview with Captain Chilembe, Head, Nelspruit Internal Tracing Unit, South African police services, Nelspruit, December 1, 1997.

We used to stay hungry. During that three weeks we only managed to get
bread for three days per week.[284]

In fact, most deportees choose not to go home or to remain in Mozambique.
Instead, they return almost immediately to South Africa for a variety of reasons:
to retrieve property left behind, to be reunited with family or friends, to return to
a job, or simply to try again to escape the desperate poverty that plagues
Mozambique. Our research and interviews suggest that undocumented migrants
deported from the greater Johannesburg area are generally deported without being
given the opportunity to retrieve their possessions. Belongings left behind are a
major impetus for returning to South Africa following deportation. As one
deportee told us in Mozambique: "I am not thinking about going back, except to
collect my belongings. If it weren't for that, I would not have to [go back]."[285]
Requests to the authorities to retrieve property often go unheeded: "When you are
arrested and you tell the police you want to go and get your things, they pay no
attention. They say 'You came here with nothing, not even money.'"[286] Since
undocumented migrants are normally arrested at their place of work or on the
street, and often have spent several years working in South Africa, they often leave
behind significant property in South Africa and are then forced to return to retrieve
their property. Once they have returned to South Africa, they will most likely
continue their previous employment, and be again at risk of arrest, possible abuse,
and deportation. As Mr. Ncuma, an official with the Mozambican Department of
Labor told Human Rights Watch:

Lots of Mozambicans are now deported who leave all their property
behind. This is now rife in Johannesburg, a very common form of abuse.

---

[284]Human Rights Watch interview with deportees, Matuba village of Chokwe,
Gaza Province, Mozambique, July 19, 1996.

[285]Human Rights Watch interview with Manuel Sibuyi, Simbe, Mozambique,
March 17, 1996.

[286]Human Rights Watch interview with Kaptine Simango, Simbe, Mozambique,
March 16, 1996.

Some even have bank accounts. That is why people come back illegally, they must collect their property.[287]

The practice of repatriating undocumented migrants without their possessions is not universal. In Cape Town, according to chief immigration officer Jurie de Wet, officials are required to ensure that undocumented migrants awaiting deportation have had the opportunity to retrieve their possessions, and undocumented migrants must sign a document saying they have been afforded the opportunity to retrieve their possessions prior to deportation.[288] According to Mr. De Wet, this procedure is required by internal guidelines of the Department of Home Affairs.[289] Even if allowed the opportunity to retrieve valuables prior to deportation, many undocumented migrants may refuse this opportunity because of the fear that their valuables may be taken from them by corrupt officials under the current system of repatriation.

Time and time again, when we concluded interviews with detainees or deportees with the question "What will you do now?," the answer was, "I will return to South Africa." Human Rights Watch often interviewed people who had been previously deported, and at detention facilities and police cells we frequently observed officials recognizing detainees whom they had previously deported. One 1995 study discussed a Mozambican who had been deported twenty-one times,[290] and Captain Van Vuuren of the South African Police Service claimed to a group of reporters in 1995 to know of a Mozambican who had boasted of having crossed the fence between Mozambique and South Africa more than one hundred times.[291] When Human Rights Watch interviewed detainees awaiting deportation at the

---

[287]Human Rights Watch interview with Mr. Ncuma, Mozambican Department of Labor, Nelspruit, December 2, 1997.

[288]Human Rights Watch interview with Mr Jurie de Wet, Chief Immigration Officer, Western Cape, Department of Home Affairs, Cape Town, December 9, 1997.

[289]Ibid.

[290]Minnaar and Hough, "Illegals in South Africa: Scope, Extent and Impact," Paper presented at the International Organization for Migration (IOM) meeting in Pretoria, August 25, 1995.

[291]Hannes de Wet, "South African border fence can't stop the hungry," *Citizen*, July 4, 1995.

Komatipoort border, all asserted that they would return to South Africa,[292] lending credence to a Mozambican newspaper report that claimed,

> It seems that people are not exaggerating when they say that more than 80 percent of the three thousand young people who get off [the train] at Ressano every Thursday morning return [to South Africa] the very same day or within two days of their repatriation, and by the same illegal routes.[293]

The fact that many undocumented migrants appear to be deported multiple times during a single year suggests that using the total number of deportations to estimate the total number of undocumented migrants in South Africa at any given time is a very unreliable method of calculation. Thus, the increase in deportations in recent years in South Africa may be due to stepped-up policing efforts rather than an increase in undocumented migration to South Africa.

Complications associated with deportation formalities often result in lengthy periods of detention, and at times make it much more difficult for a deported person to return home. In one case, a Mozambican crossed the border from the most southern area of Mozambique into South Africa at Kosi Bay, in order to buy a can of paraffin at the local South African supermarket.[294] He was arrested by the Internal Tracing Unit and had to be deported through the Lebombo border post several hundreds of miles away as this was the only border post through which Mozambicans could be repatriated, by agreement with between the South African and Mozambican governments. Since he had no money, the deportee, now several hundreds of miles away from home, decided to cross back into South Africa and work on a local farm to earn the money to return home. When he finally earned enough money to travel home, "as he was getting off the bus at Jozini he was again arrested. He had been away from his home for six months and still had to buy his can of paraffin."[295]

---

[292]Human Rights Watch interviews with detainees awaiting repatriation, Komatipoort, June 12, 1997.

[293]*Aro* (Maputo), February 8 to 22, 1996.

[294]Minnaar and Hough, *Who Goes There?*, pp. 148-49.

[295]Ibid., p. 149.

Dilapidated tents at Ga'Rankuwa refugee camp near Pretoria. The camp has been repeatedly raided by government authorities, December 1997.

V. THE TREATMENT OF REFUGEES AND ASYLUM-SEEKERS IN SOUTH AFRICA

During the apartheid era, South Africa did not accede to the various international refugee conventions and administered its refugee policy on an ad-hoc basis. For instance, South Africa accepted and granted full citizenship status to a large number of mostly white persons fleeing from Rhodesia and Mozambique as the settler colonial systems in these countries crumbled, but refused to offer a similar welcome to black Mozambicans fleeing the South African-sponsored civil war in Mozambique. To this day, South Africa remains without specific refugee legislation, administering its refugee policy according to improvised procedures under the Aliens Control Act. The improvised nature of these procedures and the lack of clear guidelines have allowed for an unacceptable degree of bureaucratic discretion which can be easily abused, as our findings indicate.

Since an agreement with UNHCR in 1993 to abide by international norms in deciding refugee status, and its ratifications of the OAU and U.N. refugee conventions in 1995 and 1996, South Africa has received a significant number of asylum-seekers. Most are young males who have fled instability in such African countries as Angola, Somalia, the Democratic Republic of Congo, Liberia, Senegal, and Ethiopia, but South Africa is also experiencing increasing refugee flows from India, Pakistan, and Bangladesh. By January 1998, the Department of Home Affairs had received 38,143 applications for refugee status since 1993, and had taken a decision on 16,282 of these, while another 21,861 remained outstanding.[296] The Department of Home Affairs currently lacks the capacity to process asylum applications on a timely basis, and it routinely takes the department more than two years to decide on an application.

---

[296]Department of Home Affairs fax to Human Rights Watch, dated January 27, 1998. A statistical analysis contained in the same fax shows that out of the 16, 385 applications considered by the department, 6,585 were rejected after consideration, 1,588 were rejected as "manifestly unfounded," 1,155 were canceled, 44 were granted immigration permits in terms of section 25 of the ACA (read with sections 28(2) and 23(a) of the ACA), 3,823 were granted temporary residence permits in terms of section 26 of the ACA (read with sections 28(2) and 23(b) of the ACA), and 1,067 were "referred." There is a slight discrepancy between these two sources, as one lists the total number of applications "finalized" at 16,282, while the other lists the number of applications "considered" at 16,385.

Asylum-Seekers in Detention

Unless their applications are suspected of being "manifestly unfounded," asylum-seekers are generally not kept in detention during the asylum determination process, which can take up to two years because of a staff shortage and a severe backlog of applications. Asylum-seekers normally receive a section 41 permit, which is a temporary (normally three-month) permit to remain in the country. "Manifestly unfounded" asylum applicants are kept in custody, because the Department of Home Affairs feels that "it would destroy all elements of Aliens Control if everyone who was arrested and detained and then applied for asylum was released."[297]

Human Rights Watch found only a few asylum-seekers in detention, mostly at relatively remote police stations. At the Komatipoort police station, we interviewed two asylum-seekers who had been in detention for a relatively long period. Jean-Pierre had fled his native Democratic Republic of Congo after his father, a former colonel in Mobutu's *Forces Armées Zairoises* (FAZ), was allegedly executed by members of the now ruling Allied Democratic Forces for the Liberation of Congo-Zaire (ADFL) in Lubumbashi on November 3, 1997.[298] He was arrested by the SANDF and brought to the Komatipoort police station on November 10, 1997, and had been in detention for more than three weeks when we visited him. He described to us how Home Affairs officials had attempted to come and interview him once, but he was out on a work site away from the police station:

> Home Affairs came last Wednesday, the 26th of November, but they had taken us to work constructing tents, so I was not here. Thursday, they told me that Home Affairs would come back on Tuesday. Today is Tuesday, but nobody has come. They still have not done the interview. So I am waiting for more than three weeks. I cannot return to Zaire because they will kill me.[299]

---

[297]Claude Schravesande, "Government Policies and Procedures," at *Asylum and Naturalisation: Policies and Practices*, Refugee Rights Consortium Workshop, November 14, 1996.

[298]Human Rights Watch interview with Jean-Pierre, Komatipoort Police Station, December 2, 1997.

[299]Ibid.

A second asylum-seeker in detention at Komatipoort police station, Ofili Chucks from Nigeria, was arrested at the border between South Africa and Mozambique on November 19, 1997, and had been in detention since that date:

> I came to South Africa on the 19th of November, I told them at the border that I wanted refugee status. So the police brought me here. Home Affairs never came to talk to me. The police tell me to go back, but I can't go back to Nigeria.... Since three weeks, we have been waiting for Home Affairs. So we are just working, working. Everyday we are working, we do construction, we wash the police men's cars, we clean the toilet. They just call us to work....They just tell me "there is no war in Nigeria, no war in Nigeria, just go home," but they don't let me tell my story.[300]

Corruption in the Asylum Process

Interviews and research conducted by Human Rights Watch suggest high levels of corruption in the refugee determination process, especially in the Johannesburg/Pretoria area.[301] Almost without fail, asylum-seekers and refugees interviewed in the Johannesburg/Pretoria region mentioned to us that they were asked for a bribe or a "fee" when they approached Home Affairs officials for documents. The alleged bribery incidents took a few familiar forms: persons were often asked for a "cool drink" after approaching officials, or they were promised an earlier interview date for a "fee," or they were approached by one of the translators who offered a speedy resolution of their application for a "fee." The process of applying for refugee status was explained by one asylum-seeker interviewed by Human Rights Watch:

> I applied at Home Affairs in Braamfontein, and my middleman was a Congolese translator. They gave me a very long period to process the application, three weeks. If you are not there when they call your name, they eliminate your papers. So you have to go every day from morning to evening, they told me. When I went out, the Congolese told me that if I could provide a "cold drink" he could help me out. He was asking 300 rands [U.S. $ 60]. Given the long wait, I bargained with him. He extorted

---

[300] Interview with Ofili Chucks, Komatipoort police station, December 2, 1997.

[301] Information about the identities of the persons interviewed in this section has been withheld because Human Rights Watch believes that our informants' refugee status could be affected if their identities are revealed.

100 rands [U.S. $ 20] from me, and then he said we were brothers. I saw a lot of Chinese, Indians, Pakistanis, and Nigerians, they just walk in and pay the cash. Everything is negotiable. They are not short of customers so they don't want to waste their time: Either you pay the money or you walk....They keep reminding you that the police will pick you up, the Congolese even told me that the police would flog me, and when you are from Africa, that makes you fearful.[302]

Many other similar accounts about bribery and extortion by Home Affairs officials were told to Human Rights Watch by refugees and asylum-seekers, including the following:

- "When I went to Home Affairs they told me they would give me an appointment in two weeks. There was a Zairian translator in the office, in Pretoria at Commissioner House. He followed me out and told me, "Why don't you give me some money, then you can come back tomorrow?" He wanted 150 rands [U.S. $ 30], but I told him I only have 20 rands [U.S. $ 4]. Finally, he accepted. He said, "Since you are my neighbor, my brother, you can come back tomorrow." I got my papers the next day."[303]

- A Somali asylum-seeker told us: "The problem is getting documents, they never give us documents. The people at Home Affairs told me one has to pay U.S. $100 to get papers. I paid US $100 for my first three-month permit. They never interview you unless you pay."[304]

- According to a Somali woman refugee, "Home Affairs, they take money to make facilitation. If you don't have papers, it is very bad. So we pay the money. They don't give you an interview unless you pay 20 rands [U.S. $ 4]. Some people, their papers expire and Home Affairs will not renew. Then people go to one of the officers at Home Affairs. They give him a bribe and get their papers. The amount depends on the person you talk to."[305]

---

[302]Human Rights Watch interview with TJ, Pretoria, December 3, 1997.

[303]Human Rights Watch interview with BR, Pretoria, December 3, 1997.

[304]Human Rights Watch interview with GM, Johannesburg, November 27, 1997.

[305]Human Rights Watch interview with SW, Johannesburg, November 27, 1997.

- A Somali asylum-seeker said: "We have to go to Home Affairs for ten to fifteen days because we didn't pay a bribe. If you give them money, it goes much faster."[306] A second Somali man told us: "When we go to the Home Affairs office there are many problems. When we have to get some papers or an interview, we have to pay a bribe. Sometimes we must queue from early morning until the next day. The bribe depends, but is normally 50 rands [U.S. $ 10]. They just extend my papers and I have to pay a bribe every time."[307]

- A Johannesburg hawker told us: "Home Affairs is the worst place in South Africa. It is a real factory of money. If you don't give them money, you don't get refugee status. Give somebody a wire [listening device] and you will see: Before giving the papers, they will ask, "Where is my soft drink?" It is full of corruption. When you get "must leave" papers, you must pay 500 to 300 rands [U.S. $ 100-60] to get it changed to a three-month permit."[308]

- A Zairian who went to the Department of Home Affairs to apply for asylum in August 1994 was asked for a bribe prior to being granted an interview, and was again asked for money at the time of his interview. A second Zairian who went to Home Affairs to apply for asylum in 1995 was told to pay 50 rands [U.S. $ 10] or he would not get an interview appointment. A third Zairian, who went for his interview in March 1996, was told to find his own translator and was forced to pay the translator a fee of 50 rands [U.S. $ 10], even though the Department of Home Affairs has undertaken to provide free translators.[309]

Corruption in the refugee determination process seems especially widespread and systemic in the Johannesburg-Pretoria area. None of the refugees we interviewed who had been processed in Cape Town claimed to have been forced to pay bribes. When we discussed our Johannesburg findings with an immigration officer in Cape

---

[306]Human Rights Watch interview with IA, Johannesburg, November 27, 1997.

[307]Human Rights Watch interview with AA, Johannesburg, November 27, 1997.

[308]Human Rights Watch interview with AN, Johannesburg, November 28, 1997.

[309]Lawyers for Human Rights, "Statements Taken from Zairian Asylum Seekers at Pretoria Central Station," dated October 4, 1996.

Town, he told us on condition of anonymity about his own experiences with asylum-seekers who had come from Johannesburg:

> When we have people coming through from Johannesburg, they often try to pay a bribe, by leaving money on the chair or something like that. Or they give you the papers with a few bills in it. They are just used to having to pay, they don't know any other way.[310]

Arbitrary, Uninformed Decisions

Because no refugee legislation currently exists in South Africa, asylum applications are being determined under a rather arbitrary ad-hoc set of procedures which are explained in Appendix A to this report. Most of the refugee advocates interviewed by Human Rights Watch complained about the often uninformed nature of decisions made by the Standing Committee on Refugee Affairs which makes the initial decision on refugee applications. The Standing Committee often seemed to rely on outdated information, and at times dismissed information about human rights abuses in certain countries by referring to the personal experiences of members of the Standing Committee in those countries.

Our own interviews and observations suggest that the refugee officers who are responsible for offering an initial evaluation of an asylum application but do not make the decision are not provided with the necessary resources to form an informed opinion about the veracity of asylum claims, or about the actual human rights situation in a particular country. Refugee officers told us that their information about various countries is obtained from the newspapers they read and from listening to BBC and CNN news. Although it is admirable that refugee officers attempt to stay informed on the situation of the numerous countries that generate asylum-seekers to South Africa, this ad-hoc method does not provide the refugee officer with the specialized information necessary to make an informed decision.

It appears that a number of asylum applications are turned down because Standing Committee members feel that the countries in question are stable and do not generate refugees. This includes asylum-seekers from Angola, which continues to be plagued by unrest and widespread human rights abuses. A refugee officer interviewed by Human Rights Watch explained how he got an angry phone call from his supervisor when he recommended a Tanzanian for refugee status:

---

[310]Human Rights Watch interview with immigration officer, Cape Town, December 9, 1997.

I told my boss that according to the U.N. principles, they had a right to be heard. But my boss said there was nothing going on in Tanzania, we are not going to accept Tanzanians here. "I've made my decision," he said, "these people are not going to fuck us around." Now the problem is with Mozambicans, Zimbabweans, Malawians, and Botswanans. We never accept any of these.[311]

Liesl Gerntholtz, senior legal officer for the South African Human Rights Commission, has expressed similar concerns about blanket denials of refugee status: "People have been deported to Mozambique without having had a chance to put their case, and in instances when they are not necessarily Mozambican."[312] Refusing to accept asylum-seekers from certain countries because they are believed to be stable is inconsistent with international law and the UNHCR Basic Agreement, which requires an individual determination of refugee status. It is entirely possible that an individual from, for example, Angola or Zimbabwe, can meet the requirements of either the U.N. or OAU definition of a refugee, even if there is no open warfare in the country at present.

On July 29, 1996, about 300 refugees and asylum-seekers from twelve African states gathered outside the offices of the UNHCR in Pretoria to protest against the unfairness of their refugee determinations, and requesting that the UNHCR assist them to resettle elsewhere.[313] After spending a night sleeping outside on the sidewalk, the police threatened to arrest the protesters, and they then moved their

---

[311]Ibid.

[312]Marion Edmunds, "Refugees Score in Fight for Asylum," *Mail & Guardian*, December 13 to 19, 1996.

[313]The demands of the refugees and asylum-seekers were the following: "(1) Assistance from the UNHCR to resettle elsewhere; (2) protection from (sic.) the South African Government of the right of rejected asylum-seekers (to remain in South Africa) until they find another country of asylum; (3) the right of rejected asylum-seekers who consider that their applications have been spoiled or given unfair decisions, to be heard by a neutral tribunal; (4) re-settlement of rejected asylum-seekers in other countries with the assistance of UNHCR; (5) asylum-seekers who have had their applications rejected because of their country of origin, like Ethiopians, to have a fair assessment of political conditions there and to be given refugee status in this country; (6) all those who are given asylum to benefit from that right like financial assistance and work opportunities." Department of Home Affairs (Subdirectorate Communications), "Asylum-Seekers, Refugees held a Demonstration," dated July 30, 1997.

protest to the Union Buildings to present a memorandum to a representative of President Mandela.

At the Union Buildings, the police and Department of Home Affairs officials arrested 106 of the protesters, releasing twenty-four the next day because their papers were in order. According to press reports, at least twenty of the arrested protesters were ultimately repatriated to the Democratic Republic of Congo in late August, a time when serious allegations of human rights abuses and massacres where being raised against the Kabila government.[314] The arrests raise serious concerns about violations of the asylum-seekers' rights to peaceful assembly, free speech, and peaceful protest, which are protected under the South African constitution and international law.[315]

Originally, the detained protesters had been kept at police stations, including the Kameelsdrift police station, but they were transferred to Pretoria Central Prison after Lawyers for Human Rights, a leading South African NGO, lodged a complaint with the South African Human Rights Commission about the conditions of detention at the police stations. At Kameelsdrift, police officials used CS tear gas on the detainees at least once. Police officials claimed this was done when the detainees were "out of control," but the detainees claimed that the tear gas was used to break a short-lived hunger strike they had organized to protest their detention and conditions in the police cells.

Jackson Mafwala was one of the persons arrested during the Union Buildings protest, and he remained in detention at Pretoria Central Prison seventy-two days

---

[314]"20 Illegal Aliens Arrested at Union Buildings to be Repatriated," *SAPA*, August 20, 1996. For details on the human rights abuse claims raised against the Kabila regime at the time, see Human Rights Watch, "Transition, War and Human Rights," *A Human Rights Watch Report*, vol. 9, no. 2(A), April 1997; Human Rights Watch & Fédération Internationale des Ligues des Droits de l'Homme, "What Kabila is Hiding: Civilian Killings and Impunity in Congo," *A Human Rights Watch Report*, vol. 9, No. 5(A), October 1997.

[315]Constitution of the Republic of South Africa (1996) Article 16 ("Everyone has the right to freedom of expression"), Article 17 ("Everyone has the right, peacefully and unarmed, to assemble, to demonstrate, to picket and to present petitions."). UDHR Article 19 ("Everyone has the right to freedom of opinion and expression; this right includes freedom to hold opinions without interference and to seek, receive and impart information and ideas through any media and regardless of frontiers"), Article 20 ("Everyone has the right to freedom of peaceful assembly and association").

later, together with twenty-four other Zairians detained at the same time.[316] He claimed that about twenty-five of the protesters had been deported by the time of our visit. The Department of Home Affairs had originally promised the detainees that their cases would be decided within thirty days, but this period had long since expired. Goma Nsika Massala from the People's Republic of Congo, was also arrested at the Union Buildings protest. He claimed that officials from the Department of Home Affairs had forced them to sign deportation papers without giving any explanations, "you are not given the chance to read the paper."[317] The officials allegedly used profanity when coercing the detainees into signing the deportation papers, saying, "You have two choices, you choose to stay in prison or you sign here and fuck off."[318]

Rubber-Stamp Appeals Process

Until quite recently, the Department of Home Affairs was unwilling to furnish reasons for denials of asylum claims. This made appeals very difficult, as denied asylum-seekers had "absolutely no idea what they were appealing against."[319] Only in December 1996, the Department of Home Affairs agreed, as part of a consent order which settled a court case brought by an asylum-seeker, to furnish applicants with reasons. However, the refugee lawyers interviewed by Human Rights Watch found that the reasons given for denials remain "flimsy" and of little help in preparing an appeal.

The Appeals Board consists of a single person, retired advocate Leach of Pretoria.[320] Human Rights Watch asked several refugee lawyers and a refugee officer about the performance of the appeals board, and none could remember a single case in which Advocate Leach had overturned a negative decision of the Standing Committee. Statistics from the Department of Home Affairs indicate that

---

[316]Human Rights Watch interview with Jackson Mafwala, Democratic Republic of Congo citizen, Pretoria Central Prison, October 11, 1996.

[317]Human Rights Watch interview with Goma Nsika Massala, People's Republic of Congo citizen, Pretoria Central Prison, October 11, 1996.

[318]Ibid.

[319]Ibid.

[320]The Department of Home Affairs has advertised for a second post for the Appeal Board, but this post has not yet been filled.

out of a total of 519 appeals considered by Advocate Leach, only two appeals (one from a Bosnian applicant and another from a Burundian applicant) were granted.[321] One lawyer, speaking on condition of anonymity, questioned the qualifications of Advocate Leach in the area of refugee law and the sources used by Advocate Leach to reach his conclusions:

> What worried us from the outset is the composition of the appeals board, which is a retired advocate from Pretoria who seems to be little more than a rubber stamp. He would often rely on atrocious hearsay. They wouldn't give us access to the information they used, which made it difficult to discredit the information. During the height of the fighting, they would say that the situation in Zaire was fine.[322]

Human Rights Watch believes that a panel consisting of several persons with experience in the area of refugee law would be a more appropriate body for the determination of asylum appeals.

Police Abuse of Refugees and Asylum-Seekers

Like undocumented migrants in South Africa, refugees and asylum-seekers often suffer abuse at the hands of an increasingly xenophobic public and police force. In some cases, asylum-seekers are the target of even more intense abuse than undocumented migrants, as they tend to come from regions farther away from South Africa (such as the Horn of Africa or the Indian subcontinent) and may sometimes be more easily identifiable because of physical appearance, mode of dress, and language. After the death of a Burundian refugee in police custody, UNHCR issued a statement addressing the rise in xenophobia in South Africa:

> UNHCR notes with alarm the increasing incidents of harassment, beatings, arbitrary arrests, assaults, and murder of asylum-seekers and refugees, and the growing problem of xenophobia in South Africa. Since December

---

[321]Department of Home Affairs, "Appeal Application—Refugee Status (Adv. Leach)," fax to Human Rights Watch dated January 27, 1998.

[322]Interview with refugee attorney, Cape Town.

1996, at least six asylum-seekers from Angola, Burundi, and Somalia have been murdered in the Western Cape province alone.[323]

In both Cape Town and Johannesburg, Human Rights Watch interviewed a number of refugees and asylum-seekers who claimed to have been assaulted and harassed by police officials. In one case, Immaculate Stuurman, a Ugandan woman refugee who was the manager of Phillipi House, a shelter for refugee women, was repeatedly insulted and maltreated after being arrested at a nightclub in Sea Point, Cape Town. The refugees were violently thrown into a police van—Ms. Stuurman had her arm twisted painfully behind her back and her neck squeezed tightly—and then driven to an unmarked building in Cape Town.[324] "The way we were driven was very bad," Ms. Stuurman told us, "They would slam on the brakes, twist and turn on the road, and it was very scary."[325] Once in the van, Ms. Stuurman noticed that her wallet was missing.

Once inside the unmarked building, the refugees were allegedly verbally abused in a racist manner by the police officers, who called them kaffirs, baboons, *makwerekwere* (a derogatory name for foreigners) and other insulting names. One of the men, an Angolan refugee, was handled roughly as the police kicked his legs apart so they could search him. After dropping the male refugees off at Woodstock police station, Ms. Stuurman and another woman were driven around for several hours and were insulted again whenever they asked what was happening. Finally, at 3 a.m., they were dropped at the Kuilsrivier police station. The next day, the same policemen came to pick the two women up and threatened to bring Ms. Stuurman to Pollsmoor prison after she refused to respond to their personal advances.[326] When they were finally brought to Home Affairs, the police officer handed Ms. Stuurman her documents, and left almost immediately. Ms. Stuurman told us how her ordeal ended:

---

[323]United Nations High Commissioner for Refugees, "UNHCR Press Statement: Death in Police Custody of an Asylum Seeker," dated June 14, 1997.

[324]Human Rights Watch interview with Immaculate Stuurman, Phillipi House, Cape Town, December 11, 1997.

[325]Ibid.

[326]Ibid.

I was shocked and did not know how he had gotten my documents. In fact, my friends had brought him my documents the evening before. Yet they had kept me in jail and treated me like a criminal the whole night. The Home Affairs man looked at my documents and asked me why I was there. I told him he should have asked the officer who brought me, not me.[327]

Ms. Stuurman reported the case to the South African Human Rights Commission, which referred the case to the Independent Complaints Directorate of the South African Police Service.

Refugees and asylum-seekers complained about the rude and aggressive manner in which they were treated by the police and the unwillingness of police officers to identify themselves. Akinjole, a Nigerian trader, told Human Rights Watch what had happened to him after he refused to show a group of police officers his documents until they identified themselves:

I asked him [the police officer] to introduce himself before I showed him my paper and this made him angry. One said in Afrikaans that they should throw me in the truck. Six of them held me and started pushing me. I said we would not solve this with force and again asked them to identify themselves to me before I showed them my paper. They started pushing me and kicking me into the truck. When we got to the truck, I told them I was going nowhere with them. If they want to see my papers, they must call immigration or identify themselves to me as immigration. And then one of them took out handcuffs and forced them unto one of my hands. Two of them were in the truck pulling on the handcuffs and the others were kicking me.[328]

Akinjole showed us his injuries, which included bruises on his legs and a deep cut on the wrist of his right hand, allegedly from being kicked on the back of his legs and having the handcuffs pulled. The police ultimately relented and identified themselves, and Akinjole showed them his documentation proving his legal status. It appears that the cause of the incident was the police's refusal to identify themselves, despite a duty to do so under the circumstances.

---

[327]Ibid.

[328]Human Rights Watch interview with Akinjole A.J. "Giant," Nigerian refugee hawker, Cape Town, December 11, 1997.

At least one asylum-seeker, Jean-Pierre Kanyangwa of Burundi, died under suspicious circumstances while in the custody of the South African police service. Mr. Kanyangwa was arrested in Cape Town at about 11 a.m., on June 2, 1997, and according to witnesses appeared in good health at the time.[329] Burundian refugees told the press that Mr. Kanyangwa was thrown in the police van "like an animal," and alleged that Mr. Kanyangwa told them before he died that he had been beaten by the police.[330] Mr. Kanyangwa was brought by police officers to the refugee office of the Department of Home Affairs in Cape Town at about 2 p.m. the same day, and was in a bad condition:

> When they arrived at the refugee office, the Burundian was suffering from stomach pains and lying on the floor....There was a foul odour coming from his body, and he had urinated in his pants.[331]

The immigration officer on duty asked Police Sergeant Kolashi, who had brought Mr. Kanyangwa to the refugee office, to take him to the hospital. Sergeant Kolashi refused, saying it was now a refugee problem, and left. Mr. Kanyangwa died on his way to the hospital. A post-mortem autopsy concluded that Mr. Kanyangwa had died from a ruptured spleen, "possibly brought on by trauma."[332] Although there was no significant external evidence of a beating, it appears that Mr. Kanyangwa was suffering from malaria which had swollen his spleen, and that his spleen could have been injured during a beating. A murder docket into the case has been opened.

While most refugees and asylum-seekers in South Africa live in private housing, there are a few church-sponsored "refugee camps" where refugees and asylum-seekers without housing can live. One such camp, the Ga'Rankuwa refugee camp outside Pretoria, was visited by Human Rights Watch. The camp houses about forty refugees from several West, North, and Central African

---

[329]Marion Edmunds, "Refugee dies at Home Affairs," *Mail & Guardian*, June 13 to 19, 1997.

[330]Ibid.

[331]Sworn affidavit of John Peter Solomon, Immigration Officer, Department of Home Affairs, dated June 6, 1997.

[332]Marion Edmunds, "Refugee dies at Home Affairs," *Mail & Guardian*, June 13 to 19, 1997.

countries in dilapidated dome tents. Residents told us how their camp had been raided on three different occasions by the Department of Home Affairs, the police, and the army. On the first occasion, residents claimed that the Department of Home Affairs had removed four Zairians from the camp who were repatriated to Zaire, including one woman named Marie Noel whom they claimed later died in the fighting in Zaire.[333] Home Affairs and the police came at about 5 a.m., and used expletives when talking to the refugees and asylum-seekers.[334] During the second visit, the camp was surrounded by military trucks at about 10 p.m., and the residents were told to stand in the rain while Department of Home Affairs officials went around writing down the names and document information for each resident.

At about 2 a.m. on November 10, 1997, a group of about fifty police officers, army personnel, and Home Affairs officials again raided the camp. "Doors were kicked in, and we were ordered at gun-point to come out of our tents with our hands on our heads like prisoners of war," Romario, an Ivorian resident of the camp, recalled, "We were then forced to sit on the bare ground at the central courtyard of our camp where the headlights of some military trucks were trained."[335] Apparently without a search warrant, the officials methodically searched the camp, going from tent to tent and even searching the toilet, ostensibly for weapons. The officials finally left after finding nothing, leaving behind torn tents and a destroyed latrine. "It was as though a hurricane had hit the camp," one resident commented.[336]

---

[333]Human Rights Watch interview with Thomas Jing, Cameroonian refugee, Ga'Rankuwa refugee camp, Pretoria, December 3, 1997.

[334]Ibid.

[335]Lawyers for Human Rights, "Raid at Ga'Rankuwa Refugee Camp," undated.

[336]Ibid.

VI. XENOPHOBIA AND ATTACKS AGAINST MIGRANTS

Since the 1994 elections, South Africa has seen a rising level of xenophobia. As in many other countries, immigrants have been blamed for a rise in violent crime, drug dealing and a rise in drug abuse, unemployment, and other social ills. Immigrants from African countries have been the target of attacks, often because they are perceived as being in direct competition with South Africans for jobs or services. In addition, African immigrants are often the target of random violence and robbery, as criminals perceive them as easy targets because they are unlikely to go to the police. The police and Home Affairs officials have shared this antagonism toward foreigners. The generally negative attitude toward foreigners encourages and condones abuses by police, army, and Home Affairs officials not only against those suspected of being undocumented migrants, but also against non-South Africans who are lawfully in the country, who can expect little or no help from the police when they themselves are victims of crime, including violent assault and theft.

Xenophobic statements by officials

As in many western countries, some politicians in South Africa are exploiting the issue of undocumented migration for their own political gain, increasing levels of xenophobia by making unfounded and explosive statements about the cost of undocumented migration and its effects on various social services and crime. The mainstream debate around illegal immigration in South Africa, focusing on the economic impact and the impact on crime of undocumented migration, has been alarmist and ill-informed.

One of the most common alarmist claims made by politicians is that the high cost of undocumented migration is endangering the transformation process currently taking place in South Africa. As pointed out earlier, Minister of Home Affairs Buthelezi stated in his first speech to the parliament that South Africa could forget about its reconstruction and development program if it did not stop the flow of migrants.[337] In his 1997 budget speech, Minister Buthelezi returned to this familiar refrain:

> With an illegal population estimated at between 2.5 million and 5 million, it is obvious that the socio-economic resources of the country, which are under severe strain as it is, are further being burdened by the presence of illegal aliens. The cost implication becomes even clearer when one makes

---

[337]See section above entitled "Migration to South Africa Today."

123

a calculation suggesting that if every illegal costs our infrastructure, say 1000 rands [U.S. $ 200] per annum, then multiplied with whatever number you wish, it becomes obvious that the cost becomes billions of rands per year.[338]

Reacting to a questionable study released in January 1998 by the Human Sciences Research Council which estimated the cost of undocumented migration at 2.75 billion rands [U.S. $ 550 million] per year, the Freedom Front and the National Party called upon the government to take stronger steps to combat undocumented migration. National Party spokesperson Daryl Swanepoel stated that "the cost [of undocumented migration] cannot be justified given the enormous pressure ... to supply our own citizens with basic services."[339] The Freedom Front said it would support "all measures" in the fight against undocumented migration.[340] The Inkatha Freedom Party (IFP) has called upon the government to take stronger steps against undocumented migrants since September 1994, threatening to organize marches and take "physical action" if the government fails to respond to the perceived crisis.[341]

Officials often make statements blaming rising levels of immigration for the rise in crime. During a recent newspaper interview, Defence Minister Joe Modise closely linked the issue of undocumented migration to the rise in crime in South Africa:

As for crime, the army is helping the police get rid of crime and violence in the country. However, what can we do? We have one million illegal immigrants in our country who commit crimes and who are mistaken by some people for South African citizens. That is the real problem. We have adopted a strict policy and have banned illegal immigration in order to

---

[338]Minister of Home Affairs, Introductory Speech: Budget Debate, National Assembly, April 17, 1997.

[339]"Illegal Immigrants Cost SA Taxpayer R2,75 Billion a Year," *SAPA*, January 4, 1998.

[340]"FF will support steps against illegal immigration," *SAPA*, January 4, 1998.

[341]Kaiser Nyatsumba, "IFP Threat of Physical Action on Illegal Immigrants," *Star*, September 14, 1994.

combat the criminals coming from neighboring states so that we can round up the criminals residing in South Africa.[342]

National Party spokesperson on home affairs Frik van Deventer has similarly linked the issues of immigration and crime, claiming that Nigerians have entered the country "in droves" since 1994 and that "eighty percent of all suspects appearing in court in Johannesburg in connection with drugs are Nigerians."[343] He blamed the African National Congress' accommodation of old solidarity friends as one of the most important causes for the rise in undocumented migration to South Africa, and he urged a more hard-line approach to the problem of undocumented migration:

> Without stricter policies and a sincere political will of the ANC government to resolve these problems, South Africa will lose the drug war and become home to criminal elements and thousands of illegal immigrants.[344]

The National Party has also blamed undocumented migrants for taking jobs away from South Africans, exacerbating poverty, and spreading diseases in South Africa.[345]

Police officials have expressed similar views of the involvement of Nigerians in drug trading, with one police captain stating in a press interview that he believed that as many as 90 percent of Nigerians who were in South Africa seeking asylum status were involved in the drug trade.[346] These statements are reinforced by constant police claims and press reports which include the number of

---

[342]"South African Defence Minister on Arms Sales," *London Al-Quds al-'Arabi*, November 19, 1997, p. 6.

[343]"Be Strict or South Africa Becomes Home to Criminals, Illegal Aliens: NP," *SAPA*, March 3, 1997.

[344]Ibid.

[345]South African Institute of Race Relations, "Illegal Immigrants also have rights," dated March 22, 1997.

[346]Blackman Ngoro, "Nigerian Drug Dealers Masquerading as Asylum Seekers," *Sunday Independent*, June 22, 1997, p.3.

undocumented migrants arrested in the overall arrest figures for "crime sweeps." By constantly linking the issue of undocumented migration to rising crime in South Africa—the latter a topic of extreme public concern—the link between these two separate issues has now become accepted as a matter of course, despite the lack of clear evidence linking undocumented migration to rising crime rates. In turn, this unfounded link between crime and migration increases resentment against migrants, and increases the potential for violent attacks against them, as shown by attacks on foreign hawkers described below. Where migrants are responsible for crime, they should be prosecuted according to law; most of those coming to South Africa are not involved in crime, but attacks on them are legitimized by statements of this type.

Not all South African politicians have joined in verbal attacks on undocumented migrants. Mpumalanga premier Matthews Phosa, for example, has spoken out against narrow nationalism, "which could easily lead to some Bantustan [homeland] mentality, undermine national unity and cohesion, or lead to some form of xenophobia."[347] Speaking on the reasons for refugee flows to South Africa, Phosa has pointed out the destructive impact of apartheid on the region's economies, arguing that "any solution to the problem of refugees, ignoring this reality, will be superficial and will not stand a chance of succeeding."[348]

Available research suggests that xenophobia among the South African public is indeed very high. A study co-authored by the Human Sciences Research Council and the Institute for Security Studies reported that 80 percent of South Africans supported stronger government efforts in controlling undocumented migration into South Africa.[349] Support for forced repatriation was found among 65 percent of respondents, while 73 percent of respondents were in favor of employer sanctions for employers who hired undocumented migrants.[350] White South Africans were found to be most hostile to migrants, with 93 percent expressing negative attitudes, compared to only 53 percent of black South Africans.[351] In May 1995, the

---

[347]"Phosa Slams 'Puppetry' Method of Premier Appointments," *SAPA*, August 23, 1997.

[348]"Apartheid Created Southern Africa Refugee Crisis," *SAPA*, June 12, 1997.

[349]"Most South Africans Hostile to Illegal Aliens: Survey," *SAPA*, June 10, 1997.

[350]Ibid.

[351]Ibid.

Southern African Bishops' Conference released an extensive report on the perceptions of migrants and refugees in South Africa. The report concluded:

> There is no doubt that there is a very high level of xenophobia in our country.... The impression is given that illegal immigrants are flooding the country and the nation's social fabric is threatened by illegals fleeing economic, political, and social upheavals in their countries. When the questions of prostitution, money laundering, arms and drug trafficking are raised, more times than not they are linked to the question of illegal immigrants.... One of the main problems is that a variety of people have been lumped together under the title of illegal immigrants, and the whole situation of demonising immigrants is feeding the xenophobia phenomenon.[352]

In particular, the report expressed concern that the unrealizable expectations of the population, bolstered by the high promises of the ANC's Reconstruction and Development Program (RDP) would soon translate into heightened xenophobia as foreigners would be blamed for the slow progress of socio-economic reform: "Indeed, this has already begun: it is not uncommon for lower-income South Africans to identify foreigners as the chief obstacle to realising the goals of the RDP."[353]

Attacks Against Foreign Hawkers

Frustrated with what they perceive as the government's inability to address the "flood" of migrants effectively, an increasing number of civil groups are suggesting and implementing their own solutions to the "problem." Some groups, such as Micro Business Against Crime and the Illegal Foreigners Action Group, have called for a boycott of businesses employing undocumented migrants and have argued that South Africans should stop buying products from foreign street traders.[354] Concerned about increasing lawlessness and tensions within local communities, the Transvaal Agricultural Union has encouraged its members to stop

---

[352]Southern African Catholic Bishops' Conference, *Report on immigrants, refugees and displaced people* (May 1995).

[353]Ibid.

[354]Gumisai Mutume, "No Immigrants Please, We Are South African," *InterPress Service*, March 21, 1997.

hiring undocumented migrants and to report known undocumented migrants to the police for deportation.[355] In a disturbing development, a group calling itself the Unemployed People of South Africa (UPSA) has threatened to take the law into its own hands and physically remove migrants from South Africa if the government fails to deport them.[356]

One of the areas of greatest tension between South Africans and foreigners has been in the informal trading sector, known as hawking. Many asylum-seekers and refugees are unable to find employment in the formal sector because of high unemployment levels, their temporary status, and because of employer prejudices, and resort to selling goods—ranging from potato chips and sodas to curios, clothes, and watches—on the street. In doing so, they sometimes enter into direct competition with locals who are either selling the same goods or would like to sell those goods. The conflict is heightened by the fact that South Africans themselves have only been allowed to engage in the informal hawking trade since apartheid restrictions were lifted in 1991.[357]

Some non-South African hawkers feel that they played an important role in developing the hawking sector in South Africa by bringing in skills they picked up in their home country, and they complain that they are now being pushed out by South African opportunists who would like to appropriate the business sectors that foreign traders developed over the years. A well-established and successful Nigerian trader in Cape Town explained how local hawkers were trying to push him and other foreign traders out of business:

> At first, we were very poor but then people started noticing that we were making money. We were progressing and having cars and such things. The local people started using our techniques, and many people wanted to become traders. We developed this thing, and now the local people want to kick us out. They say the influx of foreigners is taking their jobs, but we

---

[355]"Farmers Concerned Over Illegal Immigrants," *SAPA*, September 24, 1997.

[356]Isaac Moledi, "Foreigners must be thrown out," *Sowetan*, October 6, 1997, p.23.

[357]Sally Peberdy, "The Participation of Non-South Africans in Street Trading in South Africa and in Regional Cross-Border Trade: Implications for Immigration Policy and Customs Agreements," *Briefing Paper for the Green Paper Task Force on International Migration* (Pretoria, 1997). Available on the world-wide web at http://www.polity.org.za:80/govdocs/green_papers/migration/crossborder.html (last visited February 18, 1998).

taught them how to do business.... The locals come to tell us, "this is our country, you foreigners are taking over our country." They write us letters saying we have flooded their markets. The newcomer citizen hawkers tell us that we have to stop selling the things they sell, but we have been here for years.[358]

Whatever the competitive advantages are of foreign traders in terms of hawking experience, the local traders are increasingly reverting to a different weapon to increase their market share vis-a-vis the foreign traders: violence and other forms of intimidation.

Since at least 1994, the African Chamber of Hawkers and Independent Businessmen (ACHIB) has led a vocal campaign against foreign hawkers. ACHIB believes that 40 percent of all hawkers are foreigners.[359] ACHIB blames foreigners for rising crime, overpopulation, and falling wages, and accuses foreign hawkers of selling stolen, rotten, and expired goods.[360] ACHIB has organized a series of anti-foreigner meetings and marches, and it has successfully negotiated a "neighborhood watch" program with the police, in which ACHIB-affiliated hawkers place suspected undocumented migrants under community arrest and hand them over to the police. Considering the official anti-foreigner stance of ACHIB, Human Rights Watch feels that this cooperation between the South African police and ACHIB is inappropriate and may invite abuses.

Local hawkers have written threatening statements against foreign hawkers, have organized protest marches, and on several occasions have viciously attacked foreign hawkers. Protest marches have repeatedly deteriorated into physical violence and looting of the property of foreign hawkers in central Johannesburg, Yeoville, Germiston and Hillbrow.

In August 1997, local hawkers in Central Johannesburg attacked their foreign counterparts for two consecutive days, scattering and looting their belongings and beating the foreign traders with sticks, knobkerries [a traditional weapon consisting

---

[358]Human Rights Watch interview with Akinjole A.J. "Giant," Nigerian refugee hawking in Cape Town, December 11, 1997.

[359]Minnaar and Hough, *Who Goes There?*, p. 186.

[360]Ibid. Comments made by Lawrence Mavundle, President of ACHIB, and other ACHIB affiliated persons at the March 26, 1997, meeting between ACHIB, the Department of Home Affairs, and the South African police, attended by a Human Rights Watch representative.

of a stick with a heavy knob at the end] and sjamboks [heavy whips made out of rawhide].[361] A flyer announcing the protest obtained by Human Rights Watch stated "We want to clean the foreigners from our pavement." A South African hawker interviewed at the time vowed: "[F]oreigners flocked here after the [1994] elections and took our businesses. We will not rest until they are gone."[362] The chairperson of one local hawking group, the Inner Johannesburg Hawkers Committee, Mr. Mannekie Solomon, told the *Sowetan* newspaper that "We are prepared to push them out of the city, come what may. My group is not prepared to let our government inherit a garbage city because of these leeches."[363] More than one hundred persons were arrested on charges of participating in an illegal march after the unruly crowd broke into shops and started looting goods.

A few days later, on August 18, 1997, local hawkers attacked foreign hawkers at the Kerk Street Mall in Johannesburg, severely beating several Senegalese hawkers. Senegalese hawker Papa Demba was beaten and injured by bricks thrown at him while the crowd shouted "*Phansi makwerekwere* [a derogatory term for non-South Africans], *phansi*" (Down foreigners, down).[364] When police arrived at the scene, they advised Papa Demba to leave, but arrested only a single individual out of the group of about thirty attackers.[365] The South African Human Rights Commission issued a strong statement condemning the attacks on foreign hawkers, saying that "it is not for ordinary citizens to enforce street law, as was the case last week against the aliens."[366] Jesse Duarte, Gauteng Member of the Executive

---

[361]Patrick Phosa, "Hawkers vow to Continue CBD Protests," *Star*, August 15, 1997, p.2.

[362]Ibid.

[363]Dan Fuphe, "Hawkers Rampage," *Sowetan*, August 14, 1997.

[364]"Street Gang Attacks Foreign Hawkers," *Sowetan*, August 19, 1997, p.5.

[365]Ibid.

[366]"Hawkers' Attack Dent SA Human Rights Image: HRC," *SAPA*, August 18, 1997. The attacks were also condemned by African Methodist Bishop Mvume Dandale. "Attitude towards Africa Refugees a Source of Concern: Dandale," *SAPA*, August 17, 1997.

Council (MEC) for Safety and Security, also condemned the violence, saying that "this anarchy is totally unacceptable."[367]

The situation in Johannesburg has remained volatile since the August protests. On October 23, 1997, approximately 500 hawkers marched again in Johannesburg, chanting slogans such as "chase the *makwerekwere* out," and "down with the foreigner, up with South Africans."[368] At a rally following the march, Manikis Solomon, a representative of the Greater Johannesburg Hawkers' Planning Committee, told the crowd that,

> These people are not welcome. No country would allow the mess Johannesburg has come to. We must clean up the streets of Johannesburg of foreign hawkers. The pavements of Johannesburg are for South African citizens and not for foreigners.[369]

In November 1997, the Greater Johannesburg Hawkers Association called for a boycott of goods sold by *makwerekwere*, including Pakistanis, Chinese, Indians, Senegalese, Somalis, Nigerians, Moroccans, Zimbabweans, and Mozambicans.[370]

Attacks on hawkers are not limited to central Johannesburg. Foreign hawkers in Germiston were similarly attacked and had their property looted during a protest by local hawkers in November 1996. The local police promised to protect foreign hawkers from further attacks, but when foreign hawkers were again attacked on November 11, 1996, the police failed to protect them.[371] The chairperson of the local hawkers association, the Germiston Traders Partnership (Gemtrap), Levy Molusa, allegedly threatened one of the leaders of the foreign hawkers, Mr. Patrick Acho. Mr. Acho was later shot to death on December 30, 1996, by unidentified

---

[367]"More than 100 vendors arrested in Johannesburg," *SAPA*, August 14, 1997.

[368]Emaka Nwandiko, "Hawkers want foreigners out," *Mail & Guardian*, October 24 to 30, 1997.

[369]Ibid.

[370]Swapna Prabhakaran and Bongani Siqoko, "'Foreigners' not welcome on pavements," *Mail & Guardian*, November 21 to 27, 1997.

[371]"A Cry Against Injustice," Letter by Foreign Hawkers in Germiston to Premier of Gauteng Tokyo Sexwale, undated.

persons.[372] According to the foreign hawkers, the police showed little interest in solving the murder of Mr. Acho.

Human Rights Watch also interviewed a number of Somali hawkers who had been forced to stop hawking in Kempton Park after being threatened, and in some cases attacked, by local hawkers. A large community of several hundred Somali refugees and asylum-seekers visited by Human Rights Watch had once depended on hawking to make a meager income, but had been deprived of its only means of livelihood by violence and intimidation. Desperation abounded in the impoverished community, where men slept forty to a room in several cases. At first, many of the Somali hawkers found themselves targeted by criminal gangs that deprived them of their possessions, and they had little recourse to the police:

> We were hawking in Kempton Park. When we went to our storage space, all of our stuff was gone. Gangs took everything. People have weapons so we can't do anything. So now we can't work anymore. The police ask us if we can identify them and tell us they can't help us if we can't identify them. There is no investigation. If we can identify them, the police don't go with us. No more Somalis are hawking in Kempton Park because we are afraid.[373]

Then, in August 1997, the local hawkers protested against foreign hawkers in Kempton Park, as they had done in Johannesburg:

> The local hawkers had a strike in August, and robbed all the Somali hawkers. They kicked one Somali, and he lost three teeth. I saw the missing teeth. They also beat him with sticks. We went to the police and told them what happened. The police told us to go to Home Affairs...When I went back fifteen days later, the police refused to see me. The policeman told me, "this is not your country, go back to your own country." The police didn't try to get our property back or find out who assaulted us. When we report to the police, they don't do anything.[374]

---

[372]Ibid.

[373]Human Rights Watch interview with Iwad Achmed, Somali refugee, in Johannesburg, November 27, 1998.

[374]Human Rights Watch interview with Somali refugee, Johannesburg, November 27, 1997.

Another Somali trader was beaten and robbed by a group of about twenty South Africans around the same time in central Johannesburg, according to one source: "They took his watch and money and wallet. He was unconscious in the street at the end. A white woman helped him and took him to the police station. The police didn't help him. The gave him a letter but never did anything about the case."[375]

Foreign hawkers in Yeoville told Human Rights Watch about similar experiences of attack by local hawkers and the lack of a police response. One foreign fruit vendor in Yeoville lamented the lack of protection foreigners received from the police. "If you are a foreigner, they can do any harm to you, they can hit you. At the demonstration, they hit some people with sticks. There were so many people injured. They attacked me to rob. They took my money, 550 rands [U.S. $ 110], and my refugee papers. They hit me in the face. Two had a gun and two had knives."[376]

Foreign hawkers in both greater Johannesburg and in Cape Town complained of recent attempts by local government to exclude them from hawking licensing schemes. According to Yeoville traders, city officials had begun handing out license applications in the aftermath of the recent protests. However, foreign hawkers were not given license applications, and when one foreign hawker requested them, he was refused: "I asked about the paper but they said it is not for me. The Council sent these two people, but they don't want to talk to us."[377] A second foreign trader confirmed this practice to us, saying "the Council didn't give registration papers to the foreigners, only to the citizens."[378] Foreign hawkers in Cape Town similarly complained that police officers had told them to leave the most prosperous hawking sites, and that police officials were refusing to furnish foreign hawkers with the application forms for newly instituted licensing schemes.[379]

---

[375]Human Rights Watch interview with Sahel, Somali refugee, Johannesburg, November 27, 1997.

[376]Human Rights Watch interview with Paul, in Yeoville, November 28, 1997.

[377]Human Rights Watch interview with Musa, in Yeoville, November 28, 1997.

[378]Human Rights Watch interview with Paul, in Yeoville, November 28, 1997.

[379]Human Rights Watch interview with Cameroonian trader, Spin Street, Cape Town, December 9, 1997.

Because the police seldom intervene and investigate abuses committed against foreigners, foreign hawkers often are a favorite target for criminals, who feel that they run little risk of apprehension if they rob foreign hawkers. One Somali refugee who used to hawk in Pietersburg told Human Rights Watch how he was violently robbed twice in less than a week, and how the lack of police response had forced him out of the hawking business:

> I was selling trousers, belts, shoes and small items. One early morning, three persons overpowered me and took some of my properties, about half my goods. Five days later, two guys held me at gunpoint and took everything. I went to the police both times but they didn't do anything. He said to me, "We can't do anything but we shall try."[380]

A Nigerian hawker in Cape Town told us a similar story. He hawked chocolates at a local market, and had been repeatedly victimized by a local competitor, who used to come and steal his goods whenever he stepped away and left his female assistant to run the stall. Ultimately, he caught the offending competitor and was stabbed in the struggle which ensued. He repeatedly went to the police station, but "they never called me back, and I don't think they will do anything because I am not South African."[381] He ultimately gave up hawking, preferring to look for employment in "a safer environment where my life is not in danger. I was the last foreigner that hawked here, now it is all locals."[382]

The Deputy Minister of Home Affairs, Ms. Lindiwe Sisulu, has also suggested that asylum-seekers and refugees are trading illegally, and that South African hawkers should be given preferential treatment for hawking permits:

> South Africa's immigration policy is premised upon the notion that no immigrant should be employed at the detriment of a South African citizen.... As the Department of Home Affairs does not issue immigration or work permits to foreigners permitting them to become informal traders, those foreigners with immigration or work permits issued to them for

---

[380]Human Rights Watch interview with Somali hawker, Johannesburg, November 27, 1997.

[381]Human Rights Watch interview with Mickey, Nigerian hawker, at the Parade, Cape Town, December 11, 1997.

[382]Ibid.

employment other than hawking, have in fact illegally entered the hawking business.[383]

The Alexandra Riots against Foreigners

The rise in xenophobic sentiments among segments of the South African public has resulted in an increase in physical attacks against perceived "illegals." Migrants interviewed by Human Rights Watch—including undocumented migrants as well as asylum-seekers and refugees—repeatedly told us they were often verbally insulted on the street and often told to "go home." In some instances, this verbal abuse has escalated into physical attacks.

Some of the most serious attacks on non-South Africans occurred in the Alexandra township near Johannesburg during December 1994 and January 1995. Over a period of several weeks, gangs of South Africans tried violently to evict perceived "illegals" from the township, after blaming undocumented migrants for increased crime, sexual attacks, economic deprivation, unemployment, and other social ills. The attackers claimed to be members of the ANC, the South African Communist Party, and the South African National Civic Organization—although these organizations denied complicity and in some cases condemned the attacks. The violent campaign was known as *Buyelekhaya* or "go back home."[384] Other groups linked to the violent protests were the Concerned Residents Group of Alexandra and the Alexandra Property Owners Association. The Alexandra Property Owners Association participated in the removal campaign but attempted to distance itself from the violence accompanying the campaign by saying, "We are simply doing the job for the police by handing them [the undocumented migrants] over and asking them to be deported back to their own countries."[385]

Mozambicans, Malawians, and Zimbabweans were the primary targets of the Alexandra *Buyelekhaya* campaign. In many instances, groups of armed men evicted suspected foreigners from their homes in the township and marched them to the local police station, demanding that they be repatriated.[386] In most cases, it

---

[383]Media Release by the Deputy Minister of Home Affairs, Ms. Lindiwe Sisulu (MP), dated August 19, 1997.

[384]Minnaar & Hough, *Who Goes There?*, p. 188.

[385]Anna Cox, "Armed gangs force foreigners out of their Alexandra homes," *Star*, January 25, 1995.

[386]Tendai Dumbutshena, "Gangs Evict Zimbabweans," *Star*, January 22, 1995.

appears that the undocumented migrants were indeed repatriated, although some legal residents were released after proving their legal status to the police. The possessions of some suspected undocumented migrants were thrown into the street, while other victims told Human Rights Watch that their possessions had been stolen by members of the armed gangs when they were brought to the police station for deportation. Some of the migrants who were released by the police after proving their legal status returned to their homes only to find the locks changed, or to find armed men preventing them from entering their own homes.[387]

Many of the so-called "illegal aliens" victimized by the violent campaign were in fact long-term legal residents of South Africa. One victim, Kenneth Ngwenya, arrived in South Africa from Zimbabwe some thirty years ago. During the campaign, he was forced from his Alexandra home by a group of approximately fifteen men, who threatened to burn his taxi if he attempted to continue operating it in the township.[388] As a result, Mr. Ngwenya and his three children were driven from their home and forced to seek refuge in a squalid apartment in Hillbrow, Johannesburg. Many migrants claim to have been assaulted during the campaign, a claim bolstered by the media and television coverage of the violent events.

Although the ANC provincial leadership condemned the use of violence at the time, it appeared more ambiguous on the aim of removing migrants from the township. ANC Gauteng deputy leader Obed Bapela stated that all undocumented migrants who did not have refugee status should be removed from the country, although in a humane manner.[389] The IFP Youth Brigade similarly called for the removal of all migrants in the wake of the Alexandra events, claiming they were involved in criminal activities.[390]

---

[387]Ibid.

[388]Tendai Dumbutshena, "Hounded from their homes," *Star*, January 29, 1995.

[389]Anna Cox, "Go Home, ANC tells Illegals," *Star*, January 26, 1995.

[390]"Aliens Must Go-IFP," *Sowetan*, January 27, 1995.

VII. THE STALLED POLICY DEBATE

At the time of the first democratic elections in 1994, South Africa did not have any specific refugee legislation in place, and the new democratic government inherited an Aliens Control Act which was at odds with the Constitution and inconsistent with internationally accepted human rights norms. In order to remedy these deficiencies, the South African government appointed a Green Paper task group on international migration in late 1996 to propose a framework for a new migration policy which is in line with the rule of law, the South African Bill of Rights, and internationally accepted norms.[391] The Green Paper Task Group's mandate was defined broadly to include all areas of migration control, including refugee policy.

The Green Paper Task Group presented its draft *Green Paper on International Migration* to Minister of Home Affairs Buthelezi on May 13, 1997. Arguing that the "challenge for South Africa is to transform a racially-motivated immigration/migration system into a non-racial and rational policy response to the objective needs of the country," and that many of the clauses of the Aliens Control Act and their implementation "would probably not withstand a test of constitutionality," the green paper proposes a radical rethinking of South Africa's migration policy.[392]

The green paper proposed two separate pieces of legislation, one aimed at refugees and asylum-seekers and a second aimed at the various aspects of immigration control such as immigration, migration, and naturalization.[393]

The green paper argues that the current Aliens Control Act has elements that are inconsistent with the constitution and international obligations, particularly the wide administrative discretion that it grants to officials and because "the risk of arbitrary and unconstitutional action by the police, army, and immigration officials is greatly increased by an absence of clear procedures and guarantees set out in the

---

[391]The Green Paper Task Group's mandate is available on the world-wide web, at http://www.polity.org.za:80/govdocs/green_papers/migration/mandate.html (last visited February 18, 1998).

[392]Draft Green Paper on International Migration, presented to the Minister of Home Affairs on May 13, 1997. Available on the world-wide web at http://www.polity.org.za/govdocs/green_papers/migration/migrate.html (last visited January 20, 1998).

[393]Ibid, Section 5.4 "The Road Ahead".

legislation."[394] It recommends that the current Aliens Control Act be replaced with a new *Immigration, Naturalization and Migration Act* which complies with Constitutional and international requirements, is rights-oriented, and also puts forward an integrated and clear policy for migration in South Africa. Because of the past history of discrimination and the importance of regional cooperation, the envisioned legislation would allow special migration preferences to citizens of the SADC member states. Migration policy and enforcement would become the sole responsibility of a renamed *Department of Citizenship and Immigration Services*, ending the current blurring of responsibility between the Department of Home Affairs, the police, and the army.

The green paper argues that refugee policy should be contained in a separate piece of legislation, as it is predominantly a human rights issue and should not be subjected to immigration policy concerns. Such refugee legislation should allow for the timely determination of asylum claims by an independent body, based on the international definitions of a refugee contained in United Nations and Organization of African Unity conventions. Asylum-seekers would be allowed clear administrative justice and due process rights, including a right to appeal. The green paper also recommends that the government pursue regional, SADC-based solutions to refugee problems, and the creation of burden-sharing of refugee influxes in the region.

Human Rights Watch agrees in principle with most of the well thought-out recommendations contained in the green paper and believes that implementation of these recommendations would remedy some of the systemic abuses documented in this report. Many of the abuses discovered by our research are indeed caused by excessive administrative discretion, lack of oversight, the inconsistency of certain procedures with international and constitutional obligations, and the absence of a clear policy on migration. These deficiencies were recognized by Desmond Lockey M.P., the chair of the Parliamentary Portfolio Committee on Home Affairs, who told Human Rights Watch that his own legal advisers had told him that the deportation process violated due process rights.[395] In order to remedy these deficiencies, it is essential that revisions are made to the current legislative framework.

Sources close to the Department of Home Affairs told Human Rights Watch that the Department of Home Affairs is unhappy with the recommendations of the

---

[394]Ibid.

[395]Human Rights Watch interview with Desmond Lockey MP, New Parliament, Cape Town, December 9, 1997.

green paper and that progress on legislative reform has been stalled by the department's leadership. In order for the proposals of the green paper to be translated into legislation, the Minister of Home Affairs must appoint a white paper commission. Although the green paper was published in May 1997, the Department of Home Affairs has yet to act on the green paper's recommendation for two white paper commissions, one to deal with refugee legislation and another to deal with immigration, migration, and naturalization. In fact, the Minister of Home Affairs has been noticeably silent on the issue of legislative reform and has barely commented in public about the green paper's recommendations.

Several of the officials charged with enforcing immigration policy told Human Rights Watch that the current system of immigration control simply was not working, and that a political solution was needed. Police Captain Chilembe told Human Rights Watch that his unit could arrest a thousand persons a day if they had the capacity, but "it is a losing battle, they are always coming back....In order to win this losing battle, we must invest in Mozambique, so the people can find employment there. Mozambicans love their country, but need to work."[396] Colonel Visser, commander of the SANDF's Group 33 responsible for patrolling the Mozambican border and the lowveld area of South Africa, echoed similar sentiments: "We [the army] do not have a problem with the aliens. The politicians must wake up because a political solution is needed....The aliens are mostly docile, friendly, nice people."[397]

Unfortunately, with the 1999 general elections beginning to appear on the political horizon in South Africa, the window of opportunity for migration and refugee legislative reform is becoming increasingly smaller. In the current xenophobic climate, politicians may feel that rights-based arguments in favor of immigration reform mean lost votes. And anti-immigrant sentiments within the ruling African National Congress are becoming stronger, according to some sources. Opposition political parties such as the National Party and the Freedom Front are increasingly clamoring for a crackdown on undocumented migration, not for a more rights-based approach. Thus, there is a risk that South Africa, at least until after the crucial general elections of 1999, will continue to govern its immigration practices under legislation that is widely seen as inconsistent with international and constitutional obligations. Without legislative reform, it will be

---

[396]Human Rights Watch interview with Captain Chilembe, Head, Internal Tracing Unit Nelspruit, South African Police Services, Nelspruit, December 1, 1997.

[397]Human Rights Watch interview with Colonel Visser, Commander, Group 33, South African National Defence Forces, Komatipoort, December 2, 1997.

difficult to address the problems and abuses existing under the current system, as many of these problems and abuses stem from fundamental deficiencies in the current legislation. In the meantime, without reform, Human Rights Watch fears that migrants in South Africa will continue to suffer major and systematic human rights abuses.

APPENDIX A:
SOUTH AFRICA'S OBLIGATIONS
UNDER INTERNATIONAL AND DOMESTIC LAW

South Africa's Obligations under International Human Rights Law[398]

All persons in South Africa share a certain set of basic human rights under international law, regardless of their immigration status. Refugees have, in addition, rights based on international refugee law and the principle that persons should not be returned to a country where they fear persecution on the grounds of race, religion, nationality, membership of a particular social group, or political opinion, or which they were compelled to leave owing to external aggression, occupation, foreign domination or events seriously disturbing public order. The following section first sets out the international law relating to the rights of all persons in South Africa, and then describes the particular entitlements of refugees.

The Rights of All Persons, Citizens and Non-Citizens

International human rights law in general places obligations on states in relation to all people, not only citizens. The Universal Declaration of Human Rights (UDHR),[399] the International Covenant on Civil and Political Rights (ICCPR),[400] and the International Covenant on Economic, Social and Cultural Rights (ICESCR)[401]—together known as the "international bill of human rights" because they form the foundation of international human rights law—confer the great majority of the rights they enumerate to "everyone." The rights that have

---

[398]This section of the report is based significantly on the submission of Human Rights Watch to the Green Paper Task Force on International Migration. Human Rights Watch, "The Human Rights of Undocumented Migrants, Asylum Seekers and Refugees in South Africa," dated April 11, 1997.

[399]Proclaimed and adopted by U.N. General Assembly resolution 217A(III), December 10, 1948.

[400]International Covenant on Civil and Political Rights, adopted by U.N. General Assembly Resolution 2200 A (XXI) of December 16, 1966, entered into force March 23, 1976.

[401]International Covenant on Social, Economic and Cultural Rights, adopted by U.N. General Assembly Resolution 2200 A (XXI) of December 16, 1966, entered into force January 2, 1976.

more restricted application are those that relate directly to citizenship: in particular the right to take part in the conduct of public affairs, to vote, to stand for office, and to have equal access to public service, as well as the right of people to return to their "own" country. The UDHR, the ICCPR, and the ICESCR all enjoin states to respect and ensure the rights they set out to all the individuals within their territory without discrimination, except where the rights are expressly qualified.[402] Accordingly, although international human rights law recognizes the right of states to control their borders and to restrict entry within their territory, the fact that a person has entered a country illegally does not affect his or her rights to life, security of the person, equality before the law, or other basic civil and political rights.

The Universal Declaration of Human Rights, adopted by the United Nations General Assembly in 1948, is not a treaty to which states can become parties, but it is a statement by the international community of the minimum standards of state practice and is also regarded as an articulation of states' human rights obligations as parties to the Charter of the United Nations.[403] South Africa has not ratified either the ICCPR or ICESCR, which are treaties placing explicit and detailed obligations on parties to them, though it signed both in 1994 and is therefore considered obliged not to act against the spirit and purpose of the covenants pending ratification. Moreover, many of the rights contained in these treaties and set out in the UDHR are considered to have become part of customary international law, by which South Africa is bound simply as a member of the community of states. South Africa's constitution recognizes the importance of adhering to principles of international law, stating that "customary international law is law in

---

[402]ICCPR Articles 25 and 12. The UDHR, the ICCPR and the ICESCR all explicitly include discrimination on grounds of national origin (though not nationality) in their general prohibition of discrimination. UDHR Art. 2; ICCPR Art. 2(1); ICESCR Art. 2(2).

[403]At the time of its adoption, South Africa abstained from the vote on the UDHR, together with the Soviet Union, Byelorussia, Ukraine, and Saudi Arabia. Its abstention does not relieve South Africa of its human rights obligations as a member of the United Nations today. South Africa was a founding member of the United Nations at the time of the signing of the United Nations Charter in 1945, and has remained a member since, although it was effectively excluded from all organs of the U.N. from 1974 to 1994, in protest of the policies of apartheid. Articles 55 and 56 of the Charter commit states to promote, among other things "universal respect for, and observance of, human rights and fundamental freedoms for all without distinction as to race, sex, language or religion."

the Republic unless it is inconsistent with the Constitution or an Act of Parliament."[404]

Another declaration of the U.N. General Assembly, the 1985 *Declaration on the Human Rights of Individuals Who are not Nationals of the Country in which They Live*[405]—like the UDHR not a treaty but a statement setting out standards of practice by states—reinforces the universal application of the great majority of rights. It provides explicitly that "aliens," defined as individuals who are not nationals of the states in which they are present, shall enjoy the rights to life and security of the person; to be equal before the courts; to freedom of expression and assembly; and to freedom from torture or cruel, inhuman and degrading treatment or punishment.[406] These and other rights are repeated in a "general comment" relating to the position of undocumented migrants under the ICCPR adopted by the Human Rights Committee.[407]

South Africa is party to the Convention on the Elimination of All forms of Discrimination Against Women (CEDAW) and to the Convention on the Rights of the Child, both of which it ratified in 1995.[408] Again, CEDAW and the Convention on the Rights of the Child make no distinction between citizens and non-citizens in the rights they establish. CEDAW also provides explicitly that women and men

---

[404]Constitution of the Republic of South Africa (1996), Section 232.

[405]Adopted by General Assembly resolution 40/144 of December 13, 1985.

[406]Ibid., Articles 5 and 6.

[407]U.N. Human Rights Committee, General Comment 15: The Position of Aliens under the Covenant (Twenty-seventh session 1986), U.N. Document HRI/GEN/1/Rev.1 (1994), p.18. A General Comment of the Committee aims to clarify interpretations of the ICCPR and to serve as a guideline for assessing state compliance with the covenant. The Human Rights Committee is charged with the task of monitoring the implementation of the International Covenant on Civil and Political Rights.

[408]Convention on the Elimination of All Forms of Discrimination Against Women (CEDAW), adopted and opened for signature, ratification and accession by General Assembly Resolution 34/180 of December 18, 1979, entered into force September 3, 1981, and ratified by South Africa on December 15, 1995. The Convention on the Rights of the Child, adopted and opened for signature, ratification and accession by General Assembly Resolution 44/25 of November 20, 1989, entered into force on September 2, 1990, and ratified by South Africa on June 16, 1995.

shall have "equal rights to acquire, change or retain their nationality," and also equal rights with respect to the nationality of their children.[409]

The Rights of Detainees Generally

All those held in detention, whether nationals, non-nationals, asylum-seekers or refugees, criminally accused or convicted, should be held in conformity with the various U.N. documents setting out guidelines for minimum standards of state practice, including the Standard Minimum Rules for the Treatment of Prisoners,[410] the Body of Principles for the Protection of All Persons under Any Form of Detention or Imprisonment,[411] the Basic Principles for the Treatment of Prisoners,[412] and the Rules for the Protection of Juveniles Deprived of their Liberty.[413] These instruments provide a set of standards that are broadly in agreement with each other. For example, the Body of Principles stipulates that any detention must be "ordered by, or subject to the effective control of, a judicial or other authority," and detainees must be given "an effective opportunity to be heard promptly by a judicial or other authority"; detainees must be informed of the reason for their arrest and detention and of their rights; and they have the right to assistance of legal counsel, to be paid for by the state "where the interests of justice so require."[414] Many of these provisions are repeated in South Africa's own constitution.

The Rights of Deportees

Article 13 of the ICCPR provides that "An alien lawfully present in the territory of a State Party ... may be expelled therefrom only in pursuance of a decision

---

[409]CEDAW, Article 9.

[410]Adopted by the First United Nations Congress on the Prevention of Crime and the Treatment of Offenders, held at Geneva in 1955, and approved by the Economic and Social Council by its resolutions 663C (XXIV) of July 31, 1957 and 2076 (LXII) of May 13, 1977.

[411]Adopted by General Assembly resolution 43/173 of December 9, 1988.

[412]Adopted by General Assembly resolution 45/111 of December 14, 1990.

[413]Adopted by General Assembly resolution 45/113 of December 14, 1990.

[414]Body of Principles, Principles 4, 11, 13, 17 and 18.

reached in accordance with law and shall, except where compelling reasons of national security otherwise require, be allowed to submit the reasons against his expulsion and to have his case reviewed by, and to be represented for the purpose before, the competent authority or a person or persons especially designated by the competent authority." The U.N. Human Rights Committee, which monitors compliance by states Parties to the ICCPR, clarified the position of migrants under the covenant by stating that, while the article refers to migrants lawfully present in a country, the purpose of Article 13 is "clearly to prevent arbitrary expulsions." Therefore, "if the legality of an alien's entry or stay is in dispute, any decision on this point leading to his expulsion or deportation ought to be taken in accordance with article 13.... An alien must be given full facilities for pursuing his remedy against expulsion so that this right will in all the circumstances of his case be an effective one."[415]

The Rights of Migrant Workers

Although it has not yet come into force, the International Convention on the Protection of the Rights of All Migrant Workers and Members of Their Families,[416] which brings together and adds to provisions already contained in a number of treaties of the International Labor Organization (ILO), provides a useful standard on the protection of the rights of migrant workers.[417] The convention defines a migrant worker as "a person who is to be engaged, is engaged or has been engaged in remunerated activity in a state of which he or she is not a national,"[418] whether or not the work is carried out under the correct legal documentation; the definition is thus wider than that usually understood in the South Africa context, where the term generally refers only to those who have come under the terms of bilateral agreements with neighboring countries, especially to work in the mines, and not to

---

[415]U.N. Human Rights Committee, General Comment 15, paragraphs 9 and 10.

[416]Adopted by General Assembly Resolution 45/158 of 18 December 1990.

[417]As of the date of this report, the convention had only seven state parties (Chile, Egypt, Mexico, Morocco, Philippines, Seychelles, and Uganda) and had not yet entered into force (which requires twenty ratifications). While it is not therefore binding on South Africa or any other country in international law, it does provide a standard by which state practice can be assessed.

[418]Convention on the Protection of the Rights of All Migrant Workers, Article 2(1).

skilled workers entering the country under individual contracts. The convention explicitly confers upon both "documented" and "undocumented" migrant workers many of the rights that are already established by the International Covenant on Civil and Political Rights, and adds certain protections particularly relevant to migrants.[419]

The rights conferred on all (documented and undocumented) migrant workers include provisions that migrants and their families detained for immigration offenses must be held separately from the criminally accused or convicted; that passports may not in any circumstances be destroyed, and that identity documents, work permits and other official documentation may only be confiscated or destroyed by public officials authorized to do so by law; that migrants and their families may not be collectively expelled, but each case should be considered individually; that migrants and their families shall enjoy treatment not less favorable than that which applies to nationals in respect of remuneration and conditions of work and shall be entitled to emergency medical treatment; and that the children of migrant workers have the right to a name, registration of birth, a nationality and access to education on the basis of equality of treatment with nationals of the state concerned.[420] Documented migrant workers have certain additional rights, including the right to equality of treatment with nationals in respect of access to educational institutions, housing, social and health services, and to repatriate their earnings.[421]

Reduction of Statelessness

Both the ICCPR and the Convention on the Rights of the Child provide that every child has "the right to acquire a nationality."[422] Similarly, the Convention on

---

[419]A "documented" migrant is a migrant worker or family member who is "authorized to enter, to stay and to engage in a remunerated activity in the State of employment pursuant to the law of that State and to international agreements to which that State is a party." An "undocumented" migrant is a migrant worker or family member who does not comply with the conditions provided to be a documented migrant. Ibid. Article 5.

[420]Ibid., Articles 17(3), 21, 22, 25, 29 and 30.

[421]Ibid., Articles 43, 45 and 47.

[422]ICCPR Article 24(3); Convention on the Rights of the Child, Article 7.

the Reduction of Statelessness[423] provides that a State Party to the convention "shall grant its nationality to a person born in its territory who would otherwise be stateless" and to others born in the territory of another State Party who are unable to acquire the nationality of the state in which they were born for reasons of age or residence qualifications, if one the parents was a national of the state whose nationality is sought at the time of birth.[424] The Convention on the Status of Stateless Persons[425] guarantees certain rights for stateless people. South Africa is not a party to either of the specific conventions on statelessness, but has signed the ICCPR and is a party to the Convention on the Rights of the Child. The obligation to reduce statelessness, and in particular to ensure that children have a nationality, is of particular concern in South Africa in two respects: the status of the children of Mozambican parents born in South Africa, and the defects in the system for registering births, especially in many rural areas.

The Rights of Asylum-Seekers and Refugees
The two most important documents establishing the rights of asylum-seekers and refugees in South Africa are the 1951 U.N. Convention Relating to the Status of Refugees[426] and the 1969 Organization of African Unity (OAU) Convention Governing the Specific Aspects of Refugee Problems in Africa.[427] South Africa acceded to the U.N. Convention and its 1967 protocol on January 12, 1996, and to the OAU Convention in 1995. The two conventions provide definitions of the term

---

[423]Adopted on August 30, 1961 by a Conference of Plenipotentiaries convened pursuant to General Assembly resolution 896(IX) of December 4, 1954; entered into force December 13, 1975.

[424]Ibid., Article 1.

[425]Adopted on September 28, 1954 by a Conference of Plenipotentiaries convened by Economic and Social Council resolution 526A(XVII) of April 26, 1954; entered into force June 6, 1960.

[426]Convention Relating to the Status of Refugees, adopted by the United Nations Conference of Plenipotentiaries on the Status of Refugees and Stateless Persons on July 28, 1951, entered into force on April 22, 1954.

[427]Organization of African Unity Convention Governing the Specific Aspects of Refugee Problems in Africa, adopted by the Assembly of Heads of State and Government at its sixth ordinary session, Addis Ababa, September 10, 1969, entered into force June 20, 1974.

"refugee" and set out the principal rights of refugees in the host country, which in a number of respects are explicitly stated to be the same as those of nationals in that country. In addition, the office of the U.N. High Commissioner for Refugees (UNHCR) has published a *Handbook on Procedures and Criteria for Determining Refugee Status* and *Guidelines on the Detention of Asylum Seekers*, which are not binding on states but are considered by UNHCR to be minimum standards of state practice. The Executive Committee (ExCom) of UNHCR[428] also adopts "conclusions" from time to time, which establish further guidelines on acceptable practice.

The Definition of a Refugee

South Africa currently does not have any legislation covering the procedure for obtaining refugee status in place. Under the Basic Agreement reached between the South African government and UNHCR in 1993, South Africa agreed to abide by the definitions contained in the U.N. 1951 Convention and the 1969 OAU Convention in determining refugee status.[429] Under the U.N. Convention, a refugee is defined as,

> any person who ... owing to a well-founded fear of being persecuted for reasons of race, religion, nationality, membership of a particular social group or political opinion, is outside the country of his nationality and is unable or, owing to such fear, is unwilling to avail himself of the protection of that country; or who, not having a nationality and being outside the

---

[428]The Executive Committee of the Programme of the U.N. High Commissioner for Refugees (ExCom) is currently made up of representatives of fifty-one states, largely from those states that are important refugee-producing countries, important asylum countries or important donors to UNHCR's programs; not all members of ExCom are signatories to the 1951 U.N. Convention. The terms of reference of ExCom are to advise the High Commissioner for Refugees in the exercise of his or her functions, to approve the High Commissioner's programs and to set financial targets. While ExCom does not set legal obligations on states or on UNHCR, its conclusions on refugee protection serve as guidelines for judging government action.

[429]Letter from Claude Schravesande to Human Rights Watch, dated July 3, 1996, and Human Rights Watch telephone interview with Claude Schravesande, July 10, 1996.

country of his former habitual residence as a result of such events, is unable or, owing to such fear, is unwilling to return to it.[430]

The definition of refugee under the OAU Convention includes this description, but widens it by adding,

The term "refugee" shall also apply to every person who, owing to external aggression, occupation, foreign domination or events seriously disturbing public order in either part or the whole of his country of origin or nationality, is compelled to leave his place of habitual residence in order to seek refuge in another place outside his country of origin or nationality.[431]

An asylum-seeker is an individual who has entered a country with or without the legally required documentation, who seeks to obtain refugee status, and whose status has not yet been determined. The term is considered by UNHCR to include individuals whose application for refugee status has been rejected, where the rejection is on "purely formal grounds" (for example, when the receiving government decides that the individual can seek asylum in a safe third country); or on substantive grounds that UNHCR would not consider sufficient; or following a process for determination of refugee status that is not procedurally fair.[432] Asylum-seekers should be considered to have the same rights as refugees, until such time as it is fairly determined that they do not have refugee status.

The Right of Non-Refoulement

The central right of a refugee is not to be returned to a country in which he or she would be in danger on account of one of the grounds mentioned in the refugee conventions; this is known as the right of non-refoulement. The Universal Declaration of Human Rights provides in article 14(1) that "Everyone has the right

---

[430]Convention Relating to the Status of Refugees, Article 1(A)(2). Note that it is possible for a person to become a refugee at some time after leaving his or her own country, for example if political events at home suddenly make return unsafe.

[431]Convention Governing the Specific Aspects of Refugee Problems in Africa, Article 1(2).

[432]UNHCR, Guidelines on the Detention of Asylum Seekers, paragraph 11.

to seek and to enjoy in other countries asylum from persecution." Article 33(1) of the 1951 U.N. Convention strengthens this provision by stating that:

> No Contracting State shall expel or return ("refouler") a refugee in any manner whatsoever to the frontiers of territories where his or her life or freedom would be threatened on account of his race, religion, nationality, membership of a particular social group or political opinion.[433]

Similarly, the 1969 OAU Convention provides that "No person shall be subjected by a Member State to measures such as rejection at the frontier, return or expulsion, which would compel him to return to or remain in a territory where his life, physical integrity or liberty would be threatened"; and that "The essentially voluntary nature of repatriation shall be respected in all cases and no refugee shall be repatriated against his will."[434] Article 3(1) of the 1951 U.N. Convention against Torture and Other Cruel, Inhuman or Degrading Treatment or Punishment[435] also stipulates that the prohibition on refoulement applies to situations in which there are "substantial grounds" for believing that a person (whether or not a refugee) would be subjected to torture if returned to his or her country.

Procedures for Determining Refugee Status
In order to ensure that the right of non-refoulement is respected, it is essential that any person who faces return by the receiving government be able to challenge that decision and assert a claim for protection as a refugee in a procedurally fair hearing. UNHCR recognizes that,

---

[433]While the UDHR does not impose a duty on states to grant asylum, Human Rights Watch considers that the prohibition on expelling or returning refugees to the frontier of territories where their life or freedom would be threatened (refoulement) to be a norm of international customary law binding on all states whether or not they have ratified the 1951 U.N. Convention, and that this prohibition extends to situations in which asylum-seekers have not yet entered a state but are turned away at the border.

[434]1969 OAU Convention, Articles 2 (3) and 5 (1).

[435]Adopted by U.N. General Assembly resolution 39/46 of December 10, 1984; entry into force June 26, 1987. South Africa signed the Convention Against Torture in 1993, though it has not yet ratified the treaty.

an applicant for refugee status is normally in a particularly vulnerable situation. He finds himself in an alien environment and may experience serious difficulties, technical and psychological, in submitting his case to the authorities of a foreign country, often in a language not his own. His application should therefore be examined within the framework of specially established procedures by qualified personnel having the necessary knowledge and expertise, and an understanding of an applicants particular difficulties and needs.[436]

Accordingly, the UNHCR ExCom has made recommendations, repeated in the Handbook on Procedures, that states follow certain basic requirements in establishing their procedures:

i. The competent official (e.g., immigration officer or border police officer) to whom the applicant addresses himself at the border or in the territory of a Contracting State should have clear instructions for dealing with cases which might come within the purview of the relevant international instruments. He should be required to act in accordance with the principle of non-refoulement and to refer such cases to a higher authority.

ii. The applicant should receive the necessary guidance as to the procedure to be followed.

iii. There should be a clearly identified authority—wherever possible a single central authority—with responsibility for examining requests for refugee status and taking a decision in the first instance.

iv. The applicant should be given the necessary facilities, including the services of a competent interpreter, for submitting his case to the authorities concerned. Applicants should also be given the opportunity, of which they should be duly informed, to contact a representative of UNHCR.

v. If the applicant is recognized as a refugee, he should be informed accordingly and issued with documentation certifying his refugee status.

---

[436]UNHCR Handbook on Procedures and Criteria for Determining Refugee Status (United Nations, Geneva: 1988), p.45.

vi. If the applicant is not recognized, he should be given a reasonable time to appeal for a formal reconsideration of the decision, either to the same or to a different authority, whether administrative or judicial, according to the prevailing system.

vii. The applicant should be permitted to remain in the country pending a decision on his initial request by the competent authority referred to in paragraph (iii) above, unless it has been established by that authority that his request is clearly abusive. He should also be permitted to remain in the country while an appeal to a higher administrative authority or to the courts is pending. The competent official (e.g., immigration officer or border police officer to whom the applicant addresses himself at the border or in the territory of a Contracting State) should have clear instructions for dealing with cases which might come within the purview of the relevant international instruments. He should be required to act in accordance with the principle of non-refoulement and to refer such cases to a higher authority.[437]

The Handbook on Procedures also sets out detailed guidelines on evaluating the substance of refugee claims, including guidance on interpretation of the key phrases contained within the 1951 U.N. Convention.

Other Rights of Refugees

Aside from the right to non-refoulement, refugees have the rights of all non-citizens—which in most cases are the same as those of citizens. In addition, the 1951 U.N. Convention specifically obliges states parties to grant refugees either the same treatment as nationals of that state or, as a minimum, "the most favourable treatment accorded to nationals of a foreign country in the same circumstances" in respect of a variety of different rights. For example, refugees shall enjoy the same treatment as nationals in matters relating to access to the courts (including access to legal assistance), labor protection, public assistance, and with respect to elementary education.[438] They have the right to the same treatment as other migrants generally in respect of seeking gainful employment, access to housing or higher education. The 1969 OAU Convention is less specific, but does commit member states to "use their best endeavours ... to receive refugees and to secure the

---

[437]Handbook on Procedures, Paragraph 192.

[438]1951 U.N. Convention, Articles 16, 22, 23 & 24.

settlement of those refugees who, for well-founded reasons, are unable or unwilling to return to their country of origin or nationality."[439] Both conventions state that their provisions shall be applied without discrimination.[440]

Neither the U.N. nor the OAU refugee convention incorporate the principle of family unity into the definition of the term refugee. However, the Final Act of the U.N. Conference of Plenipotentiaries on the Status of Refugees and Stateless Persons which adopted the 1951 U.N. Convention states that the conference "Recommends Governments to take the necessary measures for the protection of the refugee's family, especially with a view to: (1) Ensuring that the unity of the refugee's family is maintained particularly in cases where the head of the family has fulfilled the necessary conditions for admission to a particular country, (2) The protection of refugees who are minors, in particular unaccompanied children and girls, with special reference to guardianship and adoption."

Detention of Asylum-Seekers and Refugees

Undocumented migrants in many countries are frequently detained pending deportation simply as a consequence of their illegal status. In the case of refugees, Article 31 of the 1951 U.N. Convention specifically provides that "States shall not impose penalties, on account of their illegal entry or presence, on refugees who, coming directly from a territory where their life or freedom was threatened ... enter or are present in their territory without authorization, provided they present themselves without delay to the authorities and show good cause for their illegal entry or presence." Furthermore, such refugees shall only be subject to restrictions of movement which are "necessary" and only until their status is regularized or until they obtain admission to another country.

The terms "coming directly," "without delay," and "good cause" should be interpreted restrictively, in favor of the asylum-seeker. The travaux préparatoires of the convention (the documents prepared in the course of its drafting) make clear that the term "coming directly" was introduced not to exclude those who had simply passed through another country in coming to the state where they applied for asylum, but only those who had "settled temporarily" in one country before entering another. Similarly, the UNHCR Guidelines on the Detention of Asylum

---

[439]1969 OAU Convention, Article II(1).

[440]In the case of the 1951 U.N. Convention, Article 3, "without discrimination as to race, religion or country of origin"; under the 1969 OAU Convention, Article IV "without discrimination as to race, religion, nationality, membership of a particular social group or political opinion."

Seekers note that "Given the special situation of a refugee, in particular the frequent fear of authorities, language problems, lack of information and general insecurity, and the fact that these and other circumstances may vary enormously from one refugee to another, there is no time limit which can be mechanistically applied associated with the term 'without delay.' ... Along with the term 'good cause' ... it must take into account all of the circumstances under which the asylum seeker fled."[441]

In accordance with article 31, the Guidelines state that "as a general rule asylum seekers should not be detained." Guideline 3 provides that:

> The permissible exceptions to the general rule that detention should normally be avoided must be prescribed by law. In such cases, detention of asylum seekers may only be resorted to, if necessary, in order:

> i. to verify identity;

> ii. to determine the elements on which the claim to refugee status or asylum is based;

> iii. to deal with cases where refugees or asylum-seekers have destroyed their travel and/or identity documents or have used fraudulent documents in order to mislead the authorities of the State in which they intend to claim asylum; or

> iv. to protect national security or public order.

Where detention of asylum-seekers is considered necessary it should only be imposed where it is reasonable to do so and without discrimination. It should be proportional to the ends to be achieved (i.e. to ensure one of the above purposes) and for a minimal period.[442]

---

[441]Guidelines, paragraphs 7 and 8.

[442]Guideline 3 is based on UNHCR ExCom Conclusion 44 "Detention of Refugees and Asylum Seekers," adopted by consensus, 1986. However, Human Rights Watch is concerned that the grounds for detention provided in Guideline 3 are too vague and undefined, and believes that states should set more precise and limited rules for detention for themselves.

Guideline 4 enumerates minimum procedural safeguards for asylum-seekers in detention, including the right to be informed of the reasons for detention; the right to challenge the lawfulness of the deprivation of liberty "before a competent, independent and impartial authority, where the individual may present his arguments either personally or through a representative"; the right to contact the local UNHCR office, other agencies, and a lawyer, and the means to make such contact.

Guideline 5 relates to the detention of children and stipulates that "minors who are asylum seekers should not be detained." If, despite this rule, children are detained, it should be "as a measure of last resort, for the shortest appropriate period of time and in accordance with the exceptions stated at Guideline 3." The guidelines refer to the Convention on the Rights of the Child, especially article 22, which provides that special measures of protection should be given to refugee children and asylum-seekers who are minors, whether accompanied or not. Children who are asylum-seekers must not be held under prison-like conditions: all efforts must be made to have them released from detention and placed in other accommodation; or, if this proves impossible, special arrangements must be made for living quarters which are suitable for children and their families. During detention, children have the right to education, preferably outside the detention premises. In addition, unaccompanied minors should have a legal guardian appointed responsible for ensuring that their interests are protected; Human Rights Watch believes that as soon as they are apprehended they should be placed in the care of the child welfare authorities, and kept out of the system applied to adult asylum-seekers.

Guideline 6 relates to conditions of detention generally and provides that "conditions of detention for asylum seekers should be humane with respect for the inherent dignity of the person," and that they should be "prescribed by law." Specifically, detainees should have the right to contact and receive visits from friends, relatives and legal counsel, the possibility to receive appropriate medical treatment and to conduct some form of physical exercise, and the possibility to continue further education or vocational training. Asylum-seekers should be held separately from those convicted of a criminal offence; in general men and women should be segregated, and children should be held apart from adults who are not their relatives. Additionally, Human Rights Watch believes that asylum-seekers in detention, who are not accused of any crime, should be segregated from those detained as a result of being accused of a criminal offence.

In summary: the language of the Guidelines indicates that in the case of asylum-seekers the detaining authority is under an obligation to show why measures short of detention are not sufficient and, even where that is the case, to detain for the shortest time necessary and in conditions consonant with human dignity.

Domestic Obligations

Constitutional Obligations

Like the international instruments, South Africa's own constitution also draws no distinction between non-citizens and citizens for most of the rights guaranteed in the bill of rights. Only the right to enter the country, to obtain a passport, to vote, to stand for office, to form a political party and other political rights are limited to citizens.[443] The South African Constitution guarantees and protects most internationally recognized human rights, and places upon the state an obligation to "respect, protect, promote and fulfil the rights in the Bill of Rights."[444] The South African Bill of Rights is considered binding on "the legislature, the executive, the judiciary and all organs of the state," and applies to all laws.[445]

A fundamental concept the South African Bill of Rights is the right to human dignity: "Everyone has inherent dignity and the right to have their dignity respected and protected."[446] The importance of this right in the South African context flows out of its particular history, in which the apartheid state daily violated the dignity of the majority black population through segregation, arbitrary detention, and various forms of abusive policies.[447] The right to freedom and security of the person is also protected by the bill of rights, in particular the right "not to be deprived of freedom arbitrarily or without just cause," the right "not to be detained

---

[443]Constitution of the Republic of South Africa (1996) Sections 19, 20, and 21.

[444]Ibid., Section 7(2).

[445]Ibid., Section 8(1).

[446]Ibid., Section 10.

[447]"The history of systematic discrimination in South Africa, from segregation through apartheid, was premised on gross invasions of human dignity. The denial of this human right, protected in many international human rights instruments, most notably the Universal Declaration of Human Rights (art. 1) and the African Charter on Human and Peoples' Rights (art. 5), was so pervasive that its inclusion [in the bill of rights], immediately after the rights to equality and life, was entirely uncontroversial." Lourens Du Plessis and Hugh Corder, *Understanding South Africa's Transitional Bill of Rights* (Cape Town: Juta, 1994), p. 149.

without trial," the right "to be free from all forms of violence from both public and private sources," the right "not to be tortured in any way," and the right "not to be treated or punished in a cruel, inhuman or degrading way."[448] In the view of Human Rights Watch, these provisions clearly place limitations on the manner in which all persons—including non-citizens—are to be treated by the various agencies involved in migrants control. In addition, the right "to be free from violence from both public and private sources" places a positive obligation on the security forces to take all possible steps to protect all persons from vigilante violence.

The South African Bill of Rights recognizes the right to just administrative action. This right includes the right to "administrative action which is lawful, reasonable and procedurally fair," the right to be given written reasons for an administrative decision which adversely affects one's rights, and the right to review of administrative action by a court or an independent tribunal.[449] As these administrative rights apply to "everyone," the South African state must respect these rights in the administration of its migration control and asylum determination systems.

A number of specific rights apply to persons in detention. Any person who is detained has a right to be informed promptly of the reason for his or her detention, to choose and consult with a legal practitioner and to have a legal practitioner assigned at the expense of the state "if substantial injustice would otherwise result" (and to be informed promptly of this right), the right to challenge the lawfulness of the detention before a court, "to conditions of detention that are consistent with human dignity, including at least exercise and the provision, at state expense, of adequate accommodation, nutrition, reading material, and medical treatment," and the right to be visited by one's spouse or partner, next of kin, religious counselor of choice, and medical practitioner of choice.[450]

In addition, the South African Bill of Rights recognizes a number of other rights relevant to the protection of migrants: the right to equality before the law and

---

[448]Constitution (1996), Section 12(1).

[449]Ibid., Section 33.

[450]Ibid., Section 35(2).

the equal protection and benefit of the law;[451] the right to life; [452]an absolute prohibition on slavery, servitude, and forced labor;[453] the right to privacy;[454] the right to freedom of conscience, religion, thought, belief and opinion;[455] freedom of expression;[456] freedom of assembly and peaceful demonstration; [457]freedom of association;[458] the right of access to "any information held by the state,"[459] and the right not to be deprived of property except in terms of a law of general application.[460]

Another area of the South African Bill of Rights which may have an impact on the rights of migrants in South Africa is its enumeration of socio-economic rights, which also apply to all persons, not just citizens. The bill of rights recognizes a number of socio-economic rights such as the right to a safe environment,[461] to adequate housing,[462] to health care, sufficient food and water and social security,[463]

---

[451]Ibid., Section 9.

[452]Ibid., Section 11.

[453]Ibid., Section 13.

[454]Ibid., Section 14.

[455]Ibid., Section 15.

[456]Ibid., Section 16.

[457]Ibid., Section 17.

[458]Ibid., Section 18.

[459]Ibid., Section 32.

[460]Ibid., Section 25.

[461]Ibid., Section 24.

[462]Ibid., Section 26.

[463]Ibid., Section 27.

to education,[464] and the right to use one's own language and to participate in the cultural life of their choice.[465] A number of rights specific to children are also entrenched in the Bill of Rights.[466] The socio-economic rights are at times subject to a progressive implementation, meaning that their implementation depends on available state funds (although implementation must take place in a non-discriminatory fashion) and their exact content, as well as their application to migrants, remains to be determined.

Since the South African constitution was only adopted in late 1996, many of the rights contained in the visionary document have not yet been interpreted by a court of law, let alone by the authoritative Constitutional Court, the highest court in South Africa. Only a single decision which deals with the rights of non-citizens has been handed down by the Constitutional Court so far.[467] In *Larbi-Odam and Others v. The Member of the Executive Council for Education (North West Province) and Another*, the Constitutional Court struck down a provincial law

---

[464]Ibid., Section 29.

[465]Ibid., Section 30.

[466]Section 28(1) of the South African Constitution recognizes the right of "every child" (defined as a person under the age of eighteen years) to "a) a name and nationality from birth; b) to family care, parental care, or appropriate alternative care when removed from the family environment; c) to basic nutrition, shelter, and basic health care services, and social services; d) to be protected from maltreatment, neglect, abuse, or degradation; e) to be protected from exploitative labor practices; f) not to be required or permitted to perform work or provide services that I) are inappropriate for a person of that child's age; or ii) place at risk the child's well-being, education, physical or mental health, or spiritual, moral, or social development; g) not to be detained except as a measure of last resort, in which case, in addition to the rights a child enjoys under sections 12 and 35, the child may be detained only for the shortest appropriate period of time, and has the right to be- I) kept separately from detained persons over the age of 18 years; and ii) treated in a manner, and kept in conditions, that take account of the child's age; h) to have a legal practitioner assigned to the child by the state, and at state expense, in civil proceedings affecting the child, if substantial injustice would otherwise result; and I) not to be used directly in armed conflict, and to be protected in times of armed conflict."

[467]A number of decisions on the rights of migrants have been handed down by lower courts under the previous interim South African Constitution of 1993. For a review and critique of these decisions, see Jonathan Klaaren, "So Far Not So Good: An Analysis of Immigration Decisions under the Interim Constitution," *South African Journal on Human Rights*, vol. 12 (Cape Town: Juta, 1996), pp. 605-616.

which prohibited foreign citizens from being permanently employed as teachers in state schools.[468] The unanimous judgment found that non-citizens were protected by the bill of rights' non-discrimination clause, and that all employment opportunities—with the limited exception of politically sensitive positions—should be available to permanent residents and South African citizens on an equal basis. It appears that the Constitutional Court's judgment reaffirms the general proposition that all rights contained in the bill of rights, with the exception of those specifically limited to citizens, provide protection to non-South Africans as well as South Africans. Thus, the treatment of undocumented migrants, asylum-seekers, refugees and other migrants in South Africa should be viewed in light of the protections provided by the constitution's bill of rights as well as against international standards. This interpretation is consistent with the preamble of the constitution, which envisions a "society based on democratic values, social justice and fundamental human rights."[469]

The Aliens Control Act

The central piece of immigration legislation in South Africa is the Aliens Control Act,[470] which has been referred to by commentators as a "draconian apartheid throwback" and "apartheid's last act."[471] The Aliens Control Act has deeply racist and anti-semitic roots in the apartheid era, and its previous versions were used during the apartheid period to exclude as "undesirables" such group as Jews, Indians, Africans and other non-whites. Under the apartheid version of migrants control, it was virtually impossible to permanently immigrate to South Africa as a non-white person, while desirable whites were welcomed:

> Immigrants were, by definition, white. The government distinguished between desirable and undesirable whites in formulating its policies. There was no immigration policy for Africans from outside the country. Africans

---

[468]*Larbi-Odam and Others v. The Member of the Executive Council for Education (North-West Province) and Another.*

[469]Ibid., preamble.

[470]Act No. 96 of 1991.

[471]Eddie Koch, "The Pass Laws Keep on Prowling," *Mail & Guardian* (Johannesburg), July 15, 1994; Jonathan Crush, "Apartheid's Last Act?," *Democracy in Action*, Vol. 10(2) (1996), pp. 12-13.

were migrants and they had to return home when they were no longer of use to South African employers.[472]

The Aliens Control Act (ACA), passed in 1991, is a consolidation of a number of earlier statutes, and has itself been amended several times since it was passed. Most recently, the ACA was amended in several major aspects by the Aliens Control Amendment Act of 1995,[473] which principally came into effect on July 1, 1996. The ACA is complicated in structure and often difficult to follow, even by those who specialize in its interpretation. As a result, practice often does not comply with the procedures established by the ACA. Human Rights Watch found significant regional variance in the procedures and forms used by different government departments and even by different branches within a department. In order to place our findings in the appropriate legislative context, the following sections aim to summarize the main provisions of the ACA.

The Deportation Process

Prohibited Persons
As the name suggests, the Aliens Control Act is mostly concerned with control of immigration into South Africa. The central element of this system of control is the concept of a "prohibited person." A prohibited person—broadly anyone who has entered the country through other than proper channels[474] or who falls within

---

[472]Sally Peberdy and Jonathan Crush, "Rooted in Racism: The Origins of the Aliens Control Act," *South African Migration Project Migration Policy Series No. 3.* Jonathan Klaaren makes a similar point: "Until 1986, South African immigration was explicitly racial, requiring that applicants for permanent residence be 'readily assimilable by the white inhabitants.' Especially from 1960, the government recruited white skilled workers, offering them permanent residence, but continued to prohibit recruited black workers from counting their time of employment towards naturalization. The effect of these policies was that permanent residence was reserved for whites and not blacks. Since the law of naturalization (as well as other legislation) depends on permanent residence status, a strong if indirect equality claim thus exists." Jonathan Klaaren, "Immigration and the South African Constitution," *South African Migration Project Policy Series No. 3.*

[473]Act No. 76 of 1995.

[474]Entering South Africa somewhere other than a designated port of entry, failing to report to an immigration officer, entering without a visa, or failing to produce satisfactory documentation upon request are grounds for being declared a prohibited person, whether or

one of a listed set of categories of undesirable types of people[475]—is liable to removal from the country and pending removal may be arrested and detained. Prior to entering the country, every person is required by the ACA to report to an immigration officer at a port of entry and satisfy the officer, who will conduct an examination under section 7 of the act, that he or she is not a prohibited person. If he or she fails to comply with these requirements or fails to satisfy the immigration officer that he or she is not a prohibited person, the immigration officer is supposed under section 9 of the act to declare that person a prohibited person and refuse them entry to the country.[476] Section 8 requires immigration officers, when they are satisfied that a person is not a prohibited person, to allow him or her to enter the Republic.

Legal Entry into the Country

The Aliens Control Act provides for three main ways for non-citizens to reside legally in the country: First, some non-South African citizens may be given permits to enter the country in the form of temporary residence permits under section 26, or immigration permits (formerly known as permanent residence

---

not that person would otherwise be legally within the country. Section 9(1) read with sections 5, 6, and 7. A person entering South Africa without a valid passport and visa is also a prohibited person unless "proved to be a South African citizen." Section 11(1).

[475] The substantive grounds cover any person who is "likely to become a public charge," who is "deemed by the Minister to be an undesirable inhabitant of or visitor to the Republic" from information received through official or diplomatic channels, who "lives or has lived on the earnings of prostitution," who has committed one of a number of crimes, or who is mentally ill or afflicted with a disease. See section 39(2) of the Act. This last ground was used from 1987 to 1991 to bar persons with AIDS or HIV from entering South Africa legally: under the predecessor section to section 39(2)(f), the Minister of Home Affairs in October 1987 declared AIDS and HIV a disease "the affliction with which will render the person a prohibited person." After considerable protest, these immigration restrictions were dropped in October 1991 without having ever been implemented. See Edwin Cameron, "Human Rights, Racism and AIDS: The New Discrimination," *South African Journal on Human Rights*, vol. 9 (Cape Town: Juta, 1993), p. 22.

[476]Alternatively, the immigration officer may issue a person suspected of being a prohibited person with a provisional permit with conditions and limitations in order to provide time for investigation of the matter and, after such investigation, declare the person to be a prohibited person if the investigation reveals evidence to this effect. In this case, the person suspected of being a prohibited person is allowed to enter the Republic while the investigation is ongoing. ACA section 10.

permits) under section 25. Historically, these permits were restricted to white immigrants,[477] and they are now restricted largely to individuals bringing skills or money into the country, and their families. Secondly, there are citizens from neighboring countries, principally Mozambique, Botswana, Lesotho and Swaziland, who enter South Africa as contract workers on the basis of bilateral agreements with the governments of those states "in accordance with a scheme of recruitment and repatriation approved by the Minister of Home Affairs."[478] These persons, largely (black) mine workers, are exempt from being considered prohibited persons for the period of their employment.[479] The third exception is those persons who have applied for asylum or been granted refugee status. Since 1993, South Africa has recognized the right of individuals to apply for refugee status, but has used the ACA and its Basic Agreement with UNHCR rather than specific refugee legislation to regulate this: asylum applicants and refugees are either granted temporary permits to enter the country under section 41, or granted an exemption from the requirements of the act on grounds of "special circumstances" under section 29. The ad-hoc procedures for examining asylum applications are described below.

Non-citizens present in South Africa without either a temporary or permanent residence permit are required to report to an immigration officer, failing which they may be arrested without warrant and deported under a warrant issued by the minister.[480] Similarly, any person with a permit who overstays the permit or acts in conflict with the conditions placed on the issue of that permit is guilty of an offence and may be dealt with as a prohibited person.[481]

---

[477]The 1937 Aliens Act, for example, echoed previous legislation by requiring that applicants for entry to South Africa should be readily assimilable with the European inhabitants of the Union. Sally Peberdy and Jonathan Crush, "Rooted in Racism: The Origins of the Aliens Control Act," *South African Migration Project Migration Policy Series No. 3.*

[478]Section 40(1)(d)(ii) and (iii).

[479]Section 40(3).

[480]Section 27. This provision does not apply to a small category of persons exempted under the South African Citizenship Act 1949. Section 27(4).

[481]Section 26(5).

Identification of Prohibited Persons

The ACA is perhaps misnamed, since certain of its most control-oriented provisions apply to citizens as well as migrants, even though a citizen should not be declared a prohibited person according to the formal provisions of the act.[482] In particular, section 7 of the act allows an immigration officer to require *any* person to produce "documentary or other evidence relative to his claim to enter or be in the Republic." The immigration officer may exercise this power over persons reporting to him upon entry or over "any other person who in the opinion of such officer is not entitled to be in the Republic."[483]

In a similar fashion, section 53(1) provides that a person may be stopped either by an immigration officer or by a police officer "who suspects on reasonable grounds that a person is an alien."[484] A person stopped is required to produce documentary evidence in support of a claim to be in the Republic lawfully. If a person stopped fails to satisfy the officer that he or she is entitled to be in the Republic, the officer may take the person into custody and detain the person, pending further investigation of their status. Such a person is not declared a prohibited person, but if "it is established" that the person is not entitled to be in the Republic, he or she is guilty of an offence and can be removed.[485]

---

[482]Section 9(3) provides that section 9, relating to the declaration of persons as prohibited persons, does not apply to South African citizens. Section 11 similarly states that a person who enters without a passport or a visa is not a prohibited person "if it is proved that he is a South African citizen."

[483]Section 7(1). If a person either fails to comply with such a request made by an immigration officer or "fails to satisfy the immigration officer that he is not a prohibited person" the immigration officer is required under section 9 to declare that person to be a prohibited person.

[484]Note that section 7 refers only to immigration officers while section 53(1) refers to both immigration officers and police officers. Section 7(1) does not have a statutory requirement of reasonable grounds. As indicated below, a number of police within internal tracing unit are also immigration officers.

[485]Section 53(2). This onus may be interpreted—at least as a matter of practice—to lie with the person to prove that they are entitled to be in South Africa rather than with the Department. Such an onus may be a difficult one to discharge for black citizens without proper documentation. As documented in this report, many black South Africans are arrested and detained for several days while their citizenship is being confirmed.

Removals

Sections 44 to 48 of the ACA provide for the removal of persons from South Africa. Most removals take place under section 44, which provides that an immigration officer may arrest without warrant, or cause to be arrested, a prohibited person found in the country, and shall "irrespective of whether such a person is arrested or not" remove or cause to be removed him or her under warrant from the minister. Pending removal, the immigration officer may order the person to be detained.[486] Removals of this type are known as "repatriations" by the Department of Home Affairs. Since many removed under this section are handled by the police or army rather than home affairs, accurate statistics for repatriations are hard to establish (see below). If, on the other hand, a person is to be removed as a result of committing an offense other than the offense of being in the country without authorization, or because his or her presence is deemed to be contrary to the public interest, then he or she is subject to what the department terms "deportation" rather than "repatriation."[487] In 1997, 851 persons were deported under deportation orders, after having been convicted of crimes in South Africa.[488] In most such cases, convicted criminals are deported after serving their sentences.

Detention of Deportees

Under the ACA, a person may be detained pending removal "in the manner and at the place determined by the Director-General" of Home Affairs,[489] although

---

[486]Section 44(1).

[487]Persons convicted of a wide range of crimes (broader than the range of crimes making one liable to declaration as a prohibited person) and sentenced to imprisonment of at least twelve months may be removed under section 45(1). Additionally, a person admitted for permanent residence who commits any offence within three years of admission may be removed if deemed by the minister to be undesirable inhabitant of the Republic. In making this determination, the minister may consider the circumstances of the offence, previous convictions, and "family affairs." Section 46(1). Persons removed under these sections are counted as deported by the Department. The act, however, refers only to "removals."

[488]Department of Home Affairs, "Removals according to Section 45, 46 and 47 of the Aliens Control Act, 1991 (Act 96 of 1991) as amended. These persons have been convicted of crimes in RSA," dated January 27, 1998.

[489]Section 44(1)(a). Section 16(1) provides that the master of a ship shall detain and remove prohibited persons found aboard that ship.

section 55 of the act, introduced in 1996, provides for certain restrictions on such detention. Currently, a suspected "prohibited person" found within South Africa and taken into custody may be detained for successive periods of forty-eight hours on the authority of an immigration officer, "for as long as may be reasonable and necessary,"[490] pending determination of his or her status. However, after the first forty-eight hours, the detainee should be informed in writing of the reasons for continued detention. The evidence gathered by Human Rights Watch suggests that this rarely happens. If an immigration officer decides that the person detained is in fact a prohibited person, he or she may be detained for an initial period of thirty days following the decision, pending removal.

Under the amendments to the ACA introduced in July 1996, detention must be reviewed after thirty days by a judge of the High Court, and may be renewed after review for successive periods of ninety days. However, as implemented by regulations passed under the act, these automatic judicial review procedures make provision only for written input by the detainee in reply to the immigration officer's reasons for detention and not for a hearing.[491] Moreover, despite the 1996 amendments to the act, there is no absolute maximum period of detention either before or after determination of status. Human Rights Watch found numerous cases were people had been kept in detention in excess of thirty days without judicial review.

Appeal and Review of Immigration Decisions and Detention
Where a person has been declared a prohibited person by an immigration officer under these procedures, there is no formal right of appeal to an independent tribunal,[492] although the act does include a provision that the immigration officer shall inform the individual of his or her right to request the minister, in writing and

---

[490]This is the same standard that existed for all detentions prior to 1 July 1996 under the predecessor to section 55.

[491]Aliens Control Regulations (28 June 1996) (No. R. 999, in GN 17253, Reg Gaz No. 5716).

[492]There had previously been such a statutory right of appeal but it was removed in 1991. *See* S. Peberdy, "An Outline of the History of South Africa's Immigration Legislation."

within three days, to review the declaration.[493] In practice, it seems that individuals are treated as prohibited persons without a "declaration" taking place. No cases are known in which the minister in fact has reviewed a decision that a person is a prohibited person. Deportees and immigration officers interviewed by Human Rights Watch were not aware of these procedures, while the Department of Home Affairs does not keep any statistics on the number of persons declared prohibited persons,[494] nor on the number of persons who take advantage of the provision allowing for review of a declaration.[495] The department has confirmed, for instance, that the 157,084 persons who were repatriated in 1995 were not legally eligible for ministerial review, and that ministerial review is also unavailable for those persons deported, for example as a result of having committed an offence other than an immigration offence or "in the public interest."[496] Indeed, the Department of Home Affairs apparently has no record of any person ever having been afforded an administrative hearing in relation to deportation or repatriation.

There is a possibility—albeit faint—of judicial review of decisions to remove a person from South Africa, that is to say of applying to the High Court for a judge to consider whether the decision was taken in accordance with the correct procedures under the relevant legislation and in accordance with the constitution.[497]

---

[493]Section 52(1). A recent case extends the applicability of the procedure for written representations to the Ministers (section 52(1)) beyond detention cases deriving from sections 9 or 10 to detention cases deriving from the provisions of section 7 where persons could be declared prohibited persons but are not and are nonetheless detained. The case might be interpreted to extend the applicability procedure to removals although it did not do so on its facts. See *Eddie Johnson v Minister of Home Affairs and Another*, Case No. 15630/1995 (CPD) (August 14, 1996) (Chetty, J.).

[494]Communication from A. Liebenberg, Home Affairs, to Jonathan Klaaren, January 26, 1997.

[495] Communication from H. Meyer, Home Affairs, to Jonathan Klaaren, January 16, 1997.

[496]Communication from H. Meyer, Home Affairs, to Jonathan Klaaren, January 16, 1997.

[497]Until the amendments brought into effect on July 1, 1996, the ACA contained a clause that purported to oust any court from inquiring into the validity of a detention conducted under the act. Indeed, this ouster clause covered all immigration matters, not just detentions. However, this provision has now been removed. (Section 55 of the Aliens

In one instance where a deportee had not been informed of his right to request ministerial review of his position the individual concerned applied to the High Court for judicial review and the court used the non-compliance as part of its reasoning that the person concerned was not a "prohibited person" in terms of the Act.[498] However, the case was only heard after the presumed migrant had been in detention for over a year, an unusually long time to wait for removal, especially since procedures have been significantly speeded up in recent years. In practice, judicial review of a declaration that a person is a prohibited person (or of a decision to remove him or her, however made, since, as mentioned above, such declarations seem not to occur in practice) is unlikely to be widely available given the rapid timing of most removals and the financial circumstances of most persons subject to removal.

Detention under the ACA, like any other detention, has since the introduction of a bill of rights in 1994 also been subject to constitutional review by the High Court.[499] As detainees, both migrants and citizens detained under the ACA are protected by section 25(1) of the interim Constitution and by section 35 of the 1996 Constitution. Constitutionally guaranteed conditions of detention include the right to consult with a legal practitioner, to be detained under conditions consonant with human dignity and to visit with family members. It is not yet clear whether the provisions of the present section 55 of the ACA, providing for automatic review of detention by a judge after thirty days, will satisfy the constitutional requirements for judicial consideration of any detention. Some lawyers working with

---

Control Act 96 of 1991, which provided: "(1) Subject to the provisions of subsection (2), no court of law shall have any jurisdiction to review, quash, reverse, interdict or otherwise interfere with any act, order, or warrant of the Minister, an immigration officer or master of a ship performed or issued under this Act and which relates to the restriction or detention, or the removal from the Republic, of a person who is being dealt with as a prohibited person. (2) If any person is detained under the provisions of this Act elsewhere than on a ship, that detention shall not be for a longer period than is under the circumstances reasonable and necessary.")

[498]*Eddie Johnson v Minister of Home Affairs and Another*, Case No. 15630/1995 (CPD) (August 14, 1996) (Chetty, J.). The Court also noted that the immigration officer had not declared Johnson a prohibited person as he was required to do by section 9(1) of the Act.

[499]One lower court has held that detention under the Aliens Control Act is an administrative or executive act or conduct granting the Supreme Court jurisdiction over its constitutionality. See *Eddie Johnson v Minister of Home Affairs and Another*, Case No. 15630/1995, (August 14, 1996), (Chetty, J.) (CPD).

immigration matters argue that a reasonable initial period of detention should be fourteen days rather than thirty days.[500]

The ACA contains no explicit power for a magistrate to grant bail, such as exists in the case of individuals charged with a criminal offence other than an immigration offence (who, under the Criminal Procedure Act must be brought before a court within forty-eight hours of their arrest) and as a consequence the magistrates' courts do not understand themselves to have jurisdiction to order the release of a person detained in terms of the Aliens Control Act. In practice, there is no systematic after-hours bail procedure with respect to detention under immigration legislation.[501] On a practical level, attorneys find that "the only way to release people so detained is to arrange an interview with immigration officials from the Dept. of Home Affairs."[502] Often station commanders of police stations do not have access to Home Affairs computers to verify the identification of a detained person; nor do they have the discretion to release such a person.[503] Some police officers do not accept that migrants can get bail under any circumstances.[504]

In addition, the interaction of immigration legislation with the ordinary South African criminal justice system creates delays within the system. Migrants charged with crimes not involving immigration may be detained by immigration officers under the Aliens Control Act as well as by the police in the exercise of their ordinary criminal jurisdiction. A person may thus have two detention orders; one by the police and another by Home Affairs. Therefore, once the police are satisfied and willing to let the person go they still have to wait to get permission from Home

---

[500]E-mail from Anton Katz to Jonathan Klaaren, July 15, 1996. In *Djama v Government of the Namibia and Others*, 1993 (1) SA 387 (NmHC), a detention over approximately two weeks was stated to be unreasonably long in the circumstances of that case.

[501]E-mail from Steve Tuson to Jonathan Klaaren, July 15, 1996; E-mail from Steve Tuson, July 19, 1996. There is such a system available in Johannesburg and elsewhere for after-hours bail in respect of persons criminally charged.

[502]E-mail from Steve Tuson to Jonathan Klaaren, July 19, 1996.

[503]Ibid.

[504]Interchange with Enquiries Officer, Hillbrow Police Station, November 30, 1996: "Illegals don't get bail. They are not South African."

Affairs.[505] In these circumstances, many magistrates are unwilling to grant bail in terms of the Criminal Procedure Act knowing that the person will remain in detention due to immigration status.

Even after the introduction of the amendments to the ACA providing for a maximum period of detention without judicial review of the detention, magistrates have read the new section 55(5) in a manner that effectively continues to oust their authority to review a detention. For instance, in Durban, a magistrate refused to grant bail to a person detained as a prohibited person under the amended Aliens Control Act, claiming that since Home Affairs had used the forms under the old version of the ACA, the ouster clause preventing the courts from inquiring into the validity of decisions made under the ACA (since repealed) was still binding upon the magistrates' courts.[506]

The Asylum Determination Process[507]

Processing of Asylum Applications

Although South Africa has since 1993 recognized the right to apply for asylum, is a party to the U.N. and OAU refugee conventions, and has in fact implemented a procedure for the recognition of refugee status, there is currently no legislation expressly regulating the asylum process. Instead, asylum-seekers are given temporary permits to remain under section 41 of the Aliens Control Act, while recognized refugees are exempted from the requirement to have a temporary or permanent residence permit, under section 28 of the Act.

The procedure for consideration of asylum applications is set out in internal documents of the Department of Home Affairs which have no statutory basis and, as a consequence, cannot be challenged in court or used as a basis for a court application. These procedures were largely developed following agreements concluded among South Africa, UNHCR and Mozambique in order to deal with the status of the estimated 350,000 Mozambicans who fled to South Africa during the course of the civil war in Mozambique.

---

[505]E-mail communication from Anton Katz, July 15, 1996.

[506]Telephone interview with S. Lockhart, August 23, 1996.

[507]This section of the report is based on the work of the Refugee Rights Project of Lawyers for Human Rights (LHR).

Application

According to the Department of Home Affairs' internal regulations, persons seeking refugee status must apply to the Department of Home Affairs as soon as they enter the country, or as soon as possible thereafter. The applicant is referred to the office of a Regional Subcommittee for Refugee Affairs where there are officials that have been trained by the Department and UNHCR to process applications for asylum. Persons are given a date for an appointment for a first interview with a standard form confirming this arrangement. No permits are granted at this stage (which means that an applicant is unable to work and may be vulnerable to arrest and detention by police who are unwilling to accept the standard form as sufficient documentation to indicate authorization to stay in the country) and the waiting period for an interview may be up to several months. According to Mr. Claude Schravesande, then-Director of Refugee Affairs,

> Where a person is in detention in terms of an offence under the Act and this person subsequently applies for asylum, he or she will continue to be detained while their application is being considered. People are detained on an ad-hoc basis, and there is no specific facility for this purpose. If one has applied for the purpose of delaying deportation, then they will not be released unless the applicant would take unreasonably long to process. In all other circumstances, one will be released.[508]

First Interview

At the first interview, the interviewer (nearly always an immigration officer from the Department of Home Affairs) completes what is called an "Eligibility Determination Form," in which the applicant is required to respond to a series of questions relevant to his or her application for asylum.[509] The department employs a limited number of persons from amongst asylum applicants or classified refugees to assist with interpretation during these interviews, though the applicant is

---

[508]Claude Schravesande, "Government Policies and Procedures," at *Asylum and Naturalisation: Policies and Practices*, Refugee Rights Consortium Workshop, November 14, 1996.

[509]While the procedure was still new, interviewers had very little understanding of what was expected of them in completing this form. Though matters appear to have somewhat improved, NGOs have expressed several outstanding concerns, particularly regarding the lack of capacity to handle the increasing number of applications, and whether immigration officers are adequately trained to do this sort of work.

generally requested to provide his or her own interpreter and a supporting statement in his or her own language. Following the interview, the applicant is provided with a temporary residence permit under section 41 of the ACA, usually for a period of three months, and has the right to work while the permit is valid.[510] The department renews this permit while the application is being processed.

Processing of Applications

Following the first interview,[511] applications are prepared by case workers at the regional offices in Cape Town, Durban, Johannesburg, and Pretoria. Decisions are split into two groups. Applications from certain countries (presently the Democratic Republic of Congo, Somalia, Burundi and Angola) are considered by the Department of Home Affairs' Regional Subcommittees. Decisions on the applications from all other countries are the responsibility of the Standing Committee, based in Pretoria and presently chaired by one of the Deputy Directors-General of the Department of Home Affairs.

The Standing Committee or Subcommittee ("Committees") decide whether the applicant fulfills the definition of a refugee contained in the 1951 U.N. Convention and 1969 OAU Convention. In addition to the Eligibility Determination Form and the applicant's statement obtained at the first interview, departmental officials rely on the UNHCR's Centre for Documentation and Research, in particular the computer database on country information, as well as the reports of international human rights organizations, the Africa Institute in Pretoria, the International Organization for Migration and on information supplied to them by South African embassies and consulates.[512] Under the Basic Agreement between UNHCR and the South African government, UNHCR is permitted to monitor the activities of the Standing Committee and Regional Subcommittees, though in practice it appears

---

[510]In practice, it is very difficult for asylum applicants to find work, given the uncertainty of their status and the short period of the temporary permits granted. Some applicants (commonly, those whose applications were eventually declared "manifestly unfounded") have received permits of only one month duration.

[511]The Department occasionally calls back an applicant for a further interview in order to clarify or confirm certain statements.

[512] As discussed in this report, officials within the Department have expressed their frustration with the difficulty in obtaining up-to-date information from the Department of Foreign Affairs on country situations, which may take up to several months.

that this rarely happens.[513] UNHCR is also consulted when the Department deems this necessary.[514]

The Standing Committee or its Subcommittees only occasionally re-interview the applicant if they wish to obtain further information or confirm specific statements made at the first interview, or in light of other information received by the Department of Home Affairs. The interviewer's "credibility statement" (part of the Eligibility Determination Form) is also taken into account, but no independent assessment of credibility is made. The committee thus depends largely on the views and diligence of the low-level immigration officials who conducted the initial interview, and give the asylum applicant no opportunity to make his or her case in person to the people actually deciding the application. After determining whether the applicant is a refugee, the department then decides whether it will grant the applicant asylum. For this the department considers those countries the applicant passed through en route to South Africa and whether (or if not for what reason) any of those countries could have provided protection.

Decisions

Officials of the Standing Committee or Regional Subcommittees make a decision whether or not to grant asylum. If the application is successful, then the department notifies the applicant and grants that person and, on request by the successful applicant, his or her family refugee status in South Africa. The applicant is granted a further section 41 permit for a period (usually six months) after which the applicant's status may be re-evaluated by the Standing Committee, though repeated renewals are usually automatic.[515] Applications can take up to two years to process.

---

[513]This is, in the view of staff at the UNHCR Regional Office in Pretoria, largely due to the office being seriously understaffed and underresourced.

[514] It is still not clear precisely under what circumstances the Department consults the UNHCR, other than in cases where the UNHCR is considered to be "better positioned" (see Gauteng Forum meeting, ante) to confirm specific statements made by the applicant.

[515]Apart from the situation of Mozambicans, whose repatriation back to Mozambique (after the government considered the situation in that country to be stable) was the subject of a tripartite agreement between the UNHCR and the governments of South Africa and Mozambique, it does not appear that the status of many refugees has been the subject of review on the basis of changed circumstances in the home country.

"Refugee Generating Countries"

Decisions on applications from certain countries are said by officials of the Department of Home Affairs to be virtually automatic. Provided applicants are able to show they are from what is referred to by the Department of Home Affairs as a "refugee generating country," their applications can be processed very quickly. The quicker procedure is apparently on the basis that, once it is established that an applicant from a country which is considered to fulfil the criteria set out in the extended definition of a refugee under the 1969 OAU Convention (including the existence of "events seriously disturbing public order in either part or the whole of [the] country"), he or she need not show individual persecution but only that he or she indeed comes from that country.

Those countries considered to be "refugee generating" by the Department of Home Affairs include Somalia and until fairly recently[516] Angola. It is not clear, despite various exchanges with officials of the Department of Home Affairs, what procedure is used to determine whether a country will be treated as "refugee generating." It is also not clear exactly what effect coming from a refugee generating country has on an individual's application, except that the chances of the application being successful are greatly increased. On the other hand, our interviews suggest that applications from certain countries, such as Tanzania, Mozambique, and most recently Angola, are automatically rejected without an individual determination being made.

"Manifestly Unfounded" Applications

If one of the department's assistant refugee officers is of the opinion that an application is *"not at all related to the refugee criteria"* or is deemed to be an *"abuse of process,"* [517] then the officer will make a recommendation that the application be declared manifestly unfounded. This recommendation is reviewed by a Deputy Director of Refugee Affairs and, should he or she support this

---

[516] Angola is no longer seen as a refugee generating country by the responsible officials in the Department of Home Affairs, and it appears that Angolans are now rejected as a matter of course.

[517] It is not clear at what point in the application process an application will be found to be manifestly unfounded, nor of what criteria are used to make this decision. Mr. Schravesande, then-Director of Refugee Affairs at the Department of Home Affairs has mentioned as examples cases of persons who are accused of ordinary criminal offences and are not deemed to be suffering from persecution. Schravesande, "Government Policies and Procedures."

determination, the applicant will be informed that he or she has been refused asylum and must leave the country. A recent consent judgment has required the Department of Home Affairs to furnish all rejected asylum applicants, included those rejected as manifestly unfounded, with reasons for their rejection.[518]

Appeal

Under the terms of this consent judgment, the Department of Home Affairs now provides reasons for all rejected asylum applicants, including those determined to be "manifestly unfounded."[519] However, according to Home Affairs officials, "manifestly unfounded" rejections are not entitled to an appeal, as the "manifestly unfounded" procedure is aimed at screening out those who should not be in the asylum seeking process.[520] The Appeals Board consists of a single retired advocate in Pretoria, Advocate Leach employed by the Department of Home Affairs, whose decisions are treated as final and binding. Out of a total of 519 appeals made so far to the Appeals Board, only two decisions were reversed on appeal.[521]

Representation

The applicant is permitted to be represented throughout the proceedings, though during the first and subsequent interviews the representative must remain silent and not intervene.[522] However, it is extremely rare that asylum-seekers are represented, given their lack of means and the NGO community's lack of capacity. A small number of rejected applications have been taken up by NGOs before the courts. Legal aid under South Africa's system for civil and criminal cases is not available for persons applying for asylum.

---

[518]Human Rights Watch interview with William Kerfoot, attorney, Legal Resources Centre, Cape Town, December 11, 1997.

[519]Marion Edmunds, "Refugees Score in Fight for Asylum," *Mail & Guardian*, December 13 to 19, 1997, p. 13.

[520]Claude Schravesande, "Government Policies and Procedures."

[521]Department of Home Affairs, "Appeal Application—Refugee Status (Adv. Leach)," fax to Human Rights Watch dated January 27, 1998.

[522]Ibid.

Rejected Applicants

Asylum-seekers whose applications are rejected are given what Home Affairs officials and asylum-seekers refer to as a "must leave" document with thirty days in which to leave South Africa. If the applicant does not leave or appeal (if it is still possible to do so) within the time period, he or she may be arrested if found and is often put into detention. Once funds are made available by the Department of Home Affairs for the repatriation, the rejected applicant is deported, although he or she is permitted to leave earlier using his or her own independent means. Those persons whose applications for asylum are rejected are subject to deportation as "prohibited persons" if they do not leave within the required period of notification (usually thirty days).[523]

These persons who are arrested and detained either before they applied for asylum or who failed to leave the country in time following a rejected application are deported to their countries of nationality. If a person does not have travel documents, then the department seeks to obtain such documents from the relevant embassy, identifying such persons as "illegal immigrants."[524] If the embassy requires the physical presence of the individual, then he or she is taken to the embassy and travel documents are eventually issued.[525] The individual is then returned to his or her country of origin once funds are made available by the Department of Home Affairs and are detained until then.[526]

------

[523]Section 43 ACA.

[524]Certain embassies, including the Democratic Republic of Congo, have started requesting a fee for the provision of travel documents.

[525]According to interviews with immigration officers and rejected asylum-seekers by Human Rights Watch at Pretoria Prison in October 1996, persons waiting to be deported have complained that the embassies are made aware that they have applied for political asylum in South Africa and as a result they fear for their lives. It is unclear whether this is a result of the applicant's admission or an immigration officer's careless statement. The Department of Home Affairs claims that its officers are under instruction not to disclose the fact that a person has applied for asylum.

[526]According to interviews with asylum-seekers held in detention at Kameelsdrift Police Station outside Pretoria in August 1996, there was one particularly worrying instance where the Department sought to deport a group of persons to Zaire without travel documents. These persons were taken to the airport with no warning in the very early hours of the morning and then kept in the back of a police vehicle for three hours in cramped conditions until it was obvious that the pilot of the aircraft would not allow those persons

ORGANIZATION OF AFRICAN UNITY CONVENTION
GOVERNING THE SPECIFIC ASPECTS OF REFUGEE PROBLEMS IN
AFRICA

Convention Governing the Specific Aspects of Refugee Problems in Africa, 1001 U.N.T.S. 45, entered into force June 20, 1974.

PREAMBLE

We, the Heads of State and Government assembled in the city of Addis Ababa, from 6-10 September 1969,

1. Noting with concern the constantly increasing numbers of refugees in Africa and desirous of finding ways and means of alleviating their misery and suffering as well as providing them with a better life and future,

2. Recognizing the need for and essentially humanitarian approach towards solving the problems of refugees,

3. Aware, however, that refugee problems are a source of friction among many Member States, and desirous of eliminating the source of such discord,

4. Anxious to make a distinction between a refugee who seeks a peaceful and normal life and a person fleeing his country for the sole purpose of fomenting subversion from outside,

5. Determined that the activities of such subversive elements should be discouraged, in accordance with the Declaration on the Problem of Subversion and Resolution on the Problem of Refugees adopted at Accra in 1965,

6. Bearing in mind that the Charter of the United Nations and the Universal Declaration of Human Rights have affirmed the principle that human beings shall enjoy fundamental rights and freedoms without discrimination,

7. Recalling Resolution 2312 (XXII) of 14 December 1967 of the United Nations General Assembly, relating to the Declaration on Territorial Asylum,

---

to board without travel documents. They were then taken back into custody.

8. Convinced that all the problems of our continent must be solved in the spirit of the Charter of the Organization of African Unity and in the African context,

9. Recognizing that the United Nations Convention of 28 July 1951, as modified by the Protocol of 31 January 1967, constitutes the basic and universal instrument relating to the status of refugees and reflects the deep concern of States for refugees and their desire to establish common standards for their treatment,

10. Recalling Resolutions 26 and 104 of the OAU Assemblies of Heads of State and Government, calling upon Member States of the Organization who had not already done so to accede to the United Nations Convention of 1951 and to the Protocol of 1967 relating to the Status of Refugees, and meanwhile to apply their provisions to refugees in Africa,

11. Convinced that the efficiency of the measures recommended by the present Convention to solve the problem of refugees in Africa necessitates close and continuous collaboration between the Organization of African Unity and the Office of the United Nations High Commissioner for Refugees,

Have agreed as follows:

Article 1 Definition of the term "Refugee"

1. For the purposes of this Convention, the term "refugee" shall mean every person who, owing to well-founded fear of being persecuted for reasons of race, religion, nationality, membership of a particular social group or political opinion, is outside the country of his nationality and is unable or, owing to such fear, is unwilling to avail himself of the protection of that country, or who, not having a nationality and being outside the country of his former habitual residence as a result of such events is unable or, owing to such fear, is unwilling to return to it.

2. The term "refugee" shall also apply to every person who, owing to external aggression, occupation, foreign domination or events seriously disturbing public order in either part or the whole of his country of origin or nationality, is compelled to leave his place of habitual residence in order to seek refuge in another place outside his country of origin or nationality.

3. In the case of a person who has several nationalities, the term "a country of which he is a national" shall mean each of the countries of which he is a national, and a person shall not be deemed to be lacking the protection of the country of which he is a national if, without any valid reason based on well-founded fear, he has not availed himself of the protection of one of the countries of which he is a national.

4. This Convention shall cease to apply to any refugee if: (a) he has voluntarily re-availed himself of the protection of the country of his nationality, or, (b) having lost his nationality, he has voluntarily reacquired it, or, (c) he has acquired a new nationality, and enjoys the protection of the country of his new nationality, or, (d) he has voluntarily re-established himself in the country which he left or outside which he remained owing to fear of persecution, or, (e) he can no longer, because the circumstances in connection with which he was recognized as a refugee have ceased to exist, continue to refuse to avail himself of the protection of the country of his nationality, or, (f) he has committed a serious non-political crime outside his country of refuge after his admission to that country as a refugee, or, (g) he has seriously infringed the purposes and objectives of this Convention.

5. The provisions of this Convention shall not apply to any person with respect to whom the country of asylum has serious reasons for considering that: (a) he has committed a crime against peace, a war crime, or a crime against humanity, as defined in the international instruments drawn up to make provision in respect of such crimes; (b) he committed a serious non-political crime outside the country of refuge prior to his admission to that country as a refugee; (c) he has been guilty of acts contrary to the purposes and principles of the Organization of African Unity; (d) he has been guilty of acts contrary to the purposes and principles of the United Nations.

6. For the purposes of this Convention, the Contracting State of Asylum shall determine whether an applicant is a refugee.

Article 2 Asylum

1. Member States of the OAU shall use their best endeavours consistent with their respective legislations to receive refugees and to secure the settlement of those refugees who, for well-founded reasons, are unable or unwilling to return to their country of origin or nationality.

2. The grant of asylum to refugees is a peaceful and humanitarian act and shall not be regarded as an unfriendly act by any Member State.

3. No person shall be subjected by a Member State to measures such as rejection at the frontier, return or expulsion, which would compel him to return to or remain in a territory where his life, physical integrity or liberty would be threatened for the reasons set out in Article I, paragraphs 1 and 2.

4. Where a Member State finds difficulty in continuing to grant asylum to refugees, such Member State may appeal directly to other Member States and through the OAU, and such other Member States shall in the spirit of African solidarity and international co-operation take appropriate measures to lighten the burden of the Member State granting asylum.

5. Where a refugee has not received the right to reside in any country of asylum, he may be granted temporary residence in any country of asylum in which he first presented himself as a refugee pending arrangement for his resettlement in accordance with the preceding paragraph.

6. For reasons of security, countries of asylum shall, as far as possible, settle refugees at a reasonable distance from the frontier of their country of origin.

Article 3 Prohibition of Subversive Activities

1. Every refugee has duties to the country in which he finds himself, which require in particular that he conforms with its laws and regulations as well as with measures taken for the maintenance of public order. He shall also abstain from any subversive activities against any Member State of the OAU.

2. Signatory States undertake to prohibit refugees residing in their respective territories from attacking any State Member of the OAU, by any activity likely to cause tension between Member States, and in particular by use of arms, through the press, or by radio.

Article 4 Non-Discrimination

Member States undertake to apply the provisions of this Convention to all refugees without discrimination as to race, religion, nationality, membership of a particular social group or political opinions.

Article 5 Voluntary Repatriation

1. The essentially voluntary character of repatriation shall be respected in all cases and no refugee shall be repatriated against his will.

2. The country of asylum, in collaboration with the country of origin, shall make adequate arrangements for the safe return of refugees who request repatriation.

3. The country of origin, on receiving back refugees, shall facilitate their resettlement and grant them the full rights and privileges of nationals of the country, and subject them to the same obligations.

4. Refugees who voluntarily return to their country shall in no way be penalized for having left it for any of the reasons giving rise to refugee situations. Whenever necessary, an appeal shall be made through national information media and through the Administrative Secretary-General of the OAU, inviting refugees to return home and giving assurance that the new circumstances prevailing in their country of origin will enable them to return without risk and to take up a normal and peaceful life without fear of being disturbed or punished, and that the text of such appeal should be given to refugees and clearly explained to them by their country of asylum.

5. Refugees who freely decide to return to their homeland, as a result of such assurances or on their own initiative, shall be given every possible assistance by the country of asylum, the country of origin, voluntary agencies and international and intergovernmental organizations, to facilitate their return.

Article 6 Travel Documents

1. Subject to Article III, Member States shall issue to refugees lawfully staying in their territories travel documents in accordance with the United Nations Convention relating to the Status of Refugees and the Schedule and Annex thereto, for the purpose of travel outside their territory, unless compelling reasons of national security or public order otherwise require. Member States may issue such a travel document to any other refugee in their territory.

2. Where an African country of second asylum accepts a refugee from a country of first asylum, the country of first asylum may be dispensed from issuing a document with a return clause.

3. Travel documents issued to refugees under previous international agreements by States Parties thereto shall be recognized and treated by Member States in the same way as if they had been issued to refugees pursuant to this Article.

Article 7 Co-operation of the National Authorities with the Organization of African Unity

In order to enable the Administrative Secretary-General of the Organization of African Unity to make reports to the competent organs of the Organization of African Unity, Member States undertake to provide the Secretariat in the appropriate form with information and statistical data requested concerning: (a) the condition of refugees; (b) the implementation of this Convention, and (c) laws, regulations and decrees which are, or may hereafter be, in force relating to refugees.

Article 8 Cooperation with the Office of the United Nations High Commissioner for Refugees

1. Member States shall co-operate with the Office of the United Nations High Commissioner for Refugees.

2. The present Convention shall be the effective regional complement in Africa of the 1951 United Nations Convention on the Status of Refugees.

Article 9 Settlement of Disputes

Any dispute between States signatories to this Convention relating to its interpretation or application, which cannot be settled by other means, shall be referred to the Commission for Mediation, Conciliation and Arbitration of the Organization of African Unity, at the request of any one of the Parties to the dispute.

Article 10 Signature and Ratification

1. This Convention is open for signature and accession by all Member States of the Organization of African Unity and shall be ratified by signatory States in accordance with their respective constitutional processes. The instruments of ratification shall be deposited with the Administrative Secretary-General of the Organization of African Unity.

2. The original instrument, done if possible in African languages, and in English and French, all texts being equally authentic, shall be deposited with the Administrative Secretary-General of the Organization of African Unity.

3. Any independent African State, Member of the Organization of African Unity, may at any time notify the Administrative Secretary-General of the Organization of African Unity of its accession to this Convention.

Article 11 Entry into force

This Convention shall come into force upon deposit of instruments of ratification by one-third of the Member States of the Organization of African Unity.

Article 12 Amendment

This Convention may be amended or revised if any member State makes a written request to the Administrative Secretary-General to that effect, provided however that the proposed amendment shall not be submitted to the Assembly of Heads of State and Government for consideration until all Member States have been duly notified of it and a period of one year has elapsed. Such an amendment shall not be effective unless approved by at least two-thirds of the Member States Parties to the present Convention.

Article 13 Denunciation

1. Any Member State Party to this Convention may denounce its provisions by a written notification to the Administrative Secretary-General.

2. At the end of one year from the date of such notification, if not withdrawn, the Convention shall cease to apply with respect to the denouncing State.

Article 14

Upon entry into force of this Convention, the Administrative Secretary-General of the OAU shall register it with the Secretary-General of the United Nations, in accordance with Article 102 of the Charter of the United Nations.

Article 15 Notifications by the Administrative Secretary-General of the Organization of African Unity

The Administrative Secretary-General of the Organization of African Unity shall inform all Members of the Organization: (a) of signatures, ratifications and accessions in accordance with Article X; (b) of entry into force, in accordance with Article XI; (c) of requests for amendments submitted under the terms of Article XII; (d) of denunciations, in accordance with Article XIII.

IN WITNESS WHEREOF WE, the Heads of African State and Government, have signed this Convention.

DONE in the City of Addis Ababa this 10th day of September 1969.

APPENDIX C:
DECLARATION ON THE HUMAN RIGHTS OF INDIVIDUALS
WHO ARE NOT NATIONALS OF THE COUNTRY
IN WHICH THEY LIVE

Declaration on the Human Rights of Individuals Who are not Nationals of the Country in which They Live, G.A. res. 40/144, annex, 40 U.N. GAOR Supp. (No. 53) at 252, U.N. Doc. A/40/53 (1985).

The General Assembly,

Considering that the Charter of the United Nations encourages universal respect for and observance of the human rights and fundamental freedoms of all human beings, without distinction as to race, sex, language or religion,

Considering that the Universal Declaration of Human Rights proclaims that all human beings are born free and equal in dignity and rights and that everyone is entitled to all the rights and freedoms set forth in that Declaration, without distinction of any kind, such as race, colour, sex, language, religion, political or other opinion, national or social origin, property, birth or other status,

Considering that the Universal Declaration of Human Rights proclaims further that everyone has the right to recognition everywhere as a person before the law, that all are equal before the law and entitled without any discrimination to equal protection of the law, and that all are entitled to equal protection against any discrimination in violation of that Declaration and against any incitement to such discrimination,

Being aware that the States Parties to the International Covenants on Human Rights undertake to guarantee that the rights enunciated in these Covenants will be exercised without discrimination of any kind as to race, colour, sex, language, religion, political or other opinion, national or social origin, property, birth or other status,

Conscious that, with improving communications and the development of peaceful and friendly relations among countries, individuals increasingly live in countries of which they are not nationals,

Reaffirming the purposes and principles of the Charter of the United Nations,

Recognizing that the protection of human rights and fundamental freedoms provided for in international instruments should also be ensured for individuals who are not nationals of the country in which they live,

Proclaims this Declaration:

Article 1

For the purposes of this Declaration, the term "alien" shall apply, with due regard to qualifications made in subsequent articles, to any individual who is not a national of the State in which he or she is present.

Article 2

1. Nothing in this Declaration shall be interpreted as legitimizing the illegal entry into and presence in a State of any alien, nor shall any provision be interpreted as restricting the right of any State to promulgate laws and regulations concerning the entry of aliens and the terms and conditions of their stay or to establish differences between nationals and aliens. However, such laws and regulations shall not be incompatible with the international legal obligations of that State, including those in the field of human rights.

2. This Declaration shall not prejudice the enjoyment of the rights accorded by domestic law and of the rights which under international law a State is obliged to accord to aliens, even where this Declaration does not recognize such rights or recognizes them to a lesser extent.

Article 3

Every State shall make public its national legislation or regulations affecting aliens.

Article 4

Aliens shall observe the laws of the State in which they reside or are present and regard with respect the customs and traditions of the people of that State.

Article 5

1. Aliens shall enjoy, in accordance with domestic law and subject to the relevant international obligation of the State in which they are present, in particular the following rights:

   (a) The right to life and security of person; no alien shall be subjected to arbitrary arrest or detention; no alien shall be deprived of his or her liberty except on such grounds and in accordance with such procedures as are established by law;

   (b) The right to protection against arbitrary or unlawful interference with privacy, family, home or correspondence;

   (c) The right to be equal before the courts, tribunals and all other organs and authorities administering justice and, when necessary, to free assistance of an interpreter in criminal proceedings and , when prescribed by law, other proceedings;

   (d) The right to choose a spouse, to marry, to found a family;

   (e) The right to freedom of thought, opinion, conscience and religion; the right to manifest their religion or beliefs, subject only to such limitations as are prescribed by law and are necessary to protect public safety, order, health or morals or the fundamental rights and freedoms of others;

   (f) The right to retain their own language, culture and tradition;

   (g) The right to transfer abroad earnings, savings or other personal monetary assets, subject to domestic currency regulations.

2. Subject to such restrictions as are prescribed by law and which are necessary in a democratic society to protect national security, public safety, public order, public health or morals or the rights and freedoms of others, and which are consistent with

the other rights recognized in the relevant international instruments and those set forth in this Declaration, aliens shall enjoy the following rights:

(a) The right to leave the country;

(b) The right to freedom of expression;

(c) The right to peaceful assembly;

(d) The right to own property alone as well as in association with others, subject to domestic law.

3. Subject to the provisions referred to in paragraph 2, aliens lawfully in the territory of a State shall enjoy the right to liberty of movement and freedom to choose their residence within the borders of the State.

4. Subject to national legislation and due authorization, the spouse and minor or dependent children of an alien lawfully residing in the territory of a State shall be admitted to accompany, join and stay with the alien.

Article 6

No alien shall be subjected to torture or to cruel, inhuman or degrading treatment or punishment and, in particular, no alien shall be subjected without his or her free consent to medical or scientific experimentation.

Article 7

An alien lawfully in the territory of a State may be expelled therefrom only in pursuance of a decision reached in accordance with law and shall, except where compelling reasons of national security otherwise require, be allowed to submit the reasons why he or she should not be expelled and to have the case reviewed by, and be represented for the purpose before, the competent authority or a person or persons specially designated by the competent authority. Individual or collective expulsion of such aliens on grounds of race, colour, religion, culture, descent or national or ethnic origin is prohibited.

Article 8

1 . Aliens lawfully residing in the territory of a State shall also enjoy, in accordance with the national laws, the following rights, subject to their obligations under article 4:

(a) The right to safe and healthy working conditions, to fair wages and equal remuneration for work of equal value without distinction of any kind, in particular, women being guaranteed conditions of work not inferior to those enjoyed by men, with equal pay for equal work;

(b) The right to join trade unions and other organizations or associations of their choice and to participate in their activities. No restrictions may be placed on the exercise of this right other than those prescribed by law and which are necessary, in a democratic society, in the interests of national security or public order or for the protection of the rights and freedoms of others;

(c) The right to health protection, medical care, social security, social services, education, rest and leisure, provided that they fulfil the requirements under the relevant regulations for participation and that undue strain is not placed on the resources of the State.

2. With a view to protecting the rights of aliens carrying on lawful paid activities in the country in which they are present, such rights may be specified by the Governments concerned in multilateral or bilateral conventions.

Article 9

No alien shall be arbitrarily deprived of his or her lawfully acquired assets.

Article 10

Any alien shall be free at any time to communicate with the consulate or diplomatic mission of the State of which he or she is a national or, in the absence thereof, with the consulate or diplomatic mission of any other State entrusted with the protection of the interests of the State of which he or she is a national in the State where he or she resides.

APPENDIX D:
INTERNATIONAL CONVENTION ON THE PROTECTION
OF THE RIGHTS OF ALL MIGRANT WORKERS
AND MEMBERS OF THEIR FAMILIES

International Convention on the Protection of the Rights of All Migrant Workers and Members of Their Families, G.A. res. 45/158, annex, 45 U.N. GAOR Supp. (No. 49A) at 262, U.N. Doc. A/45/49 (1990).

PREAMBLE

The States Parties to the present Convention,

Taking into account the principles embodied in the basic instruments of the United Nations concerning human rights, in particular the Universal Declaration of Human Rights, the International Covenant on Economic, Social and Cultural Rights, the International Covenant on Civil and Political Rights, the International Convention on the Elimination of All Forms of Racial Discrimination, the Convention on the Elimination of All Forms of Discrimination against Women and the Convention on the Rights of the Child,

Taking into account also the principles and standards set forth in the relevant instruments elaborated within the framework of the International Labour Organisation, especially the Convention concerning Migration for Employment (No. 97), the Convention concerning Migrations in Abusive Conditions and the Promotion of Equality of Opportunity and Treatment of Migrant Workers (No. 143), the Recommendation concerning Migration for Employment (No. 86), the Recommendation concerning Migrant Workers (No. 151), the Convention concerning Forced or Compulsory Labour (No. 29) and the Convention concerning Abolition of Forced Labour (No. 105),

Reaffirming the importance of the principles contained in the Convention against Discrimination in Education of the United Nations Educational, Scientific and Cultural Organization,

Recalling the Convention against Torture and Other Cruel, Inhuman or Degrading Treatment or Punishment, the Declaration of the Fourth United Nations Congress on the Prevention of Crime and the Treatment of Offenders, the Code of Conduct for Law Enforcement Officials, and the Slavery Conventions,

Recalling that one of the objectives of the International Labour Organisation, as stated in its Constitution, is the protection of the interests of workers when employed in countries other than their own, and bearing in mind the expertise and experience of that organization in matters related to migrant workers and members of their families,

Recognizing the importance of the work done in connection with migrant workers and members of their families in various organs of the United Nations, in particular in the Commission on Human Rights and the Commission for Social Development, and in the Food and Agriculture Organization of the United Nations, the United Nations Educational, Scientific and Cultural Organization and the World Health Organization, as well as in other international organizations,

Recognizing also the progress made by certain States on a regional or bilateral basis towards the protection of the rights of migrant workers and members of their families, as well as the importance and usefulness of bilateral and multilateral agreements in this field,

Realizing the importance and extent of the migration phenomenon, which involves millions of people and affects a large number of States in the international community,

Aware of the impact of the flows of migrant workers on States and people concerned, and desiring to establish norms which may contribute to the harmonization of the attitudes of States through the acceptance of basic principles concerning the treatment of migrant workers and members of their families,

Considering the situation of vulnerability in which migrant workers and members of their families frequently-find themselves owing, among other things, to their absence from their State of origin and to the difficulties they may encounter arising from their presence in the State of employment,

Convinced that the rights of migrant workers and members of their families have not been sufficiently recognized everywhere and therefore require appropriate international protection,

Taking into account the fact that migration is often the cause of serious problems for the members of the families of migrant workers as well as for the workers themselves, in particular because of the scattering of the family,

Bearing in mind that the human problems involved in migration are even more serious in the case of irregular migration and convinced therefore that appropriate action should be encouraged in order to prevent and eliminate clandestine movements and trafficking in migrant workers, while at the same time assuring the protection of their fundamental human rights,

Considering that workers who are non-documented or in an irregular situation are frequently employed under less favourable conditions of work than other workers and that certain employers find this an inducement to seek such labour in order to reap the benefits of unfair competition,

Considering also that recourse to the employment of migrant workers who are in an irregular situation will be discouraged if the fundamental human rights of all migrant workers are more widely recognized and, moreover, that granting certain additional rights to migrant workers and members of their families in a regular situation will encourage all migrants and employers to respect and comply with the laws and procedures established by the States concerned,

Convinced, therefore, of the need to bring about the international protection of the rights of all migrant workers and members of their families, reaffirming and establishing basic norms in a comprehensive convention which could be applied universally,

Have agreed as follows:

PART I SCOPE AND DEFINITIONS

Article 1

1. The present Convention is applicable, except as otherwise provided hereafter, to all migrant workers and members of their families without distinction of any kind such as sex, race, colour, language, religion or conviction, political or other opinion, national, ethnic or social origin, nationality, age, economic position, property, marital status, birth or other status.

2. The present Convention shall apply during the entire migration process of migrant workers and members of their families, which comprises preparation for migration, departure, transit and the entire period of stay and remunerated activity in the State of employment as well as return to the State of origin or the State of habitual residence.

Article 2

For the purposes of the present Convention:

1. The term "migrant worker" refers to a person who is to be engaged, is engaged or has been engaged in a remunerated activity in a State of which he or she is not a national.

2. (a) The term "frontier worker" refers to a migrant worker who retains his or her habitual residence in a neighbouring State to which he or she normally returns every day or at least once a week;

(b) The term "seasonal worker" refers to a migrant worker whose work by its character is dependent on seasonal conditions and is performed only during part of the year;

(c) The term "seafarer", which includes a fisherman, refers to a migrant worker employed on board a vessel registered in a State of which he or she is not a national;

(d) The term "worker on an offshore installation" refers to a migrant worker employed on an offshore installation that is under the jurisdiction of a State of which he or she is not a national;

(e) The term "itinerant worker" refers to a migrant worker who, having his or her habitual residence in one State, has to travel to another State or States for short periods, owing to the nature of his or her occupation;

(f) The term "project-tied worker" refers to a migrant worker admitted to a State of employment for a defined period to work solely on a specific project being carried out in that State by his or her employer;

(g) The term "specified-employment worker" refers to a migrant worker:

(I) Who has been sent by his or her employer for a restricted and defined period of time to a State of employment to undertake a specific assignment or duty; or

(ii) Who engages for a restricted and defined period of time in work that requires professional, commercial, technical or other highly specialized skill; or

(iii) Who, upon the request of his or her employer in the State of employment, engages for a restricted and defined period of time in work whose nature is transitory or brief; and who is required to depart from the State of employment either at the expiration of his or her authorized period of stay, or earlier if he or she no longer undertakes that specific assignment or duty or engages in that work;

(h) The term "self-employed worker" refers to a migrant worker who is engaged in a remunerated activity otherwise than under a contract of employment and who earns his or her living through this activity normally working alone or together with members of his or her family, and to any other migrant worker recognized as self-employed by applicable legislation of the State of employment or bilateral or multilateral agreements.

Article 3

The present Convention shall not apply to:

(a) Persons sent or employed by international organizations and agencies or persons sent or employed by a State outside its territory to perform official functions, whose admission and status are regulated by general international law or by specific international agreements or conventions;

(b) Persons sent or employed by a State or on its behalf outside its territory who participate in development programmes and other co-operation programmes, whose admission and status are regulated by agreement with the State of employment and who, in accordance with that agreement, are not considered migrant workers;

(c) Persons taking up residence in a State different from their State of origin as investors;

(d) Refugees and stateless persons, unless such application is provided for in the relevant national legislation of, or international instruments in force for, the State Party concerned;

(e) Students and trainees;

(f) Seafarers and workers on an offshore installation who have not been admitted to take up residence and engage in a remunerated activity in the State of employment.

Article 4

For the purposes of the present Convention the term "members of the family" refers to persons married to migrant workers or having with them a relationship that, according to applicable law, produces effects equivalent to marriage, as well as their dependent children and other dependent persons who are recognized as members of the family by applicable legislation or applicable bilateral or multilateral agreements between the States concerned.

Article 5

For the purposes of the present Convention, migrant workers and members of their families:

(a) Are considered as documented or in a regular situation if they are authorized to enter, to stay and to engage in a remunerated activity in the State of employment pursuant to the law of that State and to international agreements to which that State is a party;

(b) Are considered as non-documented or in an irregular situation if they do not comply with the conditions provided for in subparagraph (a) of the present article.

Article 6

For the purposes of the present Convention:

(a) The term "State of origin" means the State of which the person concerned is a national;

(b) The term "State of employment" means a State where the migrant worker is to be engaged, is engaged or has been engaged in a remunerated activity, as the case may be;

(c) The term "State of transit,' means any State through which the person concerned passes on any journey to the State of employment or from the State of employment to the State of origin or the State of habitual residence.

PART II NON-DISCRIMINATION WITH RESPECT TO RIGHTS

Article 7

States Parties undertake, in accordance with the international instruments concerning human rights, to respect and to ensure to all migrant workers and members of their families within their territory or subject to their jurisdiction the rights provided for in the present Convention without distinction of any kind such as to sex, race, colour, language, religion or conviction, political or other opinion, national, ethnic or social origin, nationality, age, economic position, property, marital status, birth or other status.

PART III HUMAN RIGHTS OF ALL MIGRANT WORKERS AND MEMBERS OF THEIR FAMILIES

Article 8

1. Migrant workers and members of their families shall be free to leave any State, including their State of origin. This right shall not be subject to any restrictions except those that are provided by law, are necessary to protect national security, public order (ordre public), public health or morals or the rights and freedoms of others and are consistent with the other rights recognized in the present part of the Convention.

2. Migrant workers and members of their families shall have the right at any time to enter and remain in their State of origin.

Article 9

The right to life of migrant workers and members of their families shall be protected by law.

Article 10

No migrant worker or member of his or her family shall be subjected to torture or to cruel, inhuman or degrading treatment or punishment.

Article 11

1. No migrant worker or member of his or her family shall be held in slavery or servitude.

2. No migrant worker or member of his or her family shall be required to perform forced or compulsory labour.

3. Paragraph 2 of the present article shall not be held to preclude, in States where imprisonment with hard labour may be imposed as a punishment for a crime, the performance of hard labour in pursuance of a sentence to such punishment by a competent court.

4. For the purpose of the present article the term "forced or compulsory labour" shall not include:

(a) Any work or service not referred to in paragraph 3 of the present article normally required of a person who is under detention in consequence of a lawful order of a court or of a person during conditional release from such detention;

(b) Any service exacted in cases of emergency or calamity threatening the life or well-being of the community;

(c) Any work or service that forms part of normal civil obligations so far as it is imposed also on citizens of the State concerned.

Article 12

1. Migrant workers and members of their families shall have the right to freedom of thought, conscience and religion. This right shall include freedom to have or to adopt a religion or belief of their choice and freedom either individually or in community with others and in public or private to manifest their religion or belief in worship, observance, practice and teaching.

2. Migrant workers and members of their families shall not be subject to coercion that would impair their freedom to have or to adopt a religion or belief of their choice.

3. Freedom to manifest one's religion or belief may be subject only to such limitations as are prescribed by law and are necessary to protect public safety, order, health or morals or the fundamental rights and freedoms of others.

4. States Parties to the present Convention undertake to have respect for the liberty of parents, at least one of whom is a migrant worker, and, when applicable, legal guardians to ensure the religious and moral education of their children in conformity with their own convictions.

Article 13

1. Migrant workers and members of their families shall have the right to hold opinions without interference.

2. Migrant workers and members of their families shall have the right to freedom of expression; this right shall include freedom to seek, receive and impart information and ideas of all kinds, regardless of frontiers, either orally, in writing or in print, in the form of art or through any other media of their choice.

3. The exercise of the right provided for in paragraph 2 of the present article carries with it special duties and responsibilities. It may therefore be subject to certain restrictions, but these shall only be such as are provided by law and are necessary:

(a) For respect of the rights or reputation of others;

(b) For the protection of the national security of the States concerned or of public order (ordre public) or of public health or morals;

(c) For the purpose of preventing any propaganda for war;

(d) For the purpose of preventing any advocacy of national, racial or religious hatred that constitutes incitement to discrimination, hostility or violence.

Article 14

No migrant worker or member of his or her family shall be subjected to arbitrary or unlawful interference with his or her privacy, family, home, correspondence or other communications, or to unlawful attacks on his or her honour and reputation. Each migrant worker and member of his or her family shall have the right to the protection of the law against such interference or attacks.

Article 15

No migrant worker or member of his or her family shall be arbitrarily deprived of property, whether owned individually or in association with others. Where, under the legislation in force in the State of employment, the assets of a migrant worker or a member of his or her family are expropriated in whole or in part, the person concerned shall have the right to fair and adequate compensation.

Article 16

1. Migrant workers and members of their families shall have the right to liberty and security of person.

2. Migrant workers and members of their families shall be entitled to effective protection by the State against violence, physical injury, threats and intimidation, whether by public officials or by private individuals, groups or institutions.

3. Any verification by law enforcement officials of the identity of migrant workers or members of their families shall be carried out in accordance with procedure established by law.

4. Migrant workers and members of their families shall not be subjected individually or collectively to arbitrary arrest or detention; they shall not be deprived o their liberty except on such grounds and in accordance with such procedures as are established by law.

5. Migrant workers and members of their families who are arrested shall be informed at the time of arrest as far as possible in a language they understand of the reasons for their arrest and they shall be promptly informed in a language they understand of any charges against them.

6. Migrant workers and members of their families who are arrested or detained on a criminal charge shall be brought promptly before a judge or other officer authorized by law to exercise judicial power and shall be entitled to trial within a reasonable time or to release. It shall not be the general rule that while awaiting trial they shall be detained in custody, but release may be subject to guarantees to appear for trial, at any other stage of the judicial proceedings and, should the occasion arise, for the execution of the judgement.

7. When a migrant worker or a member of his or her family is arrested or committed to prison or custody pending trial or is detained in any other manner:

(a) The consular or diplomatic authorities of his or her State of origin or of a State representing the interests of that State shall, if he or she so requests, be informed without delay of his or her arrest or detention and of the reasons therefor;

(b) The person concerned shall have the right to communicate with the said authorities. Any communication by the person concerned to the said authorities shall be forwarded without delay, and he or she shall also have the right to receive communications sent by the said authorities without delay;

(c) The person concerned shall be informed without delay of this right and of rights deriving from relevant treaties, if any, applicable between the States concerned, to correspond and to meet with representatives of the said authorities and to make arrangements with them for his or her legal representation.

8. Migrant workers and members of their families who are deprived of their liberty by arrest or detention shall be entitled to take proceedings before a court, in order that that court may decide without delay on the lawfulness of their detention and order their release if the detention is not lawful. When they attend such proceedings, they shall have the assistance, if necessary without cost to them, of an interpreter, if they cannot understand or speak the language used.

9. Migrant workers and members of their families who have been victims of unlawful arrest or detention shall have an enforceable right to compensation.

Article 17

1. Migrant workers and members of their families who are deprived of their liberty shall be treated with humanity and with respect for the inherent dignity of the human person and for their cultural identity.

2. Accused migrant workers and members of their families shall, save in exceptional circumstances, be separated from convicted persons and shall be subject to separate treatment appropriate to their status as unconvicted persons. Accused juvenile persons shall be separated from adults and brought as speedily as possible for adjudication.

3. Any migrant worker or member of his or her family who is detained in a State of transit or in a State of employment for violation of provisions relating to migration shall be held, in so far as practicable, separately from convicted persons or persons detained pending trial.

4. During any period of imprisonment in pursuance of a sentence imposed by a court of law, the essential aim of the treatment of a migrant worker or a member of his or her family shall be his or her reformation and social rehabilitation. Juvenile offenders shall be separated from adults and be accorded treatment appropriate to their age and legal status.

5. During detention or imprisonment, migrant workers and members of their families shall enjoy the same rights as nationals to visits by members of their families.

6. Whenever a migrant worker is deprived of his or her liberty, the competent authorities of the State concerned shall pay attention to the problems that may be posed for members of his or her family, in particular for spouses and minor children.

7. Migrant workers and members of their families who are subjected to any form of detention or imprisonment in accordance with the law in force in the State of employment or in the State of transit shall enjoy the same rights as nationals of those States who are in the same situation.

8. If a migrant worker or a member of his or her family is detained for the purpose of verifying any infraction of provisions related to migration, he or she shall not bear any costs arising therefrom.

Article 18

1. Migrant workers and members of their families shall have the right to equality with nationals of the State concerned before the courts and tribunals. In the determination of any criminal charge against them or of their rights and obligations in a suit of law, they shall be entitled to a fair and public hearing by a competent, independent and impartial tribunal established by law.

2. Migrant workers and members of their families who are charged with a criminal offence shall have the right to be presumed innocent until proven guilty according to law.

3. In the determination of any criminal charge against them, migrant workers and members of their families shall be entitled to the following minimum guarantees:

(a) To be informed promptly and in detail in a language they understand of the nature and cause of the charge against them;

(b) To have adequate time and facilities for the preparation of their defence and to communicate with counsel of their own choosing;

(c) To be tried without undue delay;

(d) To be tried in their presence and to defend themselves in person or through legal assistance of their own choosing; to be informed, if they do not have legal assistance, of this right; and to have legal assistance assigned to them, in any case where the interests of justice so require and without payment by them in any such case if they do not have sufficient means to pay;

(e) To examine or have examined the witnesses against them and to obtain the attendance and examination of witnesses on their behalf under the same conditions as witnesses against them;

(f) To have the free assistance of an interpreter if they cannot understand or speak the language used in court;

(g) Not to be compelled to testify against themselves or to confess guilt.

4. In the case of juvenile persons, the procedure shall be such as will take account of their age and the desirability of promoting their rehabilitation.

5. Migrant workers and members of their families convicted of a crime shall have the right to their conviction and sentence being reviewed by a higher tribunal according to law.

6. When a migrant worker or a member of his or her family has, by a final decision, been convicted of a criminal offence and when subsequently his or her conviction has been reversed or he or she has been pardoned on the ground that a new or newly discovered fact shows conclusively that there has been a miscarriage of justice, the person who has suffered punishment as a result of such conviction shall be compensated according to law, unless it is proved that the non-disclosure of the unknown
fact in time is wholly or partly attributable to that person.

7. No migrant worker or member of his or her family shall be liable to be tried or punished again for an offence for which he or she has already been finally convicted or acquitted in accordance with the law and penal procedure of the State concerned.

Article 19

1. No migrant worker or member of his or her family shall be held guilty of any criminal offence on account of any act or omission that did not constitute a criminal offence under national or international law at the time when the criminal offence was committed, nor shall a heavier penalty be imposed than the one that was applicable at the time when it was committed. If, subsequent to the commission of the offence, provision is made by law for the imposition of a lighter penalty, he or she shall benefit thereby.

2. Humanitarian considerations related to the status of a migrant worker, in particular with respect to his or her right of residence or work, should be taken into

account in imposing a sentence for a criminal offence committed by a migrant worker or a member of his or her family.

Article 20

1. No migrant worker or member of his or her family shall be imprisoned merely on the ground of failure to fulfil a contractual obligation.

2. No migrant worker or member of his or her family shall be deprived of his or her authorization of residence or work permit or expelled merely on the ground of failure to fulfil an obligation arising out of a work contract unless fulfilment of that obligation constitutes a condition for such authorization or permit.

Article 21

It shall be unlawful for anyone, other than a public official duly authorized by law, to confiscate, destroy or attempt to destroy identity documents, documents authorizing entry to or stay, residence or establishment in the national territory or work permits. No authorized confiscation of such documents shall take place without delivery of a detailed receipt. In no case shall it be permitted to destroy the passport or equivalent document of a migrant worker or a member of his or her family.

Article 22

1. Migrant workers and members of their families shall not be subject to measures of collective expulsion. Each case of expulsion shall be examined and decided individually.

2. Migrant workers and members of their families may be expelled from the territory of a State Party only in pursuance of a decision taken by the competent authority in accordance with law.

3. The decision shall be communicated to them in a language they understand. Upon their request where not otherwise mandatory, the decision shall be communicated to them in writing and, save in exceptional circumstances on account of national security, the reasons for the decision likewise stated. The persons concerned shall be informed of these rights before or at the latest at the time the decision is rendered.

4. Except where a final decision is pronounced by a judicial authority, the person concerned shall have the right to submit the reason he or she should not be expelled and to have his or her case reviewed by the competent authority, unless compelling reasons of national security require otherwise. Pending such review, the person concerned shall have the right to seek a stay of the decision of expulsion.

5. If a decision of expulsion that has already been executed is subsequently annulled, the person concerned shall have the right to seek compensation according to law and the earlier decision shall not be used to prevent him or her from re-entering the State concerned.

6. In case of expulsion, the person concerned shall have a reasonable opportunity before or after departure to settle any claims for wages and other entitlements due to him or her and any pending liabilities.

7. Without prejudice to the execution of a decision of expulsion, a migrant worker or a member of his or her family who is subject to such a decision may seek entry into a State other than his or her State of origin.

8. In case of expulsion of a migrant worker or a member of his or her family the costs of expulsion shall not be borne by him or her. The person concerned may be required to pay his or her own travel costs.

9. Expulsion from the State of employment shall not in itself prejudice any rights of a migrant worker or a member of his or her family acquired in accordance with the law of that State, including the right to receive wages and other entitlements due to him or her.

Article 23

Migrant workers and members of their families shall have the right to have recourse to the protection and assistance of the consular or diplomatic authorities of their State of origin or of a State representing the interests of that State whenever the rights recognized in the present Convention are impaired. In particular, in case of expulsion, the person concerned shall be informed of this right without delay and the authorities of the expelling State shall facilitate the exercise of such right.

Article 24

Every migrant worker and every member of his or her family shall have the right to recognition everywhere as a person before the law.

Article 25

1. Migrant workers shall enjoy treatment not less favourable than that which applies to nationals of the State of employment in respect of remuneration and:

> (a) Other conditions of work, that is to say, overtime, hours of work, weekly rest, holidays with pay, safety, health, termination of the employment relationship and any other conditions of work which, according to national law and practice, are covered by these terms;

> (b) Other terms of employment, that is to say, minimum age of employment, restriction on home work and any other matters which, according to national law and practice, are considered a term of employment.

2. It shall not be lawful to derogate in private contracts of employment from the principle of equality of treatment referred to in paragraph 1 of the present article.

3. States Parties shall take all appropriate measures to ensure that migrant workers are not deprived of any rights derived from this principle by reason of any irregularity in their stay or employment. In particular, employers shall not be relieved of any legal or contractual obligations, nor shall their obligations be limited in any manner by reason of such irregularity.

Article 26

1. States Parties recognize the right of migrant workers and members of their families:

> (a) To take part in meetings and activities of trade unions and of any other associations established in accordance with law, with a view to protecting their economic, social, cultural and other interests, subject only to the rules of the organization concerned;

(b) To join freely any trade union and any such association as aforesaid, subject only to the rules of the organization concerned;

(c) To seek the aid and assistance of any trade union and of any such association as aforesaid.

2. No restrictions may be placed on the exercise of these rights other than those that are prescribed by law and which are necessary in a democratic society in the interests of national security, public order (ordre public) or the protection of the rights and freedoms of others.

Article 27

1. With respect to social security, migrant workers and members of their families shall enjoy in the State of employment the same treatment granted to nationals in so far as they fulfil the requirements provided for by the applicable legislation of that State and the applicable bilateral and multilateral treaties. The competent authorities of the State of origin and the State of employment can at any time establish the necessary arrangements to determine the modalities of application of this norm.

2. Where the applicable legislation does not allow migrant workers and members of their families a benefit, the States concerned shall examine the possibility of reimbursing interested persons the amount of contributions made by them with respect to that benefit on the basis of the treatment granted to nationals who are in similar circumstances.

Article 28

Migrant workers and members of their families shall have the right to receive any medical care that is urgently required for the preservation of their life or the avoidance of irreparable harm to their health on the basis of equality of treatment with nationals of the State concerned. Such emergency medical care shall not be refused them by reason of any irregularity with regard to stay or employment.

Article 29

Each child of a migrant worker shall have the right to a name, to registration of birth and to a nationality.

Article 30

Each child of a migrant worker shall have the basic right of access to education on the basis of equality of treatment with nationals of the State concerned. Access to public pre-school educational institutions or schools shall not be refused or limited by reason of the irregular situation with respect to stay or employment of either parent or by reason of the irregularity of the child's stay in the State of employment.

Article 31

1. States Parties shall ensure respect for the cultural identity of migrant workers and members of their families and shall not prevent them from maintaining their cultural links with their State of origin.

2. States Parties may take appropriate measures to assist and encourage efforts in this respect.

Article 32

Upon the termination of their stay in the State of employment, migrant workers and members of their families shall have the right to transfer their earnings and savings and, in accordance with the applicable legislation of the States concerned, their personal effects and belongings.

Article 33

1. Migrant workers and members of their families shall have the right to be informed by the State of origin, the State of employment or the State of transit as the case may be concerning:

(a) Their rights arising out of the present Convention;

(b) The conditions of their admission, their rights and obligations under the law and practice of the State concerned and such other matters as will enable them to comply with administrative or other formalities in that State.

2. States Parties shall take all measures they deem appropriate to disseminate the said information or to ensure that it is provided by employers, trade unions or other appropriate bodies or institutions. As appropriate, they shall co-operate with other States concerned.

3. Such adequate information shall be provided upon request to migrant workers and members of their families, free of charge, and, as far as possible, in a language they are able to understand.

Article 34

Nothing in the present part of the Convention shall have the effect of relieving migrant workers and the members of their families from either the obligation to comply with the laws and regulations of any State of transit and the State of employment or the obligation to respect the cultural identity of the inhabitants of such States.

Article 35

Nothing in the present part of the Convention shall be interpreted as implying the regularization of the situation of migrant workers or members of their families who are non-documented or in an irregular situation or any right to such regularization of their situation, nor shall it prejudice the measures intended to ensure sound and equitable-conditions for international migration as provided in part VI of the present Convention.

PART IV OTHER RIGHTS OF MIGRANT WORKERS AND MEMBERS OF THEIR FAMILIES WHO ARE DOCUMENTED OR IN A REGULAR SITUATION

Article 36

Migrant workers and members of their families who are documented or in a regular situation in the State of employment shall enjoy the rights set forth in the present part of the Convention in addition to those set forth in part III.

Article 37

Before their departure, or at the latest at the time of their admission to the State of employment, migrant workers and members of their families shall have the right to be fully informed by the State of origin or the State of employment, as appropriate, of all conditions applicable to their admission and particularly those concerning their stay and the remunerated activities in which they may engage as well as of the requirements they must satisfy in the State of employment and the authority to which they must address themselves for any modification of those conditions.

Article 38

1. States of employment shall make every effort to authorize migrant workers and members of the families to be temporarily absent without effect upon their authorization to stay or to work, as the case may be. In doing so, States of employment shall take into account the special needs and obligations of migrant workers and members of their families, in particular in their States of origin.

2. Migrant workers and members of their families shall have the right to be fully informed of the terms on which such temporary absences are authorized.

Article 39

1. Migrant workers and members of their families shall have the right to liberty of movement in the territory of the State of employment and freedom to choose their residence there.

2. The rights mentioned in paragraph 1 of the present article shall not be subject to any restrictions except those that are provided by law, are necessary to protect national security, public order (ordre public), public health or morals, or the rights and freedoms of others and are consistent with the other rights recognized in the present Convention.

Article 40

1. Migrant workers and members of their families shall have the right to form associations and trade unions in the State of employment for the promotion and protection of their economic, social, cultural and other interests.

2. No restrictions may be placed on the exercise of this right other than those that are prescribed by law and are necessary in a democratic society in the interests of national security, public order (ordre public) or the protection of the rights and freedoms of others.

Article 41

1. Migrant workers and members of their families shall have the right to participate in public affairs of their State of origin and to vote and to be elected at elections of that State, in accordance with its legislation.

2. The States concerned shall, as appropriate and in accordance with their legislation, facilitate the exercise of these rights.

Article 42

1. States Parties shall consider the establishment of procedures or institutions through which account may be taken, both in States of origin and in States of employment, of special needs, aspirations and obligations of migrant workers and members of their families and shall envisage, as appropriate, the possibility for migrant workers and members of their families to have their freely chosen representatives in those institutions.

2. States of employment shall facilitate, in accordance with their national legislation, the consultation or participation of migrant workers and members of their families in decisions concerning the life and administration of local communities.

3. Migrant workers may enjoy political rights in the State of employment if that State, in the exercise of its sovereignty, grants them such rights.

Article 43

1. Migrant workers shall enjoy equality of treatment with nationals of the State of employment in relation to:

(a) Access to educational institutions and services subject to the admission requirements and other regulations of the institutions and services concerned;

(b) Access to vocational guidance and placement services;

(c) Access to vocational training and retraining facilities and institutions;

(d) Access to housing, including social housing schemes, and protection against exploitation in respect of rents;

(e) Access to social and health services, provided that the requirements for participation in the respective schemes are met;

(f) Access to co-operatives and self-managed enterprises, which shall not imply a change of their migration status and shall be subject to the rules and regulations of the bodies concerned;

(g) Access to and participation in cultural life.

2. States Parties shall promote conditions to ensure effective equality of treatment to enable migrant workers to enjoy the rights mentioned in paragraph 1 of the present article whenever the terms of their stay, as authorized by the State of employment, meet the appropriate requirements.

3. States of employment shall not prevent an employer of migrant workers from establishing housing or social or cultural facilities for them. Subject to article 70 of the present Convention, a State of employment may make the establishment of such facilities subject to the requirements generally applied in that State concerning their installation.

Article 44

1. States Parties, recognizing that the family is the natural and fundamental group unit of society and is entitled to protection by society and the State, shall take appropriate measures to ensure the protection of the unity of the families of migrant workers.

2. States Parties shall take measures that they deem appropriate and that fall within their competence to facilitate the reunification of migrant workers with their spouses or persons who have with the migrant worker a relationship that, according to applicable law, produces effects equivalent to marriage, as well as with their minor dependent unmarried children.

3. States of employment, on humanitarian grounds, shall favourably consider granting equal treatment, as set forth in paragraph 2 of the present article, to other family members of migrant workers.

Article 45

1. Members of the families of migrant workers shall, in the State of employment, enjoy equality of treatment with nationals of that State in relation to:

(a) Access to educational institutions and services, subject to the admission requirements and other regulations of the institutions and services concerned;

(b) Access to vocational guidance and training institutions and services, provided that requirements for participation are met;

(c) Access to social and health services, provided that requirements for participation in the respective schemes are met;

(d) Access to and participation in cultural life.

2. States of employment shall pursue a policy, where appropriate in collaboration with the States of origin, aimed at facilitating the integration of children of migrant workers in the local school system, particularly in respect of teaching them the local language.

3. States of employment shall endeavour to facilitate for the children of migrant workers the teaching of their mother tongue and culture and, in this regard, States of origin shall collaborate whenever appropriate.

4. States of employment may provide special schemes of education in the mother tongue of children of migrant workers, if necessary in collaboration with the States of origin.

Article 46

Migrant workers and members of their families shall, subject to the applicable legislation of the States concerned, as well as relevant international agreements and the obligations of the States concerned arising out of their participation in customs unions, enjoy exemption from import and export duties and taxes in respect of their personal and household effects as well as the equipment necessary to engage in the remunerated activity for which they were admitted to the State of employment:

(a) Upon departure from the State of origin or State of habitual residence;

(b) Upon initial admission to the State of employment;

(c) Upon final departure from the State of employment;

(d) Upon final return to the State of origin or State of habitual residence.

Article 47

1. Migrant workers shall have the right to transfer their earnings and savings, in particular those funds necessary for the support of their families, from the State of employment to their State of origin or any other State. Such transfers shall be made in conformity with procedures established by applicable legislation of the State concerned and in conformity with applicable international agreements.

2. States concerned shall take appropriate measures to facilitate such transfers.

Article 48

1. Without prejudice to applicable double taxation agreements, migrant workers and members of their families shall, in the matter of earnings in the State of employment:

(a) Not be liable to taxes, duties or charges of any description higher or more onerous than those imposed on nationals in similar circumstances;

(b) Be entitled to deductions or exemptions from taxes of any description and to any tax allowances applicable to nationals in similar circumstances, including tax allowances for dependent members of their families.

2. States Parties shall endeavour to adopt appropriate measures to avoid double taxation of the earnings and savings of migrant workers and members of their families.

Article 49

1. Where separate authorizations to reside and to engage in employment are required by national legislation, the States of employment shall issue to migrant workers authorization of residence for at least the same period of time as their authorization to engage in remunerated activity.

2. Migrant workers who in the State of employment are allowed freely to choose their remunerated activity shall neither be regarded as in an irregular situation nor shall they lose their authorization of residence by the mere fact of the termination of their remunerated activity prior to the expiration of their work permits or similar authorizations.

3. In order to allow migrant workers referred to in paragraph 2 of the present article sufficient time to find alternative remunerated activities, the authorization of residence shall not be withdrawn at least for a period corresponding to that during which they may be entitled to unemployment benefits.

Article 50

1. In the case of death of a migrant worker or dissolution of marriage, the State of employment shall favourably consider granting family members of that migrant worker residing in that State on the basis of family reunion an authorization to stay; the State of employment shall take into account the length of time they have already resided in that State.

2. Members of the family to whom such authorization is not granted shall be allowed before departure a reasonable period of time in order to enable them to settle their affairs in the State of employment.

3. The provisions of paragraphs I and 2 of the present article may not be interpreted as adversely affecting any right to stay and work otherwise granted to such family members by the legislation of the State of employment or by bilateral and multilateral treaties applicable to that State.

Article 51

Migrant workers who in the State of employment are not permitted freely to choose their remunerated activity shall neither be regarded as in an irregular situation nor shall they lose their authorization of residence by the mere fact of the termination of their remunerated activity prior to the expiration of their work permit, except where the authorization of residence is expressly dependent upon the specific remunerated activity for which they were admitted. Such migrant workers shall have the right to seek alternative employment, participation in public work schemes and retraining during the remaining period of their authorization to work, subject to such conditions and limitations as are specified in the authorization to work.

Article 52

1. Migrant workers in the State of employment shall have the right freely to choose their remunerated activity, subject to the following restrictions or conditions.

2. For any migrant worker a State of employment may:

(a) Restrict access to limited categories of employment, functions, services or activities where this is necessary in the interests of this State and provided for by national legislation;

(b) Restrict free choice of remunerated activity in accordance with its legislation concerning recognition of occupational qualifications acquired outside its territory. However, States Parties concerned shall endeavour to provide for recognition of such qualifications.

3. For migrant workers whose permission to work is limited in time, a State of employment may also:

(a) Make the right freely to choose their remunerated activities subject to the condition that the migrant worker has resided lawfully in its territory for the purpose of remunerated activity for a period of time prescribed in its national legislation that should not exceed two years;

(b) Limit access by a migrant worker to remunerated activities in pursuance of a policy of granting priority to its nationals or to persons who are assimilated to them for these purposes by virtue of legislation or bilateral or multilateral agreements. Any such limitation shall cease to apply to a migrant worker who has resided lawfully in its territory for the purpose of remunerated activity for a period of time prescribed in its national legislation that should not exceed five years.

4. States of employment shall prescribe the conditions under which a migrant worker who has been admitted to take up employment may be authorized to engage in work on his or her own account. Account shall be taken of the period during which the worker has already been lawfully in the State of employment.

Article 53

1. Members of a migrant worker's family who have themselves an authorization of residence or admission that is without limit of time or is automatically renewable shall be permitted freely to choose their remunerated activity under the same conditions as are applicable to the said migrant worker in accordance with article 52 of the present Convention.

2. With respect to members of a migrant worker's family who are not permitted freely to choose their remunerated activity, States Parties shall consider favourably granting them priority in obtaining permission to engage in a remunerated activity over other workers who seek admission to the State of employment, subject to applicable bilateral and multilateral agreements.

Article 54

1. Without prejudice to the terms of their authorization of residence or their permission to work and the rights provided for in articles 25 and 27 of the present Convention, migrant workers shall enjoy equality of treatment with nationals of the State of employment in respect of:

(a) Protection against dismissal;

(b) Unemployment benefits;

(c) Access to public work schemes intended to combat unemployment;

(d) Access to alternative employment in the event of loss of work or termination of other remunerated activity, subject to article 52 of the present Convention.

2. If a migrant worker claims that the terms of his or her work contract have been violated by his or her employer, he or she shall have the right to address his or her

case to the competent authorities of the State of employment, on terms provided for in article 18, paragraph 1, of the present Convention.

Article 55

Migrant workers who have been granted permission to engage in a remunerated activity, subject to the conditions attached to such permission, shall be entitled to equality of treatment with nationals of the State of employment in the exercise of that remunerated activity.

Article 56

1. Migrant workers and members of their families referred to in the present part of the Convention may not be expelled from a State of employment, except for reasons defined in the national legislation of that State, and subject to the safeguards established in part III.

2. Expulsion shall not be resorted to for the purpose of depriving a migrant worker or a member of his or her family of the rights arising out of the authorization of residence and the work permit.

3. In considering whether to expel a migrant worker or a member of his or her family, account should be taken of humanitarian considerations and of the length of time that the person concerned has already resided in the State of employment.

PART V PROVISIONS APPLICABLE TO PARTICULAR CATEGORIES OF MIGRANT WORKERS AND OF THEIR FAMILIES

Article 57

The particular categories of migrant workers and members of their families specified in the present part of the Convention who are documented or in a regular situation shall enjoy the rights set forth in part III and, except as modified below, the rights set forth in part IV.

Article 58

1. Frontier workers, as defined in article 2, paragraph 2 (a), of the present Convention, shall be entitled to the rights provided for in part IV that can be

applied to them by reason of their presence and work in the territory of the State of employment, taking into account that they do not have their habitual residence in that State.

2. States of employment shall consider favourably granting frontier workers the right freely to choose their remunerated activity after a specified period of time. The granting of that right shall not affect their status as frontier workers.

Article 59

1. Seasonal workers, as defined in article 2, paragraph 2 (b), of the present Convention, shall be entitled to the rights provided for in part IV that can be applied to them by reason of their presence and work in the territory of the State of employment and that are compatible with their status in that State as seasonal workers, taking into account the fact that they are present in that State for only part of the year.

2. The State of employment shall, subject to paragraph 1 of the present article, consider granting seasonal workers who have been employed in its territory for a significant period of time the possibility of taking up other remunerated activities and giving them priority over other workers who seek admission to that State, subject to applicable bilateral and multilateral agreements.

Article 60

Itinerant workers, as defined in article 2, paragraph 2 (A), of the present Convention, shall be entitled to the rights provided for in part IV that can be granted to them by reason of their presence and work in the territory of the State of employment and that are compatible with their status as itinerant workers in that State.

Article 61

1. Project-tied workers, as defined in article 2, paragraph 2 (f), of the present Convention, and members of their families shall be entitled to the rights provided for in part IV except the provisions of article 43, paragraphs I (b) and (c), article 43, paragraph I (d), as it pertains to social housing schemes, article 45, paragraph I (b), and articles 52 to 55.

2. If a project-tied worker claims that the terms of his or her work contract have been violated by his or her employer, he or she shall have the right to address his or her case to the competent authorities of the State which has jurisdiction over that employer, on terms provided for in article 18, paragraph 1, of the present Convention.

3. Subject to bilateral or multilateral agreements in force for them, the States Parties concerned shall endeavour to enable project-tied workers to remain adequately protected by the social security systems of their States of origin or habitual residence during their engagement in the project. States Parties concerned shall take appropriate measures with the aim of avoiding any denial of rights or duplication of payments in this respect.

4. Without prejudice to the provisions of article 47 of the present Convention and to relevant bilateral or multilateral agreements, States Parties concerned shall permit payment of the earnings of project-tied workers in their State of origin or habitual residence.

Article 62

1. Specified-employment workers as defined in article 2, paragraph 2 (g), of the present Convention, shall be entitled to the rights provided for in part IV, except the provisions of article 43, paragraphs I (b) and (c), article 43, paragraph I (d), as it pertains to social housing schemes, article 52, and article 54, paragraph 1 (d).

2. Members of the families of specified-employment workers shall be entitled to the rights relating to family members of migrant workers provided for in part IV of the present Convention, except the provisions of article 53.

Article 63

1. Self-employed workers, as defined in article 2, paragraph 2 (h), of the present Convention, shall be entitled to the rights provided for in part IV with the exception of those rights which are exclusively applicable to workers having a contract of employment.

2. Without prejudice to articles 52 and 79 of the present Convention, the termination of the economic activity of the self-employed workers shall not in itself imply the withdrawal of the authorization for them or for the members of their

families to stay or to engage in a remunerated activity in the State of employment except where the authorization of residence is expressly dependent upon the specific remunerated activity for which they were admitted.

PART VI   PROMOTION OF SOUND, EQUITABLE, HUMANE AND LAWFUL CONDITIONS CONNECTION WITH INTERNATIONAL MIGRATION OF WORKERS AND MEMBERS OF THEIR FAMILIES

Article 64

1. Without prejudice to article 79 of the present Convention, the States Parties concerned shall as appropriate consult and co-operate with a view to promoting sound, equitable and humane conditions in connection with international migration of workers and members of their families.

2. In this respect, due regard shall be paid not only to labour needs and resources, but also to the social, economic, cultural and other needs of migrant workers and members of their families involved, as well as to the consequences of such migration for the communities concerned.

Article 65

1. States Parties shall maintain appropriate services to deal with questions concerning international migration of workers and members of their families. Their functions shall include, inter alia:

(a) The formulation and implementation of policies regarding such migration;

(b) An exchange of information. consultation and co-operation with the competent authorities of other States Parties involved in such migration;

(c) The provision of appropriate information, particularly to employers, workers and their organizations on policies, laws and regulations relating to migration and employment, on agreements concluded with other States concerning migration and on other relevant matters;

(d) The provision of information and appropriate assistance to migrant workers and members of their families regarding requisite authorizations and formalities and arrangements for departure, travel, arrival, stay, remunerated activities, exit and return, as well as on conditions of work and life in the State of employment and on customs, currency, tax and other relevant laws and regulations.

2. States Parties shall facilitate as appropriate the provision of adequate consular and other services that are necessary to meet the social, cultural and other needs of migrant workers and members of their families.

Article 66

1. Subject to paragraph 2 of the present article, the right to undertake operations with a view to the recruitment of workers for employment in another State shall be restricted to:

(a) Public services or bodies of the State in which such operations take place;

(b) Public services or bodies of the State of employment on the basis of agreement between the States concerned;

(c) A body established by virtue of a bilateral or multilateral agreement.

2. Subject to any authorization, approval and supervision by the public authorities of the States Parties concerned as may be established pursuant to the legislation and practice of those States, agencies, prospective employers or persons acting on their behalf may also be permitted to undertake the said operations.

Article 67

1. States Parties concerned shall co-operate as appropriate in the adoption of measures regarding the orderly return of migrant workers and members of their families to the State of origin when they decide to return or their authorization of residence or employment expires or when they are in the State of employment in an irregular situation.

2. Concerning migrant workers and members of their families in a regular situation, States Parties concerned shall co-operate as appropriate, on terms agreed upon by those States, with a view to promoting adequate economic conditions for their

resettlement and to facilitating their durable social and cultural reintegration in the State of origin.

Article 68

1. States Parties, including States of transit, shall collaborate with a view to preventing and eliminating illegal or clandestine movements and employment of migrant workers in an irregular situation. The measures to be taken to this end within the jurisdiction of each State concerned shall include:

(a) Appropriate measures against the dissemination of misleading information relating to emigration and immigration;

(b) Measures to detect and eradicate illegal or clandestine movements of migrant workers and members of their families and to impose effective sanctions on persons, groups or entities which organize, operate or assist in organizing or operating such movements;

(c) Measures to impose effective sanctions on persons, groups or entities which use violence, threats or intimidation against migrant workers or members of their families in an irregular situation.

2. States of employment shall take all adequate and effective measures to eliminate employment in their territory of migrant workers in an irregular situation, including, whenever appropriate, sanctions on employers of such workers. The rights of migrant workers vis-a-vis their employer arising from employment shall not be impaired by these measures.

Article 69

1. States Parties shall, when there are migrant workers and members of their families within their territory in an irregular situation, take appropriate measures to ensure that such a situation does not persist.

2. Whenever States Parties concerned consider the possibility of regularizing the situation of such persons in accordance with applicable national legislation and bilateral or multilateral agreements, appropriate account shall be taken of the circumstances of their entry, the duration of their stay in the States of employment

and other relevant considerations, in particular those relating to their family situation.

Article 70

States Parties shall take measures not less favourable than those applied to nationals to ensure that working and living conditions of migrant workers and members of their families in a regular situation are in keeping with the standards of fitness, safety, health and principles of human dignity.

Article 71

1. States Parties shall facilitate, whenever necessary, the repatriation to the State of origin of the bodies of deceased migrant workers or members of their families.

2. As regards compensation matters relating to the death of a migrant worker or a member of his or her family, States Parties shall, as appropriate, provide assistance to the persons concerned with a view to the prompt settlement of such matters. Settlement of these matters shall be carried out on the basis of applicable national law in accordance with the provisions of the present Convention and any relevant bilateral or multilateral agreements.

PART VII APPLICATION OF THE CONVENTION

Article 72

1. (a) For the purpose of reviewing the application of the present Convention, there shall be established a Committee on the Protection of the Rights of All Migrant Workers and Members of Their Families (hereinafter referred to as "the Committee");

(b) The Committee shall consist, at the time of entry into force of the present Convention, of ten and, after the entry into force of the Convention for the forty-first State Party, of fourteen experts of high moral standing, impartiality and recognized competence in the field covered by the Convention.

2. (a) Members of the Committee shall be elected by secret ballot by the States Parties from a list of persons nominated by the States Parties, due consideration being given to equitable geographical distribution, including both States of origin

and States of employment, and to the representation of the principal legal system. Each State Party may nominate one person from among its own nationals;

(b) Members shall be elected and shall serve in their personal capacity.

3. The initial election shall be held no later than six months after the date of the entry into force of the present Convention and subsequent elections every second year. At least four months before the date of each election, the Secretary-General of the United Nations shall address a letter to all States Parties inviting them to submit their nominations within two months. The Secretary-General shall prepare a list in alphabetical order of all persons thus nominated, indicating the States Parties that have nominated them, and shall submit it to the States Parties not later than one month before the date of the corresponding election, together with the curricula vitae of the persons thus nominated.

4. Elections of members of the Committee shall be held at a meeting of States Parties convened by the Secretary-General at United Nations Headquarters. At that meeting, for which two thirds of the States Parties shall constitute a quorum, the persons elected to the Committee shall be those nominees who obtain the largest number of votes and an absolute majority of the votes of the States Parties present and voting.

5. (a) The members of the Committee shall serve for a term of four years. However, the terms of five of the members elected in the first election shall expire at the end of two years; immediately after the first election, the names of these five members shall be chosen by lot by the Chairman of the meeting of States Parties;

(b) The election of the four additional members of the Committee shall be held in accordance with the provisions of paragraphs 2, 3 and 4 of the present article, following the entry into force of the Convention for the forty-first State Party. The term of two of the additional members elected on this occasion shall expire at the end of two years; the names of these members shall be chosen by lot by the Chairman of the meeting of States Parties;

(c) The members of the Committee shall be eligible for re-election if renominated.

6. If a member of the Committee dies or resigns or declares that for any other cause he or she can no longer perform the duties of the Committee, the State Party that nominated the expert shall appoint another expert from among its own nationals for

the remaining part of the term. The new appointment is subject to the approval of the Committee.

7. The Secretary-General of the United Nations shall provide the necessary staff and facilities for the effective performance of the functions of the Committee.

8. The members of the Committee shall receive emoluments from United Nations resources on such terms and conditions as the General Assembly may decide.

9. The members of the Committee shall be entitled to the facilities, privileges and immunities of experts on mission for the United Nations as laid down in the relevant sections of the Convention on the Privileges and Immunities of the United Nations.

Article 73

1. States Parties undertake to submit to the Secretary-General of the United Nations for consideration by the Committee a report on the legislative, judicial, administrative and other measures they have taken to give effect to the provisions of the present Convention:

(a) Within one year after the entry into force of the Convention for the State Party concerned;

(b) Thereafter every five years and whenever the Committee so requests.

2. Reports prepared under the present article shall also indicate factors and difficulties, if any, affecting the implementation of the Convention and shall include information on the characteristics of migration flows in which the State Party concerned is involved.

3. The Committee shall decide any further guidelines applicable to the content of the reports.

4. States Parties shall make their reports widely available to the public in their own countries.

Article 74

1. The Committee shall examine the reports submitted by each State Party and shall transmit such comments as it may consider appropriate to the State Party concerned. This State Party may submit to the Committee observations on any comment made by the Committee in accordance with the present article. The Committee may request supplementary information from States Parties when considering these reports.

2. The Secretary-General of the United Nations shall, in due time before the opening of each regular session of the Committee, transmit to the Director-General of the International Labour Office copies of the reports submitted by States Parties concerned and information relevant to the consideration of these reports, in order to enable the Office to assist the Committee with the expertise the Office may provide regarding those matters dealt with by the present Convention that fall within the sphere of competence of the International Labour Organisation. The Committee shall consider in its deliberations such comments and materials as the Office may provide.

3. The Secretary-General of the United Nations may also, after consultation with the Committee, transmit to other specialized agencies as well as to intergovernmental organizations, copies of such parts of these reports as may fall within their competence.

4. The Committee may invite the specialized agencies and organs of the United Nations, as well as intergovernmental organizations and other concerned bodies to submit, for consideration by the Committee, written information on such matters dealt with in the present Convention as fall within the scope of their activities.

5. The International Labour Office shall be invited by the Committee to appoint representatives to participate, in a consultative capacity, in the meetings of the Committee.

6. The Committee may invite representatives of other specialized agencies and organs of the United Nations, as well as of intergovernmental organizations, to be present and to be heard in its meetings whenever matters falling within their field of competence are considered.

7. The Committee shall present an annual report to the General Assembly of the United Nations on the implementation of the present Convention, containing its own considerations and recommendations, based, in particular, on the examination of the reports and any observations presented by States Parties.

8. The Secretary-General of the United Nations shall transmit the annual reports of the Committee to the States Parties to the present Convention, the Economic and Social Council, the Commission on Human Rights of the United Nations, the Director-General of the International Labour Office and other relevant organizations.

Article 75

1. The Committee shall adopt its own rules of procedure.

2. The Committee shall elect its officers for a term of two years.

3. The Committee shall normally meet annually.

4. The meetings of the Committee shall normally be held at United Nations Headquarters.

Article 76

1. A State Party to the present Convention may at any time declare under this article that it recognizes the competence of the Committee to receive and consider communications to the effect that a State Party claims that another State Party is not fulfilling its obligations under the present Convention. Communications under this article may be received and considered only if submitted by a State Party that has made a declaration recognizing in regard to itself the competence of the Committee. No communication shall be received by the Committee if it concerns a State Party which has not made such a declaration. Communications received under this article shall be dealt with in accordance with the following procedure:

(a) If a State Party to the present Convention considers that another State Party is not fulfilling its obligations under the present Convention, it may, by written communication, bring the matter to the attention of that State Party. The State Party may also inform the Committee of the matter. Within three months after the receipt of the communication the receiving

State shall afford the State that sent the communication an explanation, or any other statement in writing clarifying the matter which should include, to the extent possible and pertinent, reference to domestic procedures and remedies taken, pending or available in the matter;

(b) If the matter is not adjusted to the satisfaction of both States Parties concerned within six months after the receipt by the receiving State of the initial communication, either State shall have the right to refer the matter to the Committee, by notice given to the Committee and to the other State;

(c) The Committee shall deal with a matter referred to it only after it has ascertained that all available domestic remedies have been invoked and exhausted in the matter, in conformity with the generally recognized principles of international law. This shall not be the rule where, in the view of the Committee, the application of the remedies is unreasonably prolonged;

(d) Subject to the provisions of subparagraph (c) of the present paragraph, the Committee shall make available its good offices to the States Parties concerned with a view to a friendly solution of the matter on the basis of the respect for the obligations set forth in the present Convention;

(e) The Committee shall hold closed meetings when examining communications under the present article;

(f) In any matter referred to it in accordance with subparagraph (b) of the present paragraph, the Committee may call upon the States Parties concerned, referred to in subparagraph (b), to supply any relevant information;

(g) The States Parties concerned, referred to in subparagraph (b) of the present paragraph, shall have the right to be represented when the matter is being considered by the Committee and to make submissions orally and/or in writing;

(h) The Committee shall, within twelve months after the date of receipt of notice under subparagraph (b) of the present paragraph, submit a report, as follows: (I) If a solution within the terms of subparagraph (d) of the present paragraph is reached, the Committee shall confine its report to a brief statement of the facts and of the solution reached; (ii) If a solution within the terms of subparagraph (d) is not reached, the Committee shall, in its report, set forth the relevant facts concerning the issue between the States Parties concerned. The written submissions and record of the oral submissions made by the States Parties concerned shall be attached to the report. The Committee may also communicate only to the States Parties concerned any views that it may consider relevant to the issue between them. In every matter, the report shall be communicated to the States Parties concerned.

2. The provisions of the present article shall come into force when ten States Parties to the present Convention have made a declaration under paragraph 1 of the present article. Such declarations shall be deposited by the States Parties with the Secretary-General of the United Nations, who shall transmit copies thereof to the other States Parties. A declaration may be withdrawn at any time by notification to the Secretary-General. Such a withdrawal shall not prejudice the consideration of any matter that is the subject of a communication already transmitted under the present article; no further communication by any State Party shall be received under the present article after the notification of withdrawal of the declaration has been received by the Secretary-General, unless the State Party concerned has made a new declaration.

Article 77

1. A State Party to the present Convention may at any time declare under the present article that it recognizes the competence of the Committee to receive and consider communications from or on behalf of individuals subject to its jurisdiction who claim that their individual rights as established by the present Convention have been violated by that State Party. No communication shall be received by the Committee if it concerns a State Party that has not made such a declaration.

2. The Committee shall consider inadmissible any communication under the present article which is anonymous or which it considers to be an abuse of the right of submission of such communications or to be incompatible with the provisions of the present Convention.

3. The Committee shall not consider any communication from an individual under the present article unless it has ascertained that:

(a) The same matter has not been, and is not being, examined under another procedure of international investigation or settlement;

(b) The individual has exhausted all available domestic remedies; this shall not be the rule where, in the view of the Committee, the application of the remedies is unreasonably prolonged or is unlikely to bring effective relief to that individual.

4. Subject to the provisions of paragraph 2 of the present article, the Committee shall bring any communications submitted to it under this article to the attention of the State Party to the present Convention that has made a declaration under paragraph 1 and is alleged to be violating any provisions of the Convention. Within six months, the receiving State shall submit to the Committee written explanations or statements clarifying the matter and the remedy, if any, that may have been taken by that State.

5. The Committee shall consider communications received under the present article in the light of all information made available to it by or on behalf of the individual and by the State Party concerned.

6. The Committee shall hold closed meetings when examining communications under the present article.

7. The Committee shall forward its views to the State Party concerned and to the individual.

8. The provisions of the present article shall come into force when ten States Parties to the present Convention have made declarations under paragraph 1 of the present article. Such declarations shall be deposited by the States Parties with the Secretary-General of the United Nations, who shall transmit copies thereof to the other States Parties. A declaration may be withdrawn at any time by notification to the Secretary-General. Such a withdrawal shall not prejudice the consideration of any matter that is the subject of a communication already transmitted under the present article; no further communication by or on behalf of an individual shall be received under the present article after the notification of withdrawal of the declaration has been received by the Secretary-General, unless the State Party has made a new declaration.

Article 78

The provisions of article 76 of the present Convention shall be applied without prejudice to any procedures for settling disputes or complaints in the field covered by the present Convention laid down in the constituent instruments of, or in conventions adopted by, the United Nations and the specialized agencies and shall not prevent the States Parties from having recourse to any procedures for settling a dispute in accordance with international agreements in force between them.

PART VIII GENERAL PROVISIONS

Article 79

Nothing in the present Convention shall affect the right of each State Party to establish the criteria governing admission of migrant workers and members of their families. Concerning other matters related to their legal situation and treatment as migrant workers and members of their families, States Parties shall be subject to the limitations set forth in the present Convention.

Article 80

Nothing in the present Convention shall be interpreted as impairing the provisions of the Charter of the United Nations and of the constitutions of the specialized agencies which define the respective responsibilities of the various organs of the United Nations and of the specialized agencies in regard to the matters dealt with in the present Convention.

Article 81

1. Nothing in the present Convention shall affect more favourable rights or freedoms granted to migrant workers and members of their families by virtue of:

   (a) The law or practice of a State Party; or

   (b) Any bilateral or multilateral treaty in force for the State Party concerned.

2. Nothing in the present Convention may be interpreted as implying for any State, group or person any right to engage in any activity or perform any act that would impair any of the rights and freedoms as set forth in the present Convention.

Article 82

The rights of migrant workers and members of their families provided for in the present Convention may not be renounced. It shall not be permissible to exert any form of pressure upon migrant workers and members of their families with a view to their relinquishing or foregoing any of the said rights. It shall not be possible to derogate by contract from rights recognized in the present Convention. States Parties shall take appropriate measures to ensure that these principles are respected.

Article 83

Each State Party to the present Convention undertakes:

(a) To ensure that any person whose rights or freedoms as herein recognized are violated shall have an effective remedy, notwithstanding that the violation has been committed by persons acting in an official capacity;

(b) To ensure that any persons seeking such a remedy shall have his or her claim reviewed and decided by competent judicial, administrative or legislative authorities, or by any other competent authority provided for by the legal system of the State, and to develop the possibilities of judicial remedy;

(c) To ensure that the competent authorities shall enforce such remedies when granted.

Article 84

Each State Party undertakes to adopt the legislative and other measures that are necessary to implement the provisions of the present Convention.

PART IX FINAL PROVISIONS

Article 85

The Secretary-General of the United Nations is designated as the depositary of the present Convention.

Article 86

1. The present Convention shall be open for signature by all States. It is subject to ratification.

2. The present Convention shall be open to accession by any State.

3. Instruments of ratification or accession shall be deposited with the Secretary-General of the United Nations.

Article 87

1. The present Convention shall enter into force on the first day of the month following a period of three months after the date of the deposit of the twentieth instrument of ratification or accession.

2. For each State ratifying or acceding to the present Convention after its entry into force, the Convention shall enter into force on the first day of the month following a period of three months after the date of the deposit of its own instrument of ratification or accession.

Article 88

A State ratifying or acceding to the present Convention may not exclude the application of any Part of it, or, without prejudice to article 3, exclude any particular category of migrant workers from its application.

Article 89

1. Any State Party may denounce the present Convention, not earlier than five years after the Convention has entered into force for the State concerned, by means of a notification writing addressed to the Secretary-General of the United Nations.

2. Such denunciation shall become effective on the first day of the month following the expiration of a period of twelve months after the date of the receipt of the notification by the Secretary-General of the United Nations.

3. Such a denunciation shall not have the effect of releasing the State Party from its obligations under the present Convention in regard to any act or omission which occurs prior to the date at which the denunciation becomes effective, nor shall denunciation prejudice in any way the continued consideration of any matter which is already under consideration by the Committee prior to the date at which the denunciation becomes effective.

4. Following the date at which the denunciation of a State Party becomes effective, the Committee shall not commence consideration of any new matter regarding that State.

Article 90

1. After five years from the entry into force of the Convention a request for the revision of the Convention may be made at any time by any State Party by means of a notification in writing addressed to the Secretary-General of the United Nations. The Secretary-General shall thereupon communicate any proposed amendments to the States Parties with a request that they notify him whether the favour a conference of States Parties for the purpose of considering and voting upon the proposals. In the event that within four months from the date of such communication at least one third of the States Parties favours such a conference, the Secretary-General shall convene the conference under the auspices of the United Nations. Any amendment adopted by a majority of the States Parties present and voting shall be submitted to the General Assembly for approval.

2. Amendments shall come into force when they have been approved by the General Assembly of the United Nations and accepted by a two-thirds majority of the States Parties in accordance with their respective constitutional processes.

3. When amendments come into force, they shall be binding on those States Parties that have accepted them, other States Parties still being bound by the provisions of the present Convention and any earlier amendment that they have accepted.

6/23/98
SLFT

Article 91

1. The Secretary-General of the United Nations shall receive and circulate to all States the text of reservations made by States at the time of signature, ratification or accession.

2. A reservation incompatible with the object and purpose of the present Convention shall not be permitted.

3. Reservations may be withdrawn at any time by notification to this effect addressed to the Secretary-General of the United Nations, who shall then inform all States thereof. Such notification shall take effect on the date on which it is received.

Article 92

1. Any dispute between two or more States Parties concerning the interpretation or application of the present Convention that is not settled by negotiation shall, at the request of one of them, be submitted to arbitration. If within six months from the date of the request for arbitration the Parties are unable to agree on the organization of the arbitration, any one of those Parties may refer the dispute to the International Court of Justice by request in conformity with the Statute of the Court.

2. Each State Party may at the time of signature or ratification of the present Convention or accession thereto declare that it does not consider itself bound by paragraph 1 of the present article. The other States Parties shall not be bound by that paragraph with respect to any State Party that has made such a declaration.

3. Any State Party that has made a declaration in accordance with paragraph 2 of the present article may at any time withdraw that declaration by notification to the Secretary-General of the United Nations.

Article 93

1. The present Convention, of which the Arabic, Chinese, English, French, Russian and Spanish texts are equally authentic, shall be deposited with the Secretary-General of the United Nations.

2. The Secretary-General of the United Nations shall transmit certified copies of the present Convention to all States.